HIP HOP
DIVAS

HIP HOP DIVAS

VIBE BOOKS

THREE RIVERS PRESS • NEW YORK

Frontispiece: Salt-N-Pepa (Ricky Powell)

Published by Three Rivers Press, New York, New York.
Member of the Crown Publishing Group.

Random House, Inc. New York, Toronto, London, Sydney, Auckland
www.randomhouse.com

THREE RIVERS PRESS is a registered trademark and the Three Rivers Press colophon is a trademark of Random House, Inc.

Printed in the United States of America

Library of Congress Cataloging-in-Publication Data
Hip hop divas / VIBE Books
    1. Hip hop.   2. Rap (Music)–History and criticism.   3. African American women
musicians.
ML3531 .H57 2001
782.421649'082–dc21   2001027985

ISBN 0-609-80836-2

10 9 8 7 6 5 4 3 2 1

First Edition

FOR ALK 1.6.00
You can't learn less. *—RBF*

Also by **VIBE** BOOKS

THE VIBE HISTORY OF HIP HOP

TUPAC SHAKUR

CONTENTS

foreword *by Mimi Valdés*

Almost everybody at my all-girl Catholic high school, St. Jean Baptiste in Manhattan, loved UTFO's "Roxanne, Roxanne." The song about three guys trying to kick it to the neighborhood hot girl put a smirk on our faces. We knew the same scenario took place every 9.2 seconds in ghettos all over the world, and that's precisely why we laughed at the brothers' antics in the song. But none of us was expecting what would come next.

I was straightening up my room the first time I heard "Roxanne's Revenge" in 1984. All of a sudden this girl Roxanne Shanté came on the radio straight dissing some cats who had a hit record. I just stood there, staring at my little silver one-speaker boombox, frozen from shock. Somehow I managed to pop in a cassette and record it. I couldn't believe someone who sounded like a teenager in my class had the nerve to make an answer to "Roxanne, Roxanne." And I couldn't believe she was cursing so much that the DJ had to keep bleeping out the words.

By morning, I had the song memorized (despite the DJ's best efforts, you could still tell what Shanté was saying). Almost every other girl at school caught the record that night, too, and we were all excited because it was so different. "Roxanne's Revenge" was a monumental moment in hip hop, marking a new level of commercial success and street credibility for the female MC. People everywhere wanted to see this young girl with the foul mouth. And pretty soon, you couldn't go anywhere in New York City without hearing her song.

Looking back, I now realize that Shanté was so revolutionary because she was the first hip hop diva. Sure, there were female rappers before her, but none had the same impact. Every fan of this still-underground music—male and female—recognized her brilliance. That fiery spark in her voice was unlike anything else out there. Her stank black-girl attitude—and the skills she used to back it up—struck fear into the hearts of the competition, and created a whole new breed of dope MC. Soon there were dozens of "Roxanne" response records from men and women trying to cash in on the drama started by this 14-year-old girl from a low-income housing project in Queens.

While Shanté might not have been anybody's idea of a role model, there's no doubt that she helped pave the way for superstars like Salt-N-Pepa and Lil' Kim and even more "positive" artists like Queen Latifah and Lauryn Hill. These women are the grande dames of a down-and-dirty culture born in park jams and basement studios. Their appeal is different from that of pop stars like Britney or Janet—though most every girl you can see on MTV draws on their flavor and power. They are the yin and the yang, the fabulous and the ferocious—hip hop divas.

A diva is, by definition, the very best. But not everyone embraces the D-word. When a VIBE writer asked Lauryn Hill about being labeled a diva, she rejected the term. "Underneath it is 'bitch,'" L replied. "Understand, it's not, 'You're dope.' It's, 'You can sing—*Bitch!*' Brothers are allowed to be kooky and zany and quirky. Diva is just so unspecific. It's like, 'What does she do? She divas.'" But there are others, like Missy "Misdemeanor" Elliott, who seem totally comfortable with the idea. "I hear divas called bitches," she has said, "but I notice the ones they call that are the ones we respect. When a man acts a certain way, he has an aggressive attitude, but when we do it, we're bitches. So being called a bitch is a strong word for a woman."

Whatever you want to call it, there's no denying that hip hop is experiencing an unprecedented explosion of female energy. And *Hip Hop Divas* is the first attempt to recognize and celebrate that explosion by tracing it all the way back to its slow-burning fuse. Just five years ago, male record execs were still repeating the self-fulfilling prophecy that female hip hop artists don't sell records. If that assumption kept proving itself—perhaps it was simply because women had very little control over their own careers. Even those who wrote their own rhymes and picked their own wardrobes were sometimes treated like novelty acts and given smaller promotional budgets than men. With Lauryn and Missy and Mary and Eve blazing the charts *and* handling their business, the ladies are running this hip hop game like never before.

That's why it's so amazing that the contributions of women in hip hop have never been taken seriously enough to be properly documented, analyzed, and put into historical perspective. This is the first book to acknowledge the triumphs and the tribulations of the women who helped shape a worldwide pop-culture revolution long before it became a billion-dollar industry.

We're all familiar with the popular stereotype of a crotch-grabbing MC boasting about his power over the ladies. But that's only half the story. Women have been doing their thing for years—from N.Y.C. to South Carolina, where

Angie Stone and Sequence were flipping cheerleader routines into rap hits, to Los Angeles, where, as Yo Yo once put it, "In the black community, rapping is like breathing."

Still, women had to fight for their space in a culture that created so much opportunity out of so few raw materials. Brothers who'd battled racism, economic deprivation, and rival crews for their chance to grab the mike were reluctant to relax their grip when sisters tried to move the crowd. The result was that, for better or worse, many women were forced to mimic the aggressive tactics of male MCs. Check out a few early records and you'll hear female rappers battling for a place in the hip hop boys' club, many using combative raps just to get a foot in the door.

The success of Roxanne Shanté created a demand that wasn't always positive for women, and there were other forces at work, too. Shanté emerged right around the time when hip hop the culture was giving way to hip hop the business venture. Lots of men saw the potential of putting out their own honey, and soon getting ripped off, exploited—even physically and mentally abused—became par for the course. The many accomplishments of women in hip hop, this age-old gender conflict. "Free the Girls," an essay by dream hampton that explores a few manifestations of this conflict, puts the rest of the book in proper context.

Despite all the woman-haters in rap, there's always been an army of women surviving and thriving in an environment that sometimes seems resentful of their very existence. Whether rhyming, deejaying, dancing, writing graffiti, throwing parties, or running record labels, women have been a part of hip hop since day one. Their story is just beginning to be told by people like Cristina Verán, a former MC whose wide-ranging report "First Ladies" reclaims a seriously neglected chapter of our cultural history.

Even after women demonstrated that they could rock the mike, major commercial success proved elusive. It wasn't until 1993 that a single by a solo female rapper—MC Lyte's "Ruffneck"—was certified gold (half a million copies sold). But at the dawn of the 21st century, the vision of Queen Latifah's funky manifesto, "Ladies First," has become a reality. Female MCs are selling millions of records and succeeding on their own terms, raising hip hop's artistic and spiritual stakes as they make music designed to counteract racism and sexism in the music industry and society at large.

The phenomenon of the hip hop diva is still so new that few people have really stopped to think about what it takes to be a female MC. She has to be fearless and feminine, sexy and classy, assertive and approachable. It takes more guts for a lady to rock the mike than a man, and then she has to rock twice as hard just to be taken seriously. She has to know when to ignore the tired misogynist insults, and when to turn the tables. Those women who manage to find their own balance are the ones who stand the test of time.

Not that every female rapper follows the same blueprint for success. Salt-N-Pepa, the fun-loving homegirls who went on to multi-platinum success, got their start when they responded to Slick Rick and Doug E. Fresh's "The Show." MC Lyte showcased her incredible storytelling skills on her debut single, "I Cram to Understand U (Sam)." Queen Latifah's Afrocentric lyrics and images helped set off a conscious movement in hip hop. Yo Yo brought a fly-girl hottie look to the masses, but let the fellas know she was not the one to be played.

While marrying the worlds of hip hop and R&B, TLC led a girl power movement that dominated both music and fashion. Mary J. Blige, the undisputed Queen of Hip Hop Soul, made ghetto fabulous music chic and stylish. The earthy sensuality of Lauryn Hill's singing voice coupled with her amazing lyrical flow launched the Fugees and created a solo sensation. Erykah Badu's spirituality and ethereal charm—not to mention her stellar songwriting—broke down the door for a new wave of soul sisters like Jill Scott and Macy Gray whose music is infused with a hip hop sensibility, even if they don't rap.

Hardrock lyrics and a tomboy attitude gave Da Brat the first platinum album by a solo female artist. Lil' Kim, Foxy Brown, and Trina popularized the image of in-your-face sexuality and high-fashion flossing with no apologies. Kim's X-rated records, provocative outfits, and modeling contracts have helped her rival Madonna as this generation's most versatile icon of female sexuality. When she stood next to Diana Ross at the MTV music awards with lavender hair and nothing but a pasty over her exposed breast—and it was Miss Ross who clearly wanted to be down with Kim, not the other way around—it was obvious that a new day had dawned for the hip hop diva. Then came futuristic Missy Elliot, who let out a joyful *hee-ha!* and proved that you didn't have to rehash the same-old same-old to sell a ton of records. Meanwhile Eve was busy proving that an MC could tackle serious female issues like spousal abuse without losing men's interest or sounding too preachy.

And the tales of female MCs keep evolving. Nowadays, these women aren't necessarily trying to prove something to men; they're rapping for their own enjoyment, to make money, and to share what they have to say. Some of the stories in *Hip Hop Divas* are tragic, but the overall triumph is simply that the best is yet to come. No one ever said being a woman is easy, but it sure is fun.

HIP HOP
DIVAS

free the girls
Or, why I really don't believe there's much of a future for hip hop, let alone women in hip hop *by dream hampton*

THROWDOWN

I remember getting jumped at the skating rink, by, like, eight girls. It started on the carpet, where you walk on the bumper part of your skates, but quickly spilled onto the rink's slippery floor. At first it was Alexis, a pretty dark-skinned girl with breasts (I had none; still don't). She grabbed one of my two French braids and spun me toward her screaming, "Yellow bitch!"

She swung. I stepped back. She missed. Her girl Tanyetta didn't, though; she punched me dead in the eye. Terrified, I still managed to bust her lip. The 15-year-old girl, who said she was Alexis's cousin and complained in the girls' bathroom that she'd had an abortion the Friday before, hit me in the back of the head with a skate and opened my scalp. Blood poured into my eye, down my cheek, into my mouth. I was on the ground now and being stomped. My pretend cousins, my real best friend Marqueila, and Skateland's security broke through the circle and peeled my battered and bruised 11-year-old self from the floor. But it was way too late.

I knew it was coming. Andre, this beautiful ninth-grader from Detroit's Martin Luther King homes, had spent the past three Saturdays trying to teach me to skate backwards. He had expensive skates and long pretty Jheri curls. I helped him write his book reports and he told me stories of all the girls he "messed with." He'd point them out while we were skating. "See that girl with the big ass?" (I didn't have one; still don't.) "She sucked my dick last night." Andre didn't turn me on; he couldn't even spell. I just wanted to be held up while I learned how to skate backwards. I was still playing with Barbies. I'm still mad at these bitches. When I cut my hair short, there is the raised scar at the crown of my skull from that skate.

I had another friend, Darius, who also had a long Carefree Curl, and used to drive a cherry-red moped. He was murdered in 1986. He would strap a giant boombox to his bike and give me rides to and from the arcade. His mother's boyfriend was from Harlem and he'd bring mix tapes of rap music back to Detroit for Darius's box. I remember the

morning he came over with this "battle rap" between Sparky D and Roxanne Shanté. They sounded as if they were in the same room but Sparky D called Shanté a crab-ass bum and accused her of giving her man fleas and gonorrhea. Shanté called her half-ass white, fat, and accused her of having a pussy that was "through" and getting fucked in the ass. Sparky came back with rhymes about Shanté being too damn black with hair that would never grow.

The girls on my block, some of whom had stepped to my defense at Skateland, loved Darius's new jam. They dubbed it and played it over and over again. Sometimes a dis from the song would make its way into our neighborhood arguments, like the time Stephanie called Naomi a crab-ass bum. One time India told me to "shut the fuck up, you half-ass white." I couldn't call her too damn black with hair that would never grow. I didn't even choke on the comeback—it never came.

I hated the way my girlfriends talked to each other, even then. In John Hughes movies the girls were scheming and cruel, but they had nothing on my friends. We were violent and abusive with one another, our deep self-hatred as visible as the tribal identification marks of a far-flung clan. We all, each and every one of us, learned to hang with boys instead, to say things like "girls ain't shit"; "you can't trust 'em." Some of us came back to our preadolescent selves, to become loving and trusting women. Some of us didn't.

SHOW STOPPA

Because they wore coordinating outfits three to four times a week for four straight years, Kenya and Shannon had to split the "Best Dressed" award in twelfth grade. In the back of the high school yearbook they are wearing twin outfits and posing in lunge positions with their hands on their hips. They're each wearing gold chains that spell the other's name. They didn't know each other before freshman year, but they sort of fell in love in Spanish class and have been best friends ever since.

When U of M turned Kenya down, Shannon forfeited her own admission and they both went to Spelman. Shannon's mom was so pissed. They pledged Delta together but their line was all fucked up when this girl died from a car crash. The school blamed it on relentless rushing. Kenya met this Morehouse boy from Queens and fell deeply in love. He spray-painted his tag on her dorm wall, then went to jail for two days when the campus guards caught him trying to sneak out of Kenya and Shannon's room with Krylon and dirty fingers.

On a trip to Lenox Mall Shannon saw Kenya's boyfriend from Queens kissing this girl from Texas and walked right up to them both and slapped the shit out of the girl. Kenya dropped the boy two hours later. They had each other's back like that.

When they attended the Al B. Sure! concert Al himself had arena security invite them backstage. He asked Shannon straight out if she wanted to fuck and she really wanted to, but Kenya gave her a look that said, "We would be so over—so *very* over—if you played yourself right now." They had each other's back like that.

Before graduating they organized a talent bazaar/charity event for a shelter that housed runaway girls. They performed "Push It" and wore matching unitards and slid under each other's legs just like Salt-N-Pepa did in their video. Shannon went to Parsons School of Design in New York for graduate school and because Kenya was unsure of her plans, she followed Shannon.

Kenya married a guy who played for the NBA a year later and Shannon designed fur coats for rappers and ball players. When Kenya's husband got some cheerleader pregnant just three weeks before she was to deliver their first baby, Shannon drove to Jersey, packed her best friend's things and moved her and her soon-come infant daughter into her one bedroom. They have each other's back like that.

BONNIE AND CLYDE

She used to be so fly, the first girl in Detroit with her own Benz. Candy-apple red and convertible, with customized plates that spelled CASH. She bought red boots to match. Red riding boots. Red Gucci boots. Red gator boots with a 24-karat gold-plated heel. She dyed her hair burgundy and had it cut into a deep asymmetrical. She modeled in the national salon competition and was on the local news when her hairdresser brought home first prize—a bronzed head with a bob. Her man was only 19 years old, but he'd opened I-95, which in the '80s became known as "Cocaine Lane," further than any other cat in the city. They say he had houses from the southwest side of Detroit to Liberty City, a neighborhood just north of where he copped his weight in Miami.

She liked to make that trip back then. She could drive all the way without stopping (he never did like to drive long distances), but he'd keep her awake with promises about the next forty years.

They were best friends. She still says that. She's eighty pounds heavier from serving 12 years of Fed time and she still calls him her best friend. She's proud of the fact that she never snitched. Doesn't seem suspicious that he served 18 months, went home, and has forgotten to put money on her books for the past 10 years. "My life is like a movie, girl. You want something to write, you should write this down." She has a girlfriend on the inside and they pass the credit card numbers they catch as telemarketers to "boosters" on the outside. I'm here to thank her for the mink she sent my godmother. She wants to talk about the '80s. How live it was. "People don't say 'live' anymore," I tell her, slightly annoyed. She wants me to remember the shopping sprees, her trips to Vegas, that flawed trip to Bogota. I remind her of her best friend who was shot in the face when she opened her apartment door, back in '90. "Mimi's daughter is pregnant," I tell her. She seems surprised that ninth-graders are still getting pregnant.

She brags that the outfit Lil' Kim was wearing on *Access Hollywood* is exactly like the one she was wearing when she got arrested. She mentioned this once already, in a letter she sent two years ago about how these little girls like Kim are rhyming about her life, about how I should do an article on her in VIBE, about how her man would've never put her on fucking Greyhound with weight. How that was beneath her even now. "But now you're wearing khaki," I tell her, "a color you hate." She accuses me of being a player hater. "People don't say that anymore," I deadpan. "Fuck you," she hisses, as she stands up, ending the visit, and gets in line to be strip-searched.

SUCKER DJS (I WILL SURVIVE)

LeShaun's from Brownsville, and she never had romantic delusions about the ghetto. She hated it and wanted out. She'd been rhyming since she could lace her shoes and a couple of times it seemed like her ticket. In 1988, a year before she had a baby boy with Sammy B from the Jungle Brothers, she had an underground smash called "Doin' It (Wild Thang)." Hers was a lilting voice that sounded sweet when she spit nasty rhymes about rough sex. When Queen Latifah and her partner Sha-Kim began their label Flavor Unit Records in 1991, they sought her out, and she was down with them for a couple of years.

In 1995 L.L. Cool J decided to do a remake of her song, called "Doin' It." She was asked to rap on the hook. It wasn't a big break, but it kept her in the game. She was in a good place in her personal life, too. She had been driving to West Virginia to visit an ex who was locked up there, but she'd recently met a man she loved. She became pregnant with his child, he made her his wife, and they moved to Maryland. She had dreams of being a rap star, but a life as a wife and mother in suburban Maryland—once a fantasy as remote as a platinum album—was coming true. Still she got on L.L.'s hook and she even rocked a few bars.

A few months before delivering her baby she learned L.L. had shot the video for "Doin' It," and had neglected to call. When she raised a little hell, even filed a lawsuit (which she settled out of court), L.L. went on *MTV News* and said he'd done her a favor, that she would have embarrassed herself trying to make a video pregnant. She was humiliated. In private she complained about the unfairness of it all, how hip hop had blown acceptable notions of sexy for men wide open; she invoked Biggie.

A couple of years later she'd settled into marriage and motherhood, and L.L. offered her, as an olive branch, a verse on a duet on his new album. She still loved hip hop, loved to rhyme, had been doing it for so long, she just couldn't hold a grudge. This time L.L. invited her to the video shoot. She hoped he'd ask her to do a couple of shows, too, and he did. He even invited her to appear on his following album. But no record deals followed, no press, no major breakthrough.

Foxy and Kim were doing well with the style she'd pioneered, but for LeShaun it was a constant chase. "I had to get my priorities straight. Hip hop's not my priority anymore. This game doesn't love me like I love it," she told me from her home in Maryland. "Just gotta let it go."

EPILOGUE

My daughter hates hip hop. It was our earliest battle, until she bent my will her way. Before the man I'd asked to be her godfather, Biggie, was murdered, I used to force it on her. Play it in the car while she was strapped in her car seat, in the house as she climbed in and out of cabinets. Then I stopped, because everything seemed some half-baked tribute to, or worse, appropriation of my friend's legacy.

Eminem doesn't occur to me, but even as I try to ease into a Common or dead prez moment she is intolerant. She calls rap "mean." Has a list of things she doesn't like in Kim's new video: "her hair, her lipstick, her dress." As we make our way down into the 125th Street subway station one evening after school, they are blasting an uncensored version of an X-rated song by Ludacris. "They're hurting me, Mommy," my daughter yells dramatically. "I know baby, sometimes a lot of bass in music make your chest hurt, like it's stretching."

"No," she insists. "They're hurting my feelings."

I want to tell her all the ways hip hop has made me feel powerful. How it gave my generation a voice, a context, how we shifted the pop culture paradigm. How sometimes it's a good thing to appear brave and fearless, even if it's just posturing. I want to suggest that maybe these rhymes about licking each other's asses are liberating. But I can't.

The Mercedes Ladies.

FIRST LADIES

Sweeter than honey

hotter than tea all the fly

guys wanna be with me

My friends tell me

"Ooh Sherri how did you

get to be a girl MC?"

fly females who rocked the mike in the '70s and '80s

by Cristina Verán

In 1980, my mom steered me toward hip hop's yellow brick road. I'll always remember the day she came home after her regular shift as "Betty the Hostess" at a pub in Englewood Cliffs, New Jersey, telling me she'd met the "The Sugar Hill Flash" (confusing the Gang with the Grandmaster, of course). The Bicycle Club was frequented by the two-martini-biz-lunch crowd from Route 9W's corporate campuses. But there was one customer who stood out from the blur of blue suits. Sugar Hill Records' grande dame, Sylvia Robinson—the label boss behind hip hop's first hit record, the Sugarhill Gang's "Rapper's Delight"—had begun lunching there with her prospective signees.

Robinson was just one of a growing number of female trailblazers who were instrumental in shaping hip hop from all angles, launching businesses, organizing parties, or creating new forms of dance, art, and music. Not only was there a proverbial good woman behind nearly every man, but a proud and significant number stood alongside their male peers, founding and building what would become a global culture from the ground up. Unfortunately, many of these foremothers' names went unrecorded, their talents all but unrecognized. And for every such pioneer, there were moms and even grandmothers whose encouragement emboldened their girl-child progeny to step into this world on equal footing with the fellas.

Though my mother certainly wasn't the most street-savvy of parents, she had cruised Egypt's Nile River, climbed Athens' Acropolis, and explored the Amazon jungles of my native Peru. And later on in life, as a single mother, she remained open to new experiences for her daughter. (This was the same woman whose appreciation of subway graffiti murals prompted her to buy me my own set of Uni-Wide art markers and a blackbook). Upon hearing her first-ever Flash tape that fateful day in 1980, she announced with missionary enthusiasm: "Cristina, you could do this, too!"

From then on, basketball, roller-skating, and, yes, even Menudo had to step aside as beats and rhymes took over my 11-year-old life.

Though I would eventually become a proud member of some of hip hop's most renowned groups, including Afrika Bambaataa's Zulu Nation, the graffiti artists collective TC5, and the dance-defining Rock Steady Crew, this chica first claimed hip hop humbly, with a neighborhood crew, a tattered college-ruled notebook, and a brain chock full o' rhymes. In those days, hip hop was all about dedication—you didn't just listen to the music, you lived it, rhymed to it, danced to it, sometimes even painted to it. Long before stylists, A&R reps, and publicists oh-so-carefully prepackaged rappers' public personas, it was love—for the culture, not money—that made this world go 'round.

My first struggle as a young MC was to find the right name to claim fame. I tried out "Vee-Ski," playing off my last initial, then "Cris Tee," for my first name. But I finally settled on Sweet Cee—a name I admittedly bit from an otherwise unimpressive tag scrawled on the corner of 175th and Fort Washington Avenue, in my Washington Heights 'hood. After all, "Sweet" *was* the translation of my Spanish nickname "Dulce," so I figured it was meant to be. I joined with my ninth-grade homegirls—Puerto Rican princesa Yvette "E-V Ski" Peña and tough but cute Irish-Italian Anne "Analdi" Walsh. We christened ourselves The Flygirls 3.

I patterned my style on the harmonizing routines of Grandmaster Caz and the Cold Crush Brothers, who cleverly grafted rhymes onto popular songs, jingle melodies, and fly original tunes. Make no mistake, I didn't want to *date* Caz—who was at least eight years older than me, anyway—I wanted to *be* Caz, to channel his sublime flow. One night when my girls and I were supposed to go to a big Cold Crush jam, they backed out at the last minute. My mom saw me crying and actually offered to go to the show with me. I was too embarrassed to take her up on it, but two things strike me about that now. First, my mom was cooler than I gave her credit for. And second, there was a time when hip hop actually was something that a mother and daughter could share.

A typical Sweet Cee/TF3 verse: "Party people, just tell me what's on your mind / Our style's so def, our words so fresh, just listen up to this rhyme / These words tell the story of our fame, fortune, and glory sending other MCs to their grave / Just sit tight, it's all right, listen to the music and you will become its slave." Of course, before we could *really* conquer the competition—to say nothing of fame or fortune—we needed a DJ.

After trying out too many wanna-be beatmeisters to mention, I connected with DJ Buddah Bless—who's now better known as TKae Mendez, the renowned recording engineer who's made hits and built sound labs for a host of hip hop headliners, including Wu-Tang Clan. Back in the day, the Mendez family's cramped apartment on 102nd Street and Central Park West was the gathering spot for notable uptown (and mostly Latino) MCs and DJs like Jay Fresh, Harry O, MC Courtland, Spanish Flash, Cee Jay, and Kurt Work—among many others. TKae's room accommodated the set of hulking wooden bunk beds he shared with his b-boy brother Larry, plus two turntables and stacks of milk crates full of 12-inches. The only decorative touches were Zulu beads (representing hip hop solidarity, *not* gang affiliations) and jam flyers haphazardly tacked to the walls. On the regular, as many as 10 guys would be perched on every available surface while TKae manned his Roland "Dr. Rhythm" drum machine and primitive 4-track recorder. Heads were already in there waiting for an at-bat when I—fearless 15-year-old that I was—reached through the iron security bars to bang on the street-level window, yelling, "Let me in! I'm an MC, too!"

A musical partnership and life-long friendship ensued from there, along with a series of *almost* record deals. The most memorable near-miss had to be the time some slimy, middle-aged label exec proposed that my 16-year-old self "spread the legs" to secure a deal. My boys threatened violence; I just told him to #%$ off.

Though my hopes for a recording contract never came to fruition, I wasn't really in the game for that. For me, it was about rhyming, about "going for what you know" and standing proud—period. I had always resisted the sidelined cheerleader roles many girls all too readily embraced. Admittedly, I aspired to the standards of style and skill set by male MCs—but that was before I heard the self-possessed poetics of a young woman named Lisa Lee. Too young to have witnessed her glorious reign over Bronx park jams in the 1970s, I felt Miss Zulu Queen speak to my MC soul from a

crackling nth-generation dubbed tape blaring from some now-forgotten homeboy's boombox in the West Bronx's Roberto Clemente Park.

It went a little something like this:

Success is the place I'm headed for
As the best MC, with rhymes galore
Swimmin' like a fish and flyin' like a bird
I got the best sound, y'all fly guys heard
I have the party in action to my satisfaction
'Cause everybody knows I'm the main attraction
I'm the girl of the world, in all the boys' dreams
And when I rock on the mike, you know they'll scream.

I snatched the tape before the kid knew what hit him (if you're reading this, sorry!). But I simply could not get enough. I was more than just a passive listener to hip hop, and finally I knew I wasn't the only woman who felt that way. But until that moment, I'd never really *thought* about female MCs before. I never stopped to consider their relative rarity and the impact they could make as women in a scene that was starting to feel a bit like a boys' club. And so, though I was already a fan of the Funky 4 + 1 More, it was only after my Lisa Lee epiphany that I finally heard—really *heard*—Sha Rock.

She started rapping in 1976, when Ford was battling Carter in the presidential race and folks were celebrating the Bicentennial of the American Revolution, oblivious to the cultural revolution taking shape in the outer boroughs of New York City. As a fresh-faced teenager, Sharon Jackson would go to parties where DJ Kool Herc was developing a style of music upon which people had yet to bestow the name hip hop.

After classes at Evander Childs High off Gunhill Road in the north Bronx (a school from which many hip hop progenitors emerged), she began writing rhymes of her own, becoming a pioneer before folks knew exactly what it was they were pioneering. This movement was still so new that just being an MC was novel enough—let alone being a girl in that role. A popular DJ from the area named Breakout invited Sha to join a new group that was being formed, and she proudly joined MCs Lil' Rodney Cee, Keith Keith, and a pre–Furious Five Rahiem. Evoking comic book superhero forces, they called themselves the Funky Four, and when their numbers increased (joined by the original Jazzy Jeff—*not* Will Smith's DJ partner—and, later, KK Rockwell), they became the Funky 4 + 1 More.

Sha Rock gained attention not only as a rare hi-profile female, but also for her command of early hip hop technology: the mighty echo chamber. She used the device to double up the end words of her rhyme stories: "I have this book from A to Z-*Z* / It's a little black book that belongs to me-*me* / It has your name, your number, and your address too-*too* / So when I want to talk, I just call up you-*you* . . ." The effect was sheer magic.

As the Funky four progressed in skill and notoriety, they started headlining at legendary clubs like the T Connection and Harlem World while still braving verbal throwdowns at park jams and community centers. "That's how I got to meet Lisa Lee," recalls Sha Rock. "Because the Funky Four had performed with Afrika Bambaataa and them at Bronx River." While some folks tried to provoke a rivalry between the two leading female MCs, they chose to form a friendship instead, occasionally tossing the mike back and forth at parties—all in fun—even as their crews battled on. Their harmonic convergence stood in stark contrast to the endless combat that became the model for female rap careers in years to come.

In 1979, the Funky 4 + 1 More's first single "Rappin' & Rockin' the House"—clocking in at an astounding 15 minutes—was released on Enjoy Records, but after an unsatisfactory experience with that label, the group left in search of greenbacks and greener pastures. Sha Rock recalls the group's excitement at being courted by the Sugar Hill label. "We went out to Jersey, to their offices, and when we saw the mansion Sylvia Robinson had, the cars that she drove, we thought, 'Man! That could be *us* one day.'" The group would deliver several years' worth of hits for this label, from "Do You Wanna Rock" to "Feel It."

The Funky 4 + 1 More was among the first hip hop acts to throw down "downtown," blasting off at Manhattan venues like the Mudd Club and the Ritz, which were filled with an eclectic mix of bohemian hipsters and punk rockers. "Our group was really the first to introduce hip hop to the white media," Sha asserts, citing *Village Voice* reporters who gave the crew props in their pages. In 1981, at the behest of Blondie's Debbie Harry, they performed their song "That's the Joint" on *Saturday Night Live*, thus becoming the first hip hop act to rock on national TV.

They always represented with style and class. "We presented a Gladys Knight and the Four Tops image," says Sha. "The guys wore suits, matching what I had on. If I wore a pink fur, they would match it with, say, a burgundy and white outfit." But like their Sugar Hill Records labelmates, the female rap trio Sequence (featuring MC Angie B, long before she became an R&B star as Angie Stone), the Funky 4 + 1 More usually had to pay for their own costumes out-of-pocket. Today's mandatory rap star perks—personal stylists, per diems, and high-fashion freebies—were still a long

way off. In fact, aside from the few hundreds they would make doing shows, Sha says they received relatively little reward for their groundbreaking careers.

In 1984, Sha Rock persuaded Sylvia Robinson to allow her to perform in the Harry Belafonte–produced movie *Beat Street*. With a newly formed all-girl trio called Us Girls, Sha joined old friends Lisa Lee—already a film veteran, having kicked a few rhymes in Charlie Ahearn's 1982 masterwork *Wild Style*—and Debbie Dee, whom Sha recalls as the first female who "really held it down as a solo artist" (she's now a preacher). *Beat Street* showcased three other notable hip hop women as well: Rock Steady b-girl Baby Love, DJ Wanda Dee, and then-rapper Brenda K. Starr, who gave Mariah Carey her first break as a backup singer, and is now a star in the salsa arena.

Though things seemed to be looking up for Sha Rock after *Beat Street*, the movie marked the beginning of the end. Neither Us Girls nor the Funky 4 (plus or minus one more) would survive past '85.

Of course, Sha wasn't the only girl who could rock. Her Evander High schoolmate, Sherri Sher, had begun having similar aspirations, inspired by Grandmaster Flash jams that took place in a schoolyard on 165th and Boston Road. At the time, teen life was all about hang-out crews, the self-organized social clubs that replaced local gangs. Sherri recalls all-female crews like the Red Devils, the Sisters Disco, and the Uptown Crew. "We were real independent and we didn't just want to be attached to a male crew," she says of her own emerging clique. "We wanted to start our own empire."

Representing for the world, they adopted the typical team uniform of homemade sweatshirts with iron-on letters spelling their chosen moniker, in this case, THE MERCEDES YOUNG LADIES. After some prompting by scratch-inventor Grand Wizard Theodore and his group the L Brothers, Sherri Sher and company made history in 1977. "We became the first all female MC and DJ crew *ever*," says Sherri, still beaming with pride almost a quarter of a century later. Their original roster included Ever Def, Zena Z, Tracey T, DJ Baby D, and RD Smiley—later joined by the L Brothers' lone sister, MC Smiley, and DJ La Spank.

"The guys out there didn't exactly welcome us with open arms," Sherri admits. With the notable exception of Afrika Bambaataa and the Zulus, she says, "they were on that male ego thing." The Ladies endured repeated attempts to sabotage their shows. One memorable fiasco took place during a gig at midtown Manhattan's Hotel Diplomat. They were onstage in their cowgirl hats, white shirts, and boots, ready to get busy. "DJ Baby Dee went to start it off with a *zigga-zigga,*" Sherri recalls, "but the turntables' connection cut off. Then, when we were about to start rhyming, our mikes cut off, too. We were left standing there and the crowd was booing us." But thanks to Baby D's tech knowledge, the night was saved, and they won the party people over with rhymes like, "We're the M-E-R, C-E-D-E-S / The girls you know with the most finesse."

Outdoor gigs in sketchy 'hoods meant braving not only the elements of nature, but also the local criminal element. While many rap crews traveled with security—the Brothers Disco, for instance, had Funky Four's back—the Mercedes Ladies handled their own problems. "Once there was even a shoot-out during the middle of our performance," Sherri Sher remembers. "But we just kept rhyming through it all. We wasn't no punk girls. We came strapped ourselves—for our own protection."

Sherri had other ways of protecting herself, too. She was always deflecting romantic overtures—often from some of the same ego-amped male peers who tried to undermine their performances. "I never dated any of those rappers who were around me," she insists. "A lot of them were stupid to me, not real boyfriend material."

Getting your dollar-due in those early days—never easy for any MC crew—could be particularly difficult for the girls in the game. When the Mercedes Ladies performed on the bill with contemporaries like the Furious Five or Dr. Jeckyll & Mr. Hyde (featuring future record exec Andre Harrell), Sherri Sher says they often got shortchanged. "Everyone else got paid," she recalls, "but we would have to almost fight the promoters or try to beat up our manager for it." When one promoter had the audacity to hand the group seven measly dollars after a show, they turned adversity into art. "Seven and a quarter and a penny to our name," Sherri once rhymed, "tryin' to put Mercedes in the Hall of Fame." But it wasn't always possible to make light of their troubles. "We used to be crying after the shows," Sherri says, "because we worked hard and we rocked the crowd, but we never got what they promised."

At one point, a fledgling mogul named Russell Simmons put the girls in the studio to record "Yes You Can-Can," an update on the Pointer Sisters classic. "We were really excited," says Sherri, "but then he gave the song to Allyson Williams, to sing instead of rap. That just crushed us." Besides the background vocals they contributed to "Don's Groove" by Donald D. (not to be confused with the Zulu

King/Rhyme Syndicate rapper of the same name) and DJ Hollywood, the Ladies never claimed their own piece of wax for posterity. While their work is still available on the vintage cassette market, like so many other key trailblazers in the evolution of hip hop, they never received anywhere close to the compensation they deserved. Then they watched as future generations of rap chicks purchased real Benzes reaping what the Mercedes Ladies had sown. "We came from the 'hood and we *more* than paid our dues," Sherri emphasizes. "But we never got our chance."

For Bronx-bred b-girl Pebblee Poo, it was breakin'—not makin' records—that begat her involvement in hip hop. She and her all-female dance group, the Non-Stop Crew, won Junior High School 122 talent shows and battled rivals at Kool Herc's Echo Park parties. The Poo earned a rep for taking no shorts from the get-go.

Rap seeped into her psyche during high school science periods, when classmates traded rhymes while banging beats on the desks. With persistent encouragement from a local MC called Dr. Bombay, Pebblee was persuaded to try her luck in the informal verbal jousting. "I started writing rhymes on these little scraps of paper," she says. "When I finally showed these things to him and my friends, they told me, 'Go on girl!'"

Spurred by her friends' support, Pebblee Poo proved she had skills and soon set her sights on conquering the scene thriving across the East River in Moneymakin' Manhattan. She had other motives for making the trek, too. Among them: "to look at the cuties." Though her own brother, DJ Master Don, was already an established hip hop icon with his crew the Death Committee, Pebblee was determined to go for hers without a hint of nepotism. She found her first real opportunity when she went to a party at the Frederick Douglass Projects on Manhattan's Upper West Side, where Mixmaster André and the Untouchables held court. Impressing the fellas with an impromptu turn at the mike, Pebblee was invited to join the pack—and accepted.

At the behest of Mixmaster André, Pebblee Poo eventually entered a big female rap contest at Mr. Cee's nightclub in Harlem. The $1,000 grand prize attracted contestants from all N.Y.C. boroughs and as far away as South Carolina. It just so happened that Harlem's own MC Missy D—a would-be rival of the Poo—was in the house by the time Pebblee entered, incognito-style. "Missy was always making statements to my brother that she could take me out," Pebblee remembers with a chuckle.

When 59 entrants had already taken their turns on the mike, the unsuspecting hosts, Ravon and Johnny-Wah, read the next name on the list in disbelief. "Ahhhhhhh shit," they shouted, "Pebblee Poo! It's gonna be on now!" Everybody in the house crowded to the front of the stage.

After a few perfunctory mike checks, Pebblee began: "One for the treble, two for the bass, come on André, let's rock this place!" He dropped the needle on her anthem—Cheryl Lynn's "Got to Be Real"—and Pebblee tore it up. "When he played that shit," she recalls, "I just went off." The crowd was screaming as she erupted with battle rhymes like: "I'm the queen with the crown and on the throne I sit / So you low-class peasant, get off my shit / I have to push this issue, yes it must be said / You could never be the Poo, so get it out of your head . . . "

No sooner had her turn ended than MC Missy D stepped to the stage with her DJ, Mr. Freeze, by her side. "She must have waited, wanting to go after me," Pebblee remembers thinking. And the crowd was impressed by her rival's set. "Don't get me wrong," Pebblee Poo says, "people were definitely feeling Missy."

Everyone anxiously awaited the announcement of a winner, but the first round was declared a tie, forcing them to go at it again. To switch up the pace, André changed the record to the Whole Darn Family's classic "Seven Minutes of Funk," yielding similar results. "I went off with that, too," Pebblee boasts. "The crowd lost their minds." She won, she believes, because of her worthy challenger's tactical error: when Missy D came back on, "she just did the exact same rhymes as before, with the same old record."

Though Pebblee only received half of the promised jackpot, the 16-year-old champion was happy with her $500, and returned home excitedly to the apartment she shared with her strict grandmother. "But she didn't want to hear about any battle," Pebblee recalls, imitating her granny's gravely voice: *You better battle your ass home by ten o'clock next time!* She presented her elder with a crumpled wad of dead presidents, but Grandma was unmoved: *Don't you stand there and tell me no lie. What boy gave you this money?* Who could blame the woman for being skeptical in those days before rappers sold soda pop on TV? "It was very hard to get her to believe there really was money out there like that."

As her rep and her raps grew stronger, Pebblee was approached after a performance at a skating rink by none other than Kool Herc, who offered her a chance to get down with his Herculords crew. (The Herculords, it should be noted, would later feature another female rapper named Sweet N Sour.) Though torn by loyalty to the Untouchables, Pebblee eventually cast her lot with Herc and returned to her original Bronx turf.

Wherever she went, Pebblee was blessed with a boyfriend who offered both encouragement and protection. "My first love was B.O.," she says of the Zulu King who was by her side for every show—and who was murdered years later. "He would always be screaming out, 'That's my girl! Do it baby!' " she recalls fondly. "We were like Bonnie and Clyde."

When her brother Don's group, reconfigured as the Masterdon Committee, was ready to throw down on wax, he finally persuaded Pebblee to make rap a family affair. When they took on top competitors of the day like the Crash Crew and Fantastic Five, Pebblee always made an impression—and not just for her rhymes. "I couldn't just look like one of the fellas," she says, describing the risqué (by 1983 standards) costume she adopted. "In one of the routines, I would be like, 'Ooh, it's hot in here,' she recalls, "and I would start to pull up this black dress I had on." Underneath was a gold-sequined outfit with matching shoes. "We weren't taking off our clothes *for real* like some girls do today, though."

The Poo's biggest claim to fame remains her snappy 1985 single "A Fly Guy." She says she was approached by Profile Records with the idea of recording an answer to "A Fly Girl" by the Boogie Boys. "They wanted to sign me as an individual artist for just that one record," Pebblee says. But she stayed true to her crew, and at her insistence, she says, "they wound up signing my whole group."

The First Ladies of the '70s and '80s were not limited to New York. West Philly's Lady B credits former 76ers guard World B. Free with introducing her to hip hop. "World and his friends all used to listen to these Kool Herc tapes," recalls the MC turned radio jock. She began rolling with the basketball star on visits to his old stomping grounds in buckwild Brownsville, Brooklyn. "At the projects on Pitkin Avenue, I'd see DJs on the turntables and hear World and them rapping," she says, "so I would grab the mike, too." While her hometown already had a rich history in the graffiti element of hip hop culture, Lady B became instrumental in transporting and popularizing other elements to Philly, especially the dance. By 1980, she was beginning to host her own breakin' competitions at area clubs.

That's when she was approached by Philadelphia radio personality Perry Johnson, who convinced her to take rhyming seriously, and brought her to T.E.C. Records. Eager to cash in on what they considered a hot fad, the label signed a deal with B, making "To the Beat Y'All" in 1980. "I took all the rhymes I knew," she recalls, "put them on three-by-five cards, and stuck those on this big board, arranging and rearranging them all night to decide which rhyme flowed better after the other." The track was completed in just one take.

"I was the one and only female here to jump on wax, to be in the game like that," she says. And the good times were very good. She earned $1,000 for her first big show—sharing the bill with Luvbug Starski at N.Y.C.'s Harlem World club, followed by gigs in Boston, Connecticut, and Upstate New York. "I rented hotel rooms just for me and my friends to go swimming," she says, "rented a car, and even bought some dookey-dope earrings."

But while shows brought in a decent income, the record label was less than forthcoming with Lady B's royalties. "I went down there with a can of black paint and sprayed it all over the office," she recounts, "all the way down the steps and on the pretty bright yellow walls. I kicked over a desk and even knocked over the water fountain." The stunt didn't help her get paid, but she says she didn't know what else to do: "That was my seventeen-year-old mentality at the time."

As the hip hop quake kept rattling Philly, Lady B saw her local fame grow and looked for ways to branch out. Spotting an opportunity, she applied for the newly vacated music director position at the jazz and blues radio station WHAT-FM. Once she got the job, she started fighting to get her favorite

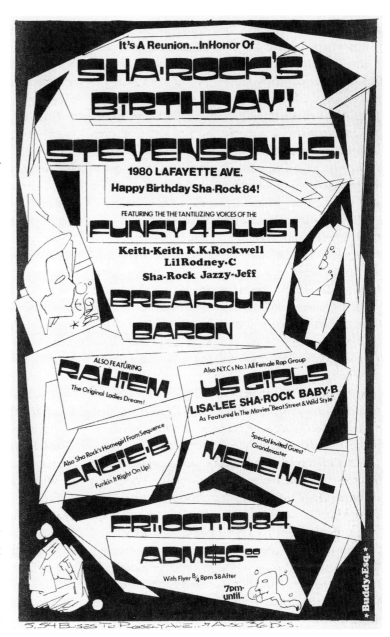

music some airtime. "I begged them to let me play stuff like Sugarhill Gang and Flash on the air," she says, "but they thought I was crazy." Sensing her determination, the station did acquiesce to B's pleas and eventually gave her a weekly slot. Her pay gradually increased from $65 to $560 a week, and the show allowed her to bring New York groups down to Philly. "Everybody came to do gigs for me, from the Treacherous Three to Soulsonic Force," B says. "And the rappers and DJs from here got more and more serious about everything."

The radio program also allowed her to bust on-air rhymes like: "When I die, they'll bury me deep / Lay two turntables at my feet / Put the mixer up near my head / So when you close the casket, I could rock the dead."

When people ask Lady B what she's proudest of achieving during two decades as an MC, radio host, and hip hop ambassador, she points not to her own accomplishments, but to the example she set for others. "I've helped little girls to have some pride in themselves," she says.

Brooklyn battle queen Doreen "Sparky D" Broadnax-Piggott was dancing in the street long before the rap bug buzzed in her ear. She says the serious action took place "at this park around my way, a lil' Madison Square Garden made of concrete called The Hole." This was the place where as many as 15 dance crews from Crown Heights to Bed-Stuy—hers was the Black Uniques—would go up against each other on the regular. The BK dance battles of Sparky's youth were different from those of your typical Bronx b-girls and b-boys, where breakers focused on footwork and floor acrobatics. "We would all be doing those Jackson 5, Dancin' Machine type of dances," Sparky explains, "with six to each crew, all dressed alike."

The Dance Masters Crew, regulars at The Hole, featured a girl on the mike named MC Baby Love (not the one from Rock Steady Crew), whom Sparky describes as "very bold and a bit arrogant" with "real witty" rhymes: "She was *it* to me." But it was a chance meeting with two other girls that steered Sparky D's course from the dance floor to the microphone. One day in a project hallway she ran into Mo Ski and City Slim and they asked her to become a part of their budding group, the Playgirls.

After-school hours were spent at one another's cribs writing rhymes and routines. A fortuitous meeting with DJ Spyder D at Powerplay Studios brought the three of them the opportunity to record a 12-inch single together called "Sophisticated Ladies (of the '80s)." The stage shows they were soon doing at clubs like The Encore in Queens and The Funhouse in Manhattan—alongside such illustrious names as Kurtis Blow, Run-DMC, and Whodini—were both sophisticated *and* streetwise. "We were bold and raw on the mike," she says, "but still *ladies,* you know."

As the spotlight grew hotter, only Sparky proved to possess the dedication hip hop demands, and the Playgirls broke up. Her solo MC career took off when she and DJ Spyder D heard Roxanne Shanté's historic dis record "Roxanne's Revenge" on the radio. "Spyder looked at me and said, 'Doreen, that's it!'" The very next day, they went into the studio and made the hard-hitting "Sparky's Turn (Roxanne You're Through)." She gives all credit to her DJ, who was then filling the role of boyfriend as well as producer. "Without Spyder, there'd be no Sparky," she says humbly. "He put my own career before his."

Overnight the battle lines were drawn on local radio airwaves. It was all about Sparky D, DJ Red Alert, and the Kiss-

FM crew versus Shanté, Marley Marl, and 'BLS. "Shanté and myself were like Muhammad Ali and Joe Frazier," Sparky recalls. "We took this thing *very* seriously, pullin' no punches." But today she bears her former rival no ill will: "She was damn good, I give her that."

Notoriety from the Roxanne rivalry earned Sparky D the first commercial endorsement by a female MC, for Mountain Dew. She went on to release a string of popular singles, including her Red Alert dedication, "He's My DJ," and "Throwdown," wherein she slashed competitors with threats to "extract the wack, take all the toys back / Grab all the duck MCs and make 'em go quack."

As fierce as the competitive posture she projected on stage was, Sparky's actions offstage bespoke an essence of womanist solidarity. She says she made sure that her female peers of the day—"including Sweet Tee, who I didn't even know at the time"—were always on the guest list at her gigs. And when she shared the bill with Salt-N-Pepa for one of their first major shows, she says they came to her asking for help. "I went over to their hotel room and just showed them what to do onstage," she recalls.

Remaining truer to the mores of hip hop than of capitalism, Sparky's loyalty to the crew who launched her dream was unshakable. "When I started making loot on my own, pulling down $3,600 for a 25-minute show," Sparky D maintains, "I made a point to always give the Playgirls money, even though we had broken up."

Not everybody had the support of a crew to lean on in hard times. Sweet Tee—who was actually the second (though better known) rapper to use that name—began her hip hop career as a sort of MC-for-hire, sought after by top producers and DJs to appear on their projects. She says she was inspired to pick up the mike by the girls who held sway during jams at Southside Queens' Forty Projects. "They didn't take it to the level of trying to record it or anything," she says, "but one girl, Double G, wrote the first rap that ever came out of my mouth."

After her own name began appearing on flyers around the way, Sweet Tee and her homegirl went to Davy DMX's house. The popular DJ invited Tee to get down on his soon-to-be hit, "One for the Treble," on which she would adopt a faux Brit accent. Of the tour that followed the single's release, Tee recalls, "The guys were running around the streets all wild, having sex in the hotel hallways." It was an eye-opening introduction to the rap-on-the-road game, but she emphasizes that as an artist, she was always respected. "Davy made it clear to everyone, 'You're not gonna be fuckin' with these young girls in my show!'" Tee recalls. "I loved him for that."

Other offers ensued, with all sorts of folks urging Tee to

get back into the studio and record a follow-up to her first song. "I never had to work that hard or go searching for opportunities," she says. "They came to me." She just happened to live on the same block as the pioneering female mouth-percussionist K-Love, who began her beat-box breakdown on the Bad Boys' big "Inspector Gadget" record with a brief introduction: "I'm short and sassy, my love's divine / My name is K-Love and I'll blow your mind." It was K-Love's manager who brought Tee her next recording opportunity. Jumping into the mid-'80s answer-track fracas, she joined a short-lived group called the Glamour Girls just long enough to record "Oh Veronica," a prefabricated response to the Bad Boys' next hit, the skeezer-dissin' gem "Veronica, Veronica." By this time the female answer-record formula was so dependable, it paid to plan your own responses in advance.

Tee's first single on the solo tip came about through a collaboration with rap Svengali Hurby Azor for Profile Records—a deal that she insists happened in "ten minutes." The first time Sweet Tee and her then DJ Jazzy Joyce performed "It's My Beat" was in 1986, at the legendary Latin Quarter nightclub near Times Square. "The place was so crowded that they asked us to come back again the following week," she recalls. When they returned, pulling up triumphant in a stretch limousine, the line of eager fans stretched around the corner and all the way down the block. By this time, she says, "the club was already packed to capacity."

Tee went on to tour with the likes of Big Daddy Kane and L.L. Cool J, impressing male and female fans with her spunky raps and her signature steelo. Though she mostly sported casual streetwear, Sweet Tee put real thought and creativity into her getups. "I used to dress in jeans and jackets with my name painted on the backside," says the hip hop glamour queen. Her long box braids were such a trademark that, according to her, "At one point, girls actually called that style 'Sweet Tee braids.'" After putting in time as a crew member and playing the role of backup in some guy's show, Tee finally became a star in her own right. "I had a good run," she says, realizing just how fortunate she was, "and I enjoyed the run I had."

Joanne Martinez, better known as the Real Roxanne, gained fame through a tour of duty in the infamous "Roxanne wars." But she wants the world to know that her personal hip hop history predates that prefab foray with the group Full Force. This Brooklyn *boricua* bombshell was out there rocking the mic as early as 1981 under the name Dimples Love. "I used to write a lot of poetry," she explains, "and I joined this group of guys from my neighborhood called Choice Emcees, who turned my poetry into rap." At the tender age of 15, she was already trekking up to Sal Abatiello's perpetually packed Disco Fever nightclub in the Bronx to set it off. "I even won a couple of trophies there," she says with a smile.

But Martinez wasn't the first recruit for the Real Roxanne role. "Full Force and UTFO originally picked this girl Elise Jacks out of the crowd at The Funhouse and put her on the mike," she recalls. "I remember even seeing her myself at Roseland." But then Full Force member Paul Anthony, a customer at the Brooklyn diner where Martinez

waited tables, took notice. This self-described "light-skinned Puerto Rican chick with red hair" soon hooked up with DJ Hitman Howie Tee and became the red-hot mama of the Full Force family—which included UTFO along with Lisa Lisa and Cult Jam—as the final, official Real Roxanne.

The Rox seduced crowds with her sexy, hip hop harem-girl style. "A lot of the clothing I wore was sort of Egyptian," she says. "The idea for my exotic eyeliner—black Cleopatra swoops—came from *I Dream of Jeannie*." Even her signature hairstyle was inspired by Barbara Eden's character on the classic sitcom. Her brash, sultry vocals on records like "Romeo" further fueled fans' fantasies: "R— for the way I like to rock / O—outstanding, I never stop /

X−rated, devastating, understanding me is too complicating / A−action on the mike / N−for the neverending suckas that bite / N−for the next, who claims the best / E− eternally putting them to rest."

She attracted attention in other ways, too. "I was always moving around, making little hand gestures in my shows," she says. "Something with my thumb and my pinky." These harmless come-ons had an unintended effect during her first L.A. performance, when she and Full Force joined Run-DMC, Force MDs, and the Fat Boys on the mid-'80s Fresh Fest tour. As she went through her usual stage routine, she noticed people in the crowd raising their hands in the air, gesturing back at her. She was quickly yanked to the side by an exasperated promoter. "Don't do that!" he scolded. "They think you're making gang signs!" It would be a few more years before Southern California's gang signifying gained wide exposure through gangsta rap groups like N.W.A. At the time, Roxanne says she knew nothing about Crips or Bloods. Fortunately, the show went on without incident. "I felt like going out there," she recalls, "and saying, 'Look, um . . . I take that back!'"

Like other ladies who did their banging on wax, Roxanne says she never had any actual animosity toward her female MC peers. But the rivalries—often orchestrated by male producers—ensured that few friendships were formed. "They would think I was this bitch because of my rap delivery, that I actually lived my life on that type of level," she says, sounding disappointed. "I guess they believed the hype."

In 1992, Roxanne herself got caught up when she released the explicit album *Go Down . . . But Don't Bite It.* "I wasn't comfortable with the messages it was putting out," she says. All the racy raps had, in fact, been written for her by Chubb Rock. "I did it because I was under pressure," she insists. "They were *not* coming from me."

Regardless of the rhymes she recited or the clothes she wore, Roxanne broke stereotypes because of who she was. Still she admits that she "felt a lot of weird vibes at times, being the only Latina MC out there." Coming up through the hip hop scene in a downtown Brooklyn neighborhood that was "always mixed" did not protect her from skeptical loudmouths with monochrome worldviews. "At that time, some black fans felt that rap belonged only to them," she states. "But we Latinos have always been a part of this."

lso defying hip hop's media-projected color barrier was Shauna Hoodes, a.k.a. Shaunie Dee, a significant white girl in the mix during the early '80s. After spending much of her childhood in Amsterdam, she and her family returned to N.Y.C. in '79, just in time for the artistic youngster to witness subway graffiti in full bloom. Mr. Magic's

WHBI radio shows gave musical context to the culture she was eagerly embracing. As fate would have it, Shauna—who lived on West 101st Street near Rock Steady Park—would soon get down with the downest of the day, dancing with the RSC's Take 1, Buck 4, Normski, and Frosty Freeze in the video for Malcolm McLaren's now-classic "Buffalo Gals" record.

"The first time I went to The Roxy was in '82," says Shauna, who felt right at home in this former roller rink where Jean-Michel Basquiat and Madonna rubbed shoulders with hip hop kids. "I'll always remember my friend Dondi [the late graffiti artist who was featured in the film *Style Wars*] walking me all through the crowd that night announcing 'Yo, everybody! This is my lil' sister Shaunie Dee!' " The Roxy DJs even tried to put her onstage to perform, she says, "but I wasn't ready yet."

By 1985 though, Shaunie's skills were sharp enough that she dared to become the first female to compete in the New Music Seminar's epic MC Battle for World Supremacy. Her opponent was a young freakazoid named Kool Keith, of Ultramagnetic MCs fame. Although he won, she represented well—and not "just for a white girl." Later on, in the early '90s, she hosted a cable-access show called *Sho Nuff Hip Hop* (her graffiti name was "Sho 101" in honor of her block).

But neither her accomplishments nor her distinguished affiliations were enough to shield Shauna from the stinging jabs of some who followed after her. When a mutual friend introduced her to Sister Souljah at an Atlantic City music conference in the early '90s, Shaunie didn't receive the warm "sisters in hip hop" greeting she was expecting. "She just stared at me with this mussed-up face, twisted her head, then proceeded to mouth off against me, just because I was white," S-Dee recalls bitterly. "I will always remember the hurt I felt in my heart at that moment. I couldn't believe that one woman could be so hateful to another woman, just like that."

Shauna's feelings were not just hurt; her faith was shaken. Undying allegiance to a cherished culture had once brought people together across racial divides. Suddenly hip hop seemed to have lost that magical power. "Sister Souljah didn't know my history at all," says Shaunie Dee, the pain still etched in her voice, "where I had been, who I knew, what I had done for the love of this culture."

s the years went by, the disappointments continued. Without either legal representation or the experience to know what compensation songwriters and performers could expect, many of rap's first ladies accepted economic exploitation as part of "paying dues." In many cases these dues accumulated interest in the bank accounts of club owners and label execs.

But in more recent times, hip hop survivors like Pebblee Poo have armed themselves with knowledge. In 1998 Master P's platinum-selling hit "Make 'Em Say UHH!" lifted the catchy hook from the Masterdon Committee's 1982 "Funkbox Party" without so much as a shout-out on the CD liner notes, much less a share of songwriting credit. Pebblee has engaged a qualified legal team and is now taking care of business.

Old-school purists lament that what was once an insider's culture has become an internationally exploited commodity, with notions like respect for tradition and diverse creativity devalued in the process. But trailblazers like Sha Rock do try to keep an open mind about the new generation of female MCs.

"I actually got a call from Lil' Kim once," she says. "There I was at two in the morning, sleeping, and Puffy's assistant rings my house, saying, 'I got Kim on the line.'" Sha remembers asking, "Kim who?" before hearing a girlish voice say, "Hi, Sha Rock. How you doing?" When she realized who she was talking to, Sha was thrilled. "Regardless of what peo-

Lest you assume that all these hip hop heroines spend their time sitting around and waxing nostalgic, think again, for their hip hop nation repatriation is at hand. Sparky D, now a nurse by profession, is working on a new album with DJ Spyder D. The Real Roxanne—recently reunited with Full Force—is busting rhymes not only in English but *en Español,* too. Sherri Sher, an administrator at Harlem Hospital, also manages younger artists, while Sweet Tee's busy writing screenplays based on her true-life showbiz adventures. Frustrated by rap's thugged-out materialism, Shaunie Dee has forged a career in the Latin music industry, working with Marc Anthony and other salsa stars. Lady B is still one of Philadelphia's best-known radio personalities on 103.9 FM, and has cofounded an organization called Rap-Sponsibility to tag CDs with stickers praising socially responsible lyrics. And as for Pebblee Poo, who held down a job at the phone company throughout her MC career and for the past 21 years, she's recently begun working on tracks with Grandmaster Flash. When she, Sherri Sher, and Lady B showed up at a conference for

"Just because they say that sex sells, you don't have to take off all your clothes," says Pebblee Poo. "If you can rap and draw everyone's attention, you've got it made."

ple may say about her," says the veteran MC, bestowing props, "I love myself some Lil' Kim." During their conversation, Kim expressed an interest in meeting her MC elder one day, saying it would be "an honor." To Sha that feeling is clearly mutual.

But not all of hip hop's female pioneers are quite so taken with the promiscuous posturing of the rap industry's dollar-sign divas. Pebblee Poo has this advice for aspiring female MCs: "Just because they say that sex sells, you don't have to take off all your clothes. If you can rap and draw everyone's attention, if you have that 'umph,' you got it made." For this battle-tested veteran it all comes down to believing in one's own skills: "Just be yourself," she says.

Lady B joins the Poo in lamenting the rise of lingerie-clad lyricists. "I wish they had kept it as risqué as, say, Salt-N-Pepa," says the radio jock, who actually took Puff Daddy to task about Lil' Kim's image during an on-air interview. "That was the perfect mix of sexy and cute," she reminisces, "that 'I'm proud to be a woman' attitude that says, 'Hey, look at me! I'm sexy, but I'm not a slut.'"

the Hip Hop Hall of Fame in February 2001, they truly looked as fit and fabulous as they did back in their heyday, nearly two decades ago.

"Can you imagine," asks Sha Rock with a laugh, "someone's parents rapping?" But the rhymes she's recorded with her own daughter, 20-year-old MC Tee Rock—who's already opened for Guru, Doug E. Fresh, and dead prez—are no joke. The first song they did was entitled (what else?) "Like Mother, Like Daughter."

Listening to Sha Rock talk about hip hop, it's clear that her affection for the culture she discovered so long ago is as strong as ever. "Here I am, already in my late thirties, but I know I'll be fifty or eighty and still have this love for hip hop," she says. "When you grow up in it, you just don't lose it. The music stays with you."

As somebody whose mother inspired many of my own hip hop adventures, I have to agree. As long as we remember those Mistresses of Ceremony—women who gave birth to a culture and nurtured future generations of fierce MCs—the spirit of this music will stay with all of us, too.

WOMEN ON WAX *by Cristina Verán*

While names like Latifah and Lil' Kim come quickly to mind when the subject of female MCs arises, and Roxanne Shanté is widely credited as being the first solo superstar, few people recognize that not one or two, but more than *60* records came out between 1978 and 1986 that featured female MCs, DJs, and even a human beat box. Whether on the solo tip or as part of groups like Funky 4 + 1 More and the Masterdon Committee, these fly foremothers merit the same respect received by their male peers in hip hop history. You better recognize.

PAULETTE TEE AND SWEET TEE
"Vicious Rap" (Paul Winley Records, 1978)
"Rhymin' and Rappin'" (Paul Winley Records, 1979)

Born into the Winley family's Harlem-based recording empire, these school-age sisters could flow to the beat with ease, dropping the first female voices ever heard on a 12-inch rap record.

LADY B
"To the Beat Y'All" (TEC Records, 1979)

This record made one Philadelphia female into a hip hop star, which she parlayed into a successful (and still going) career as the city's on-air hostess with the mostest hip hop flavor.

AFRIKA BAMBAATAA AND THE COSMIC FORCE (FEATURING LISA LEE)
"Zulu Nation Throwdown, Vol. 1" (Paul Winley Records, 1980)

"Chitty-chitty bang-bang / We are your main thang / Listen to this song that I'm gonna sang-sang." MC Lisa truly held her own with hip hop superhero Afrika Bambaataa and Cosmic Force crewmates Prince Ikey C, Ice Ice, and Chubby Chub.

FUNKY 4 + 1 MORE (FEATURING SHA ROCK)
"Rappin' and Rockin' the House" (Enjoy, 1979)
"That's the Joint" (Sugar Hill, 1981)
"Do You Want to Rock (Before I Let Go)" (Sugar Hill, 1982)
"Feel It" (Sugar Hill, 1984)

Sha Rock was the "plus one" giving you more on the mike, catching raves from South Bronx schoolyards to NBC's *Saturday Night Live* with her winning charm and lyrics like: "I'm lookin for a fella that I can't call jive / Doin' something for himself, workin 9 to 5 / You gotta dress nice, you gotta look fine / To have Sha Rock you know I'm one of a kind."

VARIOUS ARTISTS (FEATURING SHA ROCK)
"Live Convention '81 at the T-Connection & Celebrity Club" (Disco Wax, 1981)

On this rare mixtape-on-wax pressing, Sha appears with the Harmonizing 3 on a track called "Different Strokes for Different Folks."

US GIRLS (FEATURING SHA ROCK, LISA LEE, AND DEBBIE DEE)
"Us Girls" (*Beat Street* soundtrack) (Atlantic, 1984)

Rap's first female supergroup, Us Girls combined three legends who appeared in the film and on the soundtrack to *Beat Street*. Their lyrical theme was female solidarity, a concept that seems sadly out of date in the age of bling-bling: "Us Girls are the best of friends / When one ain't got no money the other one lends."

DEBBIE DEE
"Tom, Dick, and Harry" (label unknown, 1985)

A raw record dissing run-of-the-mill, ne'er-do-well men by the former Us Girl, whom Sha Rock calls "the first solo female MC" back in the '70s.

SEQUENCE
"Funk You Up" (Sugar Hill, 1979)
"Monster Jam" (with Spoonie Gee) (Sugar Hill, 1980)
"And You Know That" (Sugar Hill, 1980)
"Funky Sound" (Sugar Hill, 1981)
"Simon Says" (Sugar Hill, 1982)
"I Don't Need Your Love" (Sugar Hill, 1982)
"Here Comes the Bride" (Sugar Hill, 1982)
"I Just Want to Know" (Sugar Hill, 1983)
"Funk You Up '85" (Sugar Hill, 1984)
"Control" (Sugar Hill, 1985)

This former singing group came to N.Y.C. from "down south" to find fame as the first rap divas on Sugar Hill. Long before Angie Stone made audiences swoon with her singing, she was MC Angie B, joining MC Blondie and Cheryl the Pearl in this sultry trio.

CHERYL THE PEARL
"Don't You Sit Back Down" (Spring, 1986)

This Sequencer's solo effort, coming too little too late in the game to cash in on her group's fame, appeared on a label founded by the family of future Loud Records honcho Steve Rifkind.

BLONDIE
"Rapture" (Chrysalis, 1981)

Yes, Blondie was a white punk band, but when Debbie Harry bigged up Fab 5 Freddy and Grandmaster Flash, rapping lyrics about painting trains and rocking parties, there could be no doubt that hip hop's crossover process had begun—*and ya don't stop.*

SILVER STAR
"Eeei-Eeei-O" (Enjoy, 1982)

Nasty, naughty nursery rhymes about Old MacDonald and the rest of his freaky farm fam from this one-shot all-girl crew.

SYLVIA
"It's Good to Be the Queen" (Sugar Hill, 1982)

Though MC-ing was not her vocation, Sugar Hill Records president Sylvia Robinson—a singer-songwriter since the 1960s—came out with this first-ever female response record to Mel Brooks's rap novelty "It's Good to Be the King." Given her stature at the hit-making label, Mrs. Robinson can truly be called the first queen of the rap biz.

DONALD D. (FEATURING MERCEDES LADIES)
"Don's Groove" (Elektra, 1984)

After years of rocking live shows, the ladies represented—as background vocalists—on this jam by a male rapper (not to be confused with the Zulu King and erstwhile Ice-T cohort of the same name).

MASTERDON COMMITTEE
"Funk Box Party" (Enjoy, 1982)
"Musicgram" (Enjoy, 1984)
"Funkbox Party II" (Profile, 1985)

Pebblee Poo was the sister of the late Harlem DJ Master Don, and a sometime member of the Committee, who shines on these three cuts. "Funk Box" was making the crowds say "Uhh, na-nah na-naaaah" 15 years before Master P took a big bite of their style.

PEBBLEE POO
"A Fly Guy" (Profile, 1985)

This takin'-no-shorts reply to the Boogie Boys hit "A Fly Girl" was Pebblee's only release as a solo artist.

BEE SIDE
"Change the Beat" (featuring Fab 5 Freddy) (Celluloid, 1982)
"The Wildstyle" (with Afrika Bambaataa) (Time Zone, 1983)

Dripping with savoir-faire, this artsy white chick (aka Ann Boyle) rhymed in French for these early electro–hip hop hits.

DIMPLES DEE
"Sucker DJs (I Will Survive)" (Partytime, 1983)

This no-nonsense Queens MC was down with Marley Marl back in the day, joining forces with the super-DJ/producer to create their first track on wax: "I'm 5 foot five, stayin' alive / In this world Dimples Dee will sure enough survive."

MAIN ATTRACTION (FEATURING DIMPLES DEE, CHINA DOLL, AND PARADISE)
"Masters of the Scratch" (with the Fearless Four's DJs O.C. and Crazy Eddie) (Next Plateau, 1984)
"Lost for Words" (Easy Street, 1985)

Dimples' all-female crew Main Attraction came out on two vinyl releases showcasing their bubbly, harmonizing compositions, but lack of promotional support kept them from achieving greater renown.

THE PLAYGIRLS
"Our Picture of a Man" b/w "Sophisticated Ladies (of the '80s)" (Sutra, 1984)

This brazen trio from the projects of Brownsville, Brooklyn—Sparky D, Mo Ski, and City Slim—rocked the mike to the delight of the patrons at legendary clubs like The Funhouse and The Roxy.

SPARKY D

"Sparky's Turn (Roxanne You're Through)" (Nia, 1985)
"Sparky D vs. The Playgirls" (Nia, 1985)
"He's My DJ (Red Alert)" (Nia, 1985)
"Throwdown" (Nia, 1985)

This girl was no joke. When she wasn't putting her competition (the Real Roxanne or Roxanne Shanté) in check, she was name-checking DJs Red Alert and Spyder D. "Mathematically applied, I'm equaled by none," she said, and who could doubt her?

MC CHIEF & SEXY LADY

"Beef Box" (4 Sight Records, 1984)

This obscure duo on a South Florida label snatched Wendy's advertising slogan "Where's the beef?" for this decent track's catchphrase.

ROXANNE SHANTÉ

"Roxanne's Revenge" (Pop Art, 1984)
"Queen of Rox" (Pop Art, 1985)
"Bite This" (Pop Art, 1985)
Def Mix Vol. 1 (Pop Art, 1985)
"The Def Fresh Crew" (Cold Chillin', 1986)

UTFO's song about a girl named Roxanne gave this spunky Queens teen her chance to shine. DJ Marley Marl provided the musical foundation for a string of hard-rocking hits, occasionally accompanied by Juice Crew compadres like Biz Markie.

THE REAL ROXANNE

"The Real Roxanne" (Select, 1984)
"Romeo" b/w "Roxanne's Groove" (Select, 1985)
"United" (featuring Lisa-Lisa) (Columbia, 1985)
"Bang Zoom (Let's Go-Go)" b/w "Howie's Teed Off" (Select, 1986)

First UTFO did the record, then they went out and found a girl to play the part. Their first choice didn't work out but fortunately producers Full Force came across this fly Latina to fill her shell-toes. To distinguish herself from the clones, Rox let you know that "I'm the Real Roxanne, let's get it straight / And all the other perpetrating ones are fake."

SUPER NATURE

"Show Stoppa (Is Stupid Fresh)" (Pop Art, 1985)

Hurby "Luv Bug" Azor wrote and produced this blistering answer to Doug E. Fresh and Slick Rick's hits "The Show" and "La Di Da Di," which also marked the first appearance of two women who called themselves "the Salt and Pepper MCs." More about them later.

MIRACLE MIKE & THE LADIES OF THE '80S

"Outta Control" (Sugar Hill, 1985)

A one-shot record and crew from the Sugar Hill farm team that never quite blew up.

DYNASTY & MIMI

"Dynasty Rap" b/w "Won't You Be My Lady" (Jive, 1985)
"Rappers Revenge" (Jive, 1985)

Mimi was the standout in this male/female rhyme team, a confident counterpart to MC Dynasty (twin brother of Whodini's MC Ecstasy). Well before today's obsession with flossing, they played the roles of battling billionaires Blake and Alexis Carrington from the prime-time soap *Dynasty*.

BAD BOYS (FEATURING K LOVE)

"Bad Boys" (a.k.a. Inspector Gadget) (Starlite, 1985)
"Veronica" (Starlite, 1985)
"Mission" (a.k.a. Mission Impossible) (Starlite, 1985)

K Love represented as the first female beat box on wax, showin' and provin' during her vocal percussion cameos on these TV-hook-flipping hits.

E-VETTE MONEY

"E-Vette's Revenge" (Slice, 1986)

A retort to L.L. Cool J's "Dear Yvette," this Philly homegirl (now, like Lady B, a popular radio host in her hometown) taunts the G.O.A.T. with questions about his sexuality, because, as she explained, "No one gets away with what you said about me."

DAVY DMX (FEATURING SWEET TEE)
"One for the Treble" (mid-'80s)

Southside Queens MC Sweet Tee made her first appearance on a record with this New York DJ star, saluting him in a faux Brit accent: "Davy D, you are the best / Rock this beat on the DMX ('cause it is so fresh)."

GLAMOUR GIRLS (FEATURING SWEET TEE AND CRAIG G AS THE HUMAN BEAT BOX)
"Oh Veronica" (Pop Art, 1986)

These saucy rapstresses joined the rauchy rumor brigade about the Bad Boys' mythical Veronica and her allegedly loose caboose.

THE UNDERCOVER LOVERS
"Undercover Lovers" (York's Records, 1986)

These "three young super ladies, rockin' in the '80s" had a fun harmonizing flow but their way-underground label, owned by controversial religious leader Dr. Malachi Z. York, couldn't deliver the fame their skills should have earned.

SWEET TRIO (FEATURING DJ JAZZY JOYCE)
"Non-Stop" (Tommy Boy, 1986)

This short-lived female crew, now best remembered for introducing Joyce's skills to the world, rapped tough-girl rhymes that made this record a favorite of party-pleasing DJs.

SWEET TEE & JAZZY JOYCE
"It's My Beat" (Profile, 1986)

The homegirl-next-door staked her claim, joining forces with the old-school turntable wizardress for this classic jam, which inquired, in poetic cadence: "How shall I rock thee? / Let me count the ways . . ."

ROXA NNE SHANTE

*I'm just
the devastating
always rockin'
always have the
niggas clockin'
everybody notice
me the
R-O-X-A-N-N-E*

Photograph by David Corio

we used to do it out in the park

by Sacha Jenkins

"Shanté is my name from birth," says the modestly dressed woman in the nondescript diner in the heart of Jackson Heights, Queens. "My mother named me Shanté after a cheap wine that she used to like. It was made by Martini & Rossi, and it used to cost $1.98. They stopped making it in '73."

Once upon a time she was the fly MC, empress of prime-time battle rhymes, Lolita Shanté Gooden, better known as Roxanne Shanté. Now she sips a Coke (no Moët) and reflects on the life she left behind. The stage name came from her first record, released when she was just 14 years old.

"What's so funny is we tend to live out our names," she says. "My other name is Lolita—which means lover of older men. That's why whenever a young girl is involved with an older man they call her Lolita. Like Amy Fisher was the 'Long Island Lolita.'"

A beehive-haired waitress asks if she wants the usual. "No thanks, just a bowl of soup," says Shanté. She's wearing a simple denim outfit, a far cry from the tailor-made Louis Vuitton jumpsuits she'd been known to sport in her MC years. "My son's father was eighteen years my elder. He was from Queensbridge, just like all my babies' fathers," adds the mother of two with an open chuckle. Her thoughts return for a moment to the massive Long Island City housing project and hip hop mecca, renowned for its deep concentration of flow-masters. Back before Mobb Deep, before the whole Juice Crew, the first MC to blow up big out of the Bridge was hip hop's universally recognized First Lady, Roxanne Shanté.

"I went all the way around the world, and came back and got another man from Queensbridge," she says, shaking her shoulder-length ponytail (the trademark Shanté 'do). "Queensbridge does that to you. Every rapper from Queensbridge has kids with somebody from Queensbridge. It's a magnet. You work so hard to get out of it, to become suc-cessful—just to go back." Though Shanté's new home in the Heights is a good three miles from her native QB, the old 'hood is still very close to heart.

"Queensbridge is the largest housing complex in the United States—and that's just spooky," reminisces the former wild child who's put the days of rapping, scrapping, and beating on tables behind her. "It never seemed that big when I lived there. There are ninety-six buildings, and there ain't one that I haven't been in."

Hip hop luminaries like producer supreme Marley Marl, blue-collar rapsmiths MC Shan, Tragedy, and Craig G. (known collectively as the almighty Juice Crew), and QB's favorite son—multiplatinum supastar Nasir "Nasty Nas" Jones—come back to Queensbridge for some of that 'round-the-way love as often as possible. They can't help it. It's the rhythm of a people so closely quartered that reels them home; the same power that made them not just rappers, but fully rounded, verbally versatile microphone controllers.

For despite budget cuts, body bags, and baseheads, there flourishes in Queensbridge an inconceivable amplitude of storytelling and beat-composing genius. Maybe it's the giant Con Edison electrical plant next to River Park that charges the minds of these word slingers, or maybe the East River's swirling might helps keep the turntables spinning. Maybe it's the isolation, the view of the Manhattan skyline across the river, the feeling of being just *on the verge*. Whatever the reason, no other expanse of concentrated 'hoodscape is responsible for a parallel pool of raw, natural artistry.

Queensbridge has been this way since 1976: in the summertime, her DJs—some working two crusty turntables from the core of their bedrooms, echo chambers blaring, homemade, def-defining speakers dangling out their windows—would pump Kraftwerk or the Treacherous Three well into the wee hours of the night. Little girl QB resident Shanté was your average shorty who loved to play tag and handball in the various parks that lined the Bridge's labyrinthine landscape. There was nothing hotter than the complimentary breakbeat bombardment that blazed those sweltering streets.

Can it be that it was all so simple then? Save for the exceptional Friday- and Saturday-night rap shows mixed by the likes of Kool DJ Red Alert or Mr. Magic (and later, Marley himself), the broadcasted boom-bap that now crowds the TV and radio dial was nonexistent through the early to mid-'80s. It took legions of boisterous Noo Yawkers—MCs, DJs, pop-lockers, break dancers, and subway bombers—to keep the party shinin' underneath the cloud cover of a dying, yet still powerful, musical style called disco. Meanwhile inside Queensbridge's microcosmic universe, the music that would be called hip hop was the soundtrack of daily life.

So folks rapped for themselves, rapped while busting out twisted Double Dutch jump-rope maneuvers, rapped for beer and cheers on forest green benches. And in 1984, Lolita Shanté Gooden decided to rap for designer jeanswear.

"Marley worked at the Sergio Valente factory," Shanté recalls of her earliest interactions with one of rap music's true all-stars, Marlon "Marley Marl" Williams. The groundbreaking producer/engineer offered Shanté a pair of pricey dungarees in exchange for her rhyme time. Marley had some experience with female rappers. His first-ever release was the 1983 12-inch single "Sucker DJs," voiced by Dimples D, another daughter of QB.

But the man responsible for underground gems like "The Symphony" and, later, L.L. Cool J's classic LP *Mama Said Knock You Out,* did not make good on his promise to 14-year-old Shanté that day. "I rapped for some Sergios that I never got," she says earnestly.

What she, and every other self-respecting head-nodder in the world, would receive instead was a gift more precious than a pair of $35 slacks. Roxanne Shanté and Marley Marl were about to transmit hip hop's rawest frequency—the mortal-combat zone of the dozens, snaps, and battle raps—to party peoples everywhere.

That first phat joint was "Roxanne's Revenge" (Pop Art, 1984), which responded to (and dissed to all hell) UTFO's radio killer, "Roxanne, Roxanne" (a playful ditty about a hard-to-obtain neighborhood hottie). Marley was supposedly mad at UTFO for missing a gig. Whatever the motive, Shanté's debut was a defining moment in hip hop—the birth of the gangsta bitch as we know it. Like the Coffys and Cleopatra Joneses of blaxploitation screen fame, Shanté was simply not having it.

"I was buggin' on the fact that she dissed UTFO like that," says Brooklyn Juice Crew representative Masta Ace, who remembers when a low-budget "Roxanne's Revenge"

video (featuring Shanté stepping out of a limo in a fur coat) showed up on the cable show Video Music Box. "Most people knew who she was before they knew who Marley was. Cats on the street thought she was fly with that white fur."

Shanté jumped from recording studio to the airwaves in no time. "She paved the way for female MCs like Foxy Brown and Lil' Kim to be feminine and cute but still have that attitude and street mentality," says Ace with admiration. "She had skills; she took on all battles." Shanté was a ghetto girl with a mike and an audience who wasn't afraid to say what was on her mind. If that made her a bitch then so be it. Her whirlwind bulldozer flow had rap stars twice her size—and twice her age—by the gonads. Shanté's merciless attack on UTFO was powerful enough to set off the longest-running series of answer records in the annals of hip hop, an ongoing "battle on wax" that resulted in over 90 different releases jumping on the trend, from "The Real Roxanne" all the way to "Roxanne Is a Man."

"Revenge" was also Shanté's fast ticket out of the ghetto. The whole world wanted to see her, and she traded in the local park-jam and talent-show scene for mini-tours and spot dates around the country. "I can remember flying to *three* places in one day," she says with a grin. Shanté the survivor had run away from home at 13 for reasons she'd rather not say. She will say that rap was the catalyst that launched the blast-off: "I got my own place when I was fourteen, moved into this basement out in Jamaica, Queens. I stopped going to school during the second marking period of the ninth grade because I had a lot of tours happening." This little girl had, in theory, become a grown-ass woman who did real adult things.

"I was fourteen years old when I got my first $5,000. Do you know what $5,000 in tens looks like?" says a smiling Shanté. That hefty purse was her reward for rocking the two big Manhattan hot spots—The Funhouse and The Roxy—in one mammoth night. "Roxanne's Revenge" was huge, and fans and foes alike fought their way inside to hear the squeaky-voiced chick kick lines like "I'm just the devastating always rockin' / Always have the niggas clockin' / Everybody notice me / The R-O-X-A-N-N-E."

"I took that $5,000 to my mom's house," she says, "and put it in the freezer in a brown paper bag. Then my mom opens up the freezer and starts to scream—'Girl, who's looking for this money?'—because for a time, I was a thief. Then I explained the whole music thing to her. She had no idea about what I was into. I went out into the world at thirteen and I came home the next year and was like, 'Ma, this is what I make. And I make this two, three times a week.'"

The rap loot was good, and Shanté's dream rap team—the chiefly Queensbridgian, diversely talented Juice Crew (the collective that would inspire Rza's Wu-Tang Clan)—was in full effect with Big Daddy Kane, Biz Markie, Kool G. Rap, MC Shan, Craig G., T.J. Swan, Masta Ace, and of course DJ Marley Marl on the wheels of steel. But make no mistake: from 1985 through 1989, Roxanne Shanté's traveling dram-o-rama was the top-billing heavyweight event on the road.

"I sung for everybody else in the Juice Crew to eat and live," she says without a drop of bitterness. "I never once said, 'Oh, I'm Shanté, give me more.' I took my money and divided it up equally—like as if everybody was a star. If there was five of us who went out, I split my money five ways."

Being the only girl in the Crew also had its benefits. "The fellas weren't used to having someone like me around," she recalls with fondness in her voice. "It's nothing like it is now. It wasn't about . . . fucking. I was Roxanne Shanté, but I was like their little sister."

For the girl who left home at a tender age, the Juice Crew were like family. "She was lil' sister, momma, and one of the guys all wrapped up in one," says Ace. "We had her back, she had ours, and she could hold her own against any competition—male or female. She was one of the best female 'off the top of the head' rappers ever."

"Shanté's contribution to the Juice Crew gave the team a balance not seen in groups in that era," says Tragedy, a.k.a. The Intelligent Hoodlum, reaching out via e-mail. "She opened us up to a female audience. And she was a female who could actually spit! Her impact on hip hop is tremendous; her presence represented the femme side of hip hop."

"Shanté was the foundation of the Juice Crew in my estimation," adds Masta Ace. "If she had not done her thing on that 'Roxanne's Revenge' record maybe people wouldn't have continued to listen to the artists to follow. Most people don't know that records like 'Roxanne's Revenge' and 'Queen of Rox' were not written." If you listen carefully, you can hear the slight pauses as her brain formulates the next scathing line. It's that unpolished sound that makes connoisseurs of the MC's art give Shanté maximum thanks and praise. Few have the personality, tonality, and guts to project the pure *charge* that Shanté emits on 12-inches like "Def Fresh Crew," "Live On Stage," and "Have a Nice Day."

But Shanté was a hip hop mega-star in the tradition of pop mega-stars who didn't necessarily pen all their own tunes. "I was a *rapper,* not a writer," she says without apology. "Give me a beat, give me a mike, let me do my thing. When rap got more structured, where you had to do things within a certain time limit, where you had to set up choruses . . ." Her voice gets louder as the memories flow. "We didn't have no chorus before. I didn't know how to stop at eight bars; stop at sixteen. I just went through. Any record where I'm rapping straight through from beginning to end—

I wrote it. Any record where it stops and there's a chorus—Big Daddy Kane, Kool G. Rap, or MC Shan wrote it. But it's not about who writes a song," she says proudly. "It's who sings the shit out of it."

Hers was the voice that even non-hip hoppers recognized—she was the bitch who took potshots at UTFO during prime-time radio slots. In some regions, Shanté even headlined over the multiplatinum, chocolate boy band New Edition. "That Roxanne thing was so hot," she says with a smile, "that 'Candy Girl' just couldn't stand up to it."

For a few legendary nights, Rox and her on-wax rivals UTFO and the Real Roxanne shared the same stage, settling the vinyl wars hand to hand. There was no shortage of people who would pay good money to see the beef sizzle. Bowlegged Lou of Full Force (the group that produced and sang on records by UTFO and the Real Roxanne) recalls one of those confrontations:

"I'll never forget it," he says. "Our Roxanne came on first and she was doing her thing and the audience started laughing. I was in back wondering, Why are these people laughing? So I walked up front and right down by the steps that lead to the stage was Shanté. She was sitting there cracking up at the Real Roxanne's performance, and everyone was laughing along with her. This was back in the days when the battling shit was going crazy. Shanté was bad. She had one of the biggest dis records in rap. But today we're real tight."

Tight or not, UTFO threatened suit against Cold Chillin' for unauthorized samples in "Roxanne's Revenge," then settled out of court. They eventually got their names listed on future pressings of the record. According to Shanté, they also refused to do shows with her. "I would dis UTFO and them *sooo* bad," she says with a smile. "I'd talk about their clothes, stuff like that. And because I was good at doing freestyles, they just couldn't take it," Shanté says. "Eventually, it would be just me going out there."

The queen-bitch position wasn't the easiest gig available in the hip hop classifieds, but somebody had to do it. Shanté didn't always whistle while she worked, though. "It bothered me that as much as people loved me, a lot of people hated me," she admits. "I would always wonder, like, well, if people really don't like me, why are my shows so packed? Do all of these people come here just to *hate* me?" That was when an old friend broke it down for her. "You're the person who people love to hate," they said. "Just like [*Dynasty*'s] Alexis Carrington. Everyone loved Krystle, but if Alexis wasn't in the episode, then it wasn't a good episode." Shanté could live with the comparison to Joan Collins.

"I was like, as long as I'm Alexis; as long as I get to wear these Gucci boots and Gucci clothes, then so be it. As long as I could have these Guess suits in every color, and bombers and sheepskins and big door-knocker earrings till my earlobes ripped, bamboos with my name on 'em . . ." She pauses to laugh, then she's all business. "As long as I was getting paid for it, I felt fine."

It was all gravy until a hectic tour schedule started to get the better of her. And at this point, the 16-year-old Lolita was eating for two. "I was in Philadelphia," she recalls. "I was expecting my son Kareem." But her manager was unmoved. "He pulled some real Ike Turner shit, like 'I don't care if you sick; you gonna get onstage.' But I was *so* sick. I remember this lady was like, 'Come on, she's a little girl. You can see that she's sick.' I damn near looked like Tina Turner with tears in my eyes. They said, 'No, no, no–she can go out there and do one song.' I think from that day on, I stopped liking performing."

For a while thereafter, nobody had much luck getting Shanté to do things she didn't want to do. She was not only growing tired of the physical performance end of rap, but the business was starting to aggravate her, too. She felt cheated. Swindled. Shanté started to really not give a fudge.

"Getting me in the studio was almost impossible. I would turn down tour dates–or agree to dates then not show up. I'd disappear for days. I was just real"–she pauses to find the perfect word–"ghetto." Things began falling apart, and Shanté didn't know where to turn. "My management was the record company," she says, "this one sniffed coke with that one. The promoters were usually friends and family." But the Shanté show wasn't about to be canceled. There was money to be made, and her little man to feed.

"I was sixteen," she says, swirling a straw in her bubbly drink. "I just had my son–he was only a couple of weeks old and it was time for me to go back out on tour. I wanted to sit home and play with him, you know? And they was like, 'Nah, you goin' on tour with Eric B. and Rakim.'" The tour would also include L.L. Cool J, Whodini–and Shanté's pint-sized hype-man Kareem.

"I kept my son on the road until I couldn't anymore," she recalls. "I would take him everywhere I went. He was at the photo shoot, so he wound up on the back of the album (*Bad Sister,* Warner Bros., 1989). I don't remember him crying or teething, I don't remember having to potty-train him–he just stopped wearing Pampers one day. He

THE QUEEN OF ROX

ROXANNE SHANTE

Mr. Magic Enterprises, Ltd.
Production * Management * Promotion
Rapp Attack Radio Syndication
P.O. Box 671   New York, N.Y. 10040

was what God sent me to keep me from turning to drugs or anything. Because I was so into him. He didn't care if I sang or not–he just wanted to be with me."

Occasional bouts of secondhand cheeba smoke and booming beats didn't seem to faze the little fella, though Mom did have her concerns. "I wasn't even sure if he was gonna be able to hear, the way we used to play music," Shanté says. "He'd sit in the studio, blasting to three in the morning. I'd lay him on a jacket; he'd sleep in the corner. That was my homie. Wherever I went, he had to go."

Then without warning Kareem's father took her to court seeking custody on the grounds that the showbiz lifestyle was bad for the child. "He had told the judge I took the baby away on tour and the baby's surrounded by drugs. But when we got in the court, the judge was like, 'Okay, she's seventeen and you're thirty-five?' The judge was like, 'Man, I should be lockin' you up! She's only seventeen. She's showing me how she pays all the bills, how she takes care of the house . . . and you want to stop that?'"

The case was thrown out, and Roxanne's baby pa managed to stay out of custody. The QB couple hadn't been on the best terms to begin with, but the court battle left their relationship seriously strained. "No one makes decisions about my child but me," she says. "And that still stands today. Because fathers come and fathers go."

Sure enough, the next year Shanté became a single mother by way of unfortunate circumstance. "Kareem's father got killed when my son was five," she says. Poppa was a drug dealer who fell prey to the code of the streets. "Even though I didn't have too much emotion for him, I got a limousine, dressed the baby up in a really nice black suit and we went to the funeral out of respect. It was sad. My son didn't understand what was going on at the time. He was like, 'Why are we here? Come on Shanté, let's go. . . .'"

It was about that time when Shanté felt a change sweep through her body. Something told her that it was time to change her lifestyle, to make wiser life decisions.

The culture of hip hop was evolving into the business of rap: a multizillion-dollar commodities market hotter than well-fed pork bellies. From platinum teeth to silver-washed velour sweats, CD-ROMs to the silver screen, the way of

daughter Tajzae. "I have to live right," she says. "Hip hop was not gonna let me live right. I just wanted to bow out gracefully." Her bow was short and bittersweet. There were scores of challengers stepping up to try and topple the original Big Mama and her merry Juice Crew. They wouldn't let Shanté have a moment's rest.

"Every female rapper who came out felt like they had this Shanté thing to prove," she says, perplexed. "If someone didn't know what to make a record about, they would make it about Roxanne Shanté."

Then came the epic rivalry between the Juice Crew and Boogie Down Productions from the South Bronx. Suddenly it looked like Queensbridge was fully entrenched in World War III. Everybody knew that the Bronx was where living legends like Kool Herc, Bambaataa, Grandmaster Flash, and Hollywood started this whole hip hop thing. Nobody ever expected quiet-ass Queens to step up with credible beats and rhymes.

But then came MC Shan's "The Bridge" (a song that was

"Every female rapper who came out felt like they had this Shanté thing to prove," she says, perplexed. "If someone didn't know what to make a record about, they would make it about Roxanne Shanté."

life that evolved from street-speak was moving on up to Wall Street. Forget about the tight blue Sergios or the lint-strewn burgundy Lee twills that were once the shit. Today's young MCs (more of them female than ever) were waxing poetic about the finer things that cash affords: diamond-infected platinum jewelry, designer clothes, luxury cars, sparkling vintage.

Although a few rhyme-sayers did go on to get seriously paid, it was the machine itself—which produces, manufactures, and distributes the toonage, and often feasts off its young—that was truly raking in the Trump dough.

Having peeped the real mathematics behind the glitz and glamour, Shanté soon found herself raging against said machine. "It's not about the money," she says, preaching showbiz heresy. "No, I'm not filthy rich, but I will be comfortable forever because I planned it that way. Shanté is not struggling. Shanté is not hungry. Shanté is quite happy."

The first step toward happiness came when she put a priority on living well for herself, her son Kareem and her

recorded for a local block party and never intended for a wider audience). When it got released in 1986, Bronx loyalists thought the Kangol-domed MC was spewing some bizarre pro-Queens revisionist history.

Kris "KRS-One" Parker of Boogie Down Productions struck a blow in defense of his favorite borough, smearing mud on the face of the Bridge with "The South Bronx" (B-Boy, 1986). Suddenly it was The Roxanne Wars Part *Deux*, only now the stakes were higher. This wasn't just crew-on-crew beef. We're talking the whole Bronx borough (plus, of course, all them Bronx sympathizers) against one giant public housing development on the coast of Queens.

There were rules to the battling game, a code of honor that said don't talk about anybody's mama, keep the beef on wax. MCs rarely fouled out while rapping for sport. But sometimes things did get personal. Unfortunately for Shanté, one of the most memorable (and vile) comments BDP launched at the Juice Crew impacted against her body—hard. "After KRS did that 'Shanté is only good for steady fuckin'

line' ["The Bridge Is Over," B-Boy, 1987],
people saw that as another invitation to go
at me," she says.

It seemed like open season on Shanté.
West Coast speed-rapping females called J.J.
Fad dissed her on 1987's "Anotha Ho /
Anotha Tramp," which became one of their
biggest sellers. Shanté hit 'em back with
"Wack It" and "Skeezer" and J.J. Fad eventually became just that. But it was the prin-
ciple of the thing that bothered Shanté. "It
was like, 'If you can get at Shanté, you'll be
famous," she observes. Like Pacino in *Godfather III,* just when she thought she could
storm troop out of the beef, they kept
pulling her back in.

As with the UTFO / Real Roxanne situation, people wanted to see two posses—the
Juice Crew and BDP—at each other's throats
onstage. Records were made on both sides,
some "battles" were staged; the Queen of
the Juice Crew took more hits than a fat
piñata in Tijuana. But that's how the game
was played, and Shanté understood better
than anyone. She took her lumps—just as
she had from day one—and kept movin'.

Most rap nerds will tell you that BDP
won the war with the Juice Crew. Die-hards from
the Q-borough may disagree, but either way, these
fireworks marked the beginning of the end for the once massive J.C. Before long Tony Kane, G. Rap, Biz, and Ace—who
were not reared in Queensbridge—started to distance themselves from the clique. Meanwhile Shanté wasn't too pleased
with the dough she was seeing.

"I didn't start making albums until the late 1980s, isn't
that funny?" she muses. "I was queen of the 12-inch. Everybody else was making albums, but I think Cold Chillin' felt
like, it's better for Shanté to keep making 12-inches because
she won't think that we owe her a lot of money," she says
with a laugh. "Everybody else is talkin' 'bout, 'Yo, I'm getting $50,000 for my album . . .'"

Then in a flash, the '80s were gone and the Juice Crew's
collective well had pretty much run dry. But through all the
ups and downs it was the drama—the public thirst for Roman
gladiator-esque battle—that kept Roxanne Shanté in the
public eye. And even without her posse, somehow the Dra-
matics just kept coming to Shanté's door.

In 1992, she was invited to appear on a new talk show
called *Jane.* "They put me in the Green Room with no TV

monitor, no nothin'," she recalls. "They just told me the
show was about in women in hip hop. Talk shows weren't
that big then, so we wasn't thinkin' it was about to be Jerry
Springer upstairs," says Shanté, who had recently released
her *Bitch Is Back* EP (Livin' Large/Cold Chillin'). On the
spicy track "Big Mama," the still-feisty rapper had served
up some choice words for pretty much every female MC
who mattered at that time. "I dig ditches for you bitches,"
Shanté taunted on the song, "While I collect riches / And
leave you with a head full of stitches." But that tune was the
last thing on her mind for a TV appearance.

Meanwhile back at the studio, the stage was set for a sneak
attack. "I hear Jane say, 'We have another guest who may
not agree with everything. She's the mother of rap.'" Shanté
relates the action blow by blow, like an episode of *WWF
Smackdown.* "The crowd starts booing, then I walk out there
and see MC Lyte, Yo Yo, Nikki D. I said, Wait a minute. . . .
But my pride would not let me turn around and walk away."
The air was thick. Shanté felt as if she'd just been ambushed.
"That Queensbridge in me was like 'Yo, if they're gonna
jump me, then they're just gonna jump me,'" she says coolly.

"Then Lyte says, 'She attacked my femininity.' I said,

'Let's be real: do you like men? You don't like men. It's no secret.'" The audience started to lose it.

(Lyte now says that Shanté's record—which described Lyte as a lesbian in need of "a good piece of dick"—was symptomatic of men controlling a woman's career. "She hadn't been out in a long time," says Lyte. "Granddaddy IU produced the record and wrote all the lyrics to it. I just felt like, Damn. It could be sisterhood existing within hip hop. And in fact there was, but just by her doing that, she sort of omitted herself from a family within a family. I mean I've done dis records, and I still do. I understand the essence of hip hop and where dis records come from, but a record like that—I don't think it was called for.")

Shanté kept piling on the insults. "At the time, I was really slim and Yo Yo was thick. So I was like, 'And what, you don't need to lose weight?' I was like, 'Yeah, I said it. So now everybody wants to fight about it?'"

The trash-talking barrage raged on, and the audience's loyalties began to shift. "As it went on, the crowd was like 'Yeah, Shanté!' when before, nobody was with me," she

She's right. Elevation is the ultimate high. Lolita Shanté Gooden—who graduated from Marymount University in 1995—is all about rising. She says she's called a truce with most of her hip hop adversaries. "I love KRS to death. I was always a fan of his anyway. And he was one of the first people outside of my family to hug me and say that he was proud of me for going to college and doing what I did," she says. "I broke down in that hug."

The woman in the diner who's almost finished her soup now calls herself Dr. Lolita Shanté Gooden. She sees 25 clients on the regular, and these days she's only good for steady healing. "In order to become a psychiatrist, you have to be able to write prescriptions, so I was at Cornell University for a little while," Shanté explains. "But then I realized that I don't even wanna write prescriptions—there's a quick fix for everything. Instead, I went and looked into the Yoruba religion, and I found it fascinating. So I incorporated some of those rituals and some other ideas and came up with this Shanté thing. We do a little of the Santería/botanica thing; you name it."

"I don't do pity parties," says Dr. Lolita Shanté Gooden. "Someone will say, 'I was abused,' and I say 'Yeah? My ribs were broken and I was left in a house to die.'"

says. "Then one guy stood up and says, 'You know what? Y'all don't understand, Jane Pratt did this just for the ratings.' I said, 'Yeah? But she won't even have the show after this.' And I got up and left." When she returned home, Roxanne promptly complained to her manager, Benny Medina (the mind behind Jennifer Lopez and Will Smith). The *Jane* show was off the air four weeks later. "That just goes to show," Shanté says, sucking her Coke dry. "It's not how powerful you are, it's how politically connected you are."

It's said that time heals all wounds, and when the master battler ran into a former foe, Shanté was big enough to put down the sword in the name of sistahood. "I saw Yo Yo a few months later," recalls Roxanne, who tried to squash any hard feelings.

"I went up to her and said, 'Uh . . . so how are you?' She was like 'I'm fine.' She asked how my baby was. I said, 'Great.' Then I said, 'You know what? In this business, you have to learn to let go in order to elevate.' She said, 'Yeah, I am.' I said, 'All right.' Then I walked away."

If her practice is far from traditional, maybe that's because she's always done her own thing. But there are women she relates to, strong survivors who've seen the depths of despair and climbed back up to the mountain top. "Sometimes we pop in the Tina Turner story—*What's Love Got to Do With It?*—and we will sit there and watch Ike Turner," she says, "and then get the strength from where Tina did. I struggled so hard to get things right for myself, so if I can help others . . . whatever it takes." Shanté's brown eyes become warmer as she speaks. "So many nights, I needed somebody to talk to and there wasn't anybody I could turn to—so I found myself talking to trees. I found myself sitting up in churches of any religious denomination; I would walk in and say, 'Well, if God is here, then let *Him* hear me.'

The former tomboy who once said, "Girls and me don't get along" has had a change of heart. "I only deal with women," she says. "It's not like I have strange men calling me for sex therapy late at night. I find that women, because they deal with emotion, they think with consideration."

But please don't assume that Shanté's gone soft. Never that. "I don't do pity parties," she says, that Queensbridge sass stretching out. Then Shanté unexpectedly opens up, as though the Rox herself was in a therapy session. "Someone will say 'I was getting beatings, I was abused.' And I say 'So was I.' Now what else? 'Well, he beats me.' And I say, 'Yeah? My ribs were broken and I was left in a house to die.'"

Shanté's brand of tough love is strictly for those who understand how to keep it real. "It gets deep," she admits. "Some women have said that I'm a tad bit harsh, that they didn't need that type of reality check."

Can the good doctor prescribe an appropriate reality check for the current crop of rap chicks? "All you females today who are industry angry," she says scornfully, "if you take off your clothes, then that's what you'll be seen as. If you want to be treated as an MC, then come as an MC."

Monie Love, another MC who caught some flak on "Big Mama," remembers Shanté fondly, despite everything. "With women today, there is far less unity," says Monie. "Seems like they all hate each other. We were not hating. You know who, out of all the female rappers, use'ta hate? Roxanne Shanté. Roxanne Shanté was the only hating force. But I loved her for it. She inspired me one hundred percent, because it was art. That's how we all saw it. Keep it in the art."

All the same, Shanté knows that many sisters in rhyme will forever equate her name with Big Mac meat. As recently as 2000, a female group called the Deadly Venoms were throwing her name around on record. But she insists she wasn't tempted for a minute to come out of retirement and chin-check 'em. "It's sad," she says. "Because I like all the female rappers. I do. There's not one that I can say I don't like. But they shouldn't be thinking about me, period. They should be thinking about their lawyers, their contracts, their managers—that's what they should be thinking about.

"To say, Oh yeah, Shanté, I look up to her, she's dope, she's one of the first to do this—if you say it, then thank you. I appreciate it. And if you don't, I still appreciate it. Because regardless of what you do, you will still always be a reflection of me. It'll always come up. And I like that."

And how would the '80s version of Roxanne Shanté hold up in today's ride-or-die hip hop climate?

"Shit, in this day and age Shanté would have been shot," she says with a happily sarcastic giggle. "Don't you think?"

SALT N PEPA

My mike sounds nice check one, my mike sounds nice check two, my mike sounds nice check three, are you ready?

the queens from queens

by Harry Allen

"Security. Wanda."

In her twenty-odd years of life, Deidre Roper has heard far more melodious voices coming out of speakers. Right now, though, this bland, disembodied utterance is music to her ears. Deidre, known as Dee Dee to her friends and as Salt-N-Pepa's DJ Spinderella to her fans, is out looking at houses today with her youngest sister, Andrea, and "Realtor to the Stars!" Joanne English. As they slide past the video-cam eyeballing English's hunter green Isuzu Rodeo, Dee Dee mentally notes that, should she and her daughter Christenese decide to call this townhouse development their new home, only those who appease Checkpoint Wanda will get past these burly gates.

As Joanne hunts for parking, Spin scans the medium-six-figures, rust-colored dwellings—Patrick Ewing lives here, as does Lil' Kim—mega-parsecs from the Louis H. Pink Houses, the East New York, Brooklyn, projects that she and her family once called home. It's a perfect, cloudless day as we enter the contemporary dwelling with its parquet wooden floors, a two-story-high skylight over the kitchen, and a sauna, with gym, in the basement.

Then, Andrea makes a twisted discovery. Peering into a bathroom, she says, unaffectedly, "It's got two toilets."

Dee looks at the second porcelain bowl and its upward-pointed nozzle. "She's so ghetto," Dee Dee states, amused. "That's not two toilets."

"What is it?"

"It's a *bidet*," says Joanne, the agent.

"A bih-DAY?" Andrea repeats. "What do you do with it?"

Dee Dee, unsure: "It's a . . . uh . . . they have that in Europe a lot."

The upward nozzle. Andrea takes the next best leap of faith. "You use it for the face?"

Umm . . . not quite. But then again, we've come a long way from the Pink Houses, a place where everything is real, especially the basics. Who could have guessed that in some American homes, the essentials would include a separate bathroom fixture solely for the washing of one's genitals?

As distant as the Pink Houses are from a certain bidet, though, the journey of Salt-N-Pepa—Cheryl "Salt" James, Sandra "Pepa" Denton, and Roper—winds farther still. Theirs is a story that, from almost any oblique angle, has the gleam and sparkle of awesome triumph. On the face of it, all three women, the products of working-class black families with roots in the South and the Caribbean, and raised in New York City's Brooklyn and Queens boroughs, should be leading average, inconspicuous, inconsequential lives.

Instead, these creators of four definitive hip hop works—*Hot, Cool & Vicious, A Salt with a Deadly Pepa, Black's Magic,* and the quintuple platinum *Very Necessary*—numerous gold and platinum singles—"Tramp," "My Mic Sounds Nice," "Push It," "Shake Your Thang," "Expression," "Whatta Man," "Shoop"—and seemingly a yellow brick road full of awards, have become tireless, ageless representatives for the dreams and ideals of two generations of avid believers.

In the years since they released their debut dis, "The Show Stoppa," in 1985, they have grown to embody distinct, unique, and previously incompatible personae, both public and private: artists, entertainers, single mothers, sex objects, Christians, feminists, businesswomen, AIDS activists and spokespersons, philanthropists, global hip hop ambassadors. It's no wonder pro-femmes like the acid comic Roseanne adore these women. Not just 'cause they're cute and spunky and hip, but because they—Lilith Fair be damned—*ballsily* represent the fibrous interconnectedness and strength of womyn, doing so with that brassy finesse that only black women possess—the strength that sisters have developed, not only to survive, but, as the Bible says, to bear each other up, lest one dash her foot against a stone. (Small wonder Lil' Kim refers to S&P as her "angels.") Salt-N-Pepa state an unrepentant womanist agenda in the strongest musical terms, envoys for the empathy, warmth, and holiness of black femininity.

Still, a woman's work is never done. *Brand New*—a.k.a. *Flavor in Ya Ear*—their fifth and still most recent album (1997), is a collection of sweetly R&B-saturated sets; a smooth, solid, commercial piece of work. But you've never seen player-haters (a term that wasn't widespread in 1993 when *Very Necessary,* their last hit album, came out) cock their derbied heads with greater smugness than they do when the topic of Salt-N-Pepa's relevance is discussed. Even many with supposedly more beneficent attitudes think that, well, like glue horses, it's time to put these fine mares out to pasture.

To which we, the faithful, might say, Salt-N-Pepa have a fine and cherished tradition of biting your expectations in the ass. Keep a first-aid kit handy.

Oh, and one more thing, haters: Watch your back. A Grammy is bigger than you'd expect and can be used as a weapon if necessary. I'd never seen a real one until today, poking around Dee Dee's living room shortly after her house hunt. "Best Rap Performance by A Duo or Group, 'None of Your Business,' 1994," this one reads. Other curios include an MTV Music Award, gold and platinum plaques, ceramic figurines, a picture of Dee Dee at the age of one day, a framed photo from *Entertainment Weekly* of S&P diva-ing at Woodstock, and their Matthew Rolston *Very Necessary* soft-focused glamour portrait—her favorite of the group (and mine).

Later, we'll trek out to her Queens-based beauty salon, She Things. Then afterward, we'll pick up Christy—the offspring of Dee Dee's defunct union with Boston Celtics point guard Kenny Anderson—from her afternoon karate class. In a black Dolce & Gabbana dress, Spin, high cheekbones and all, looks delicate, sitting slenderly on the one piece of furniture in the room—a futon—her faintly almond-shaped eyes alternately looking straight ahead, then straight at me, as we speak.

As pink turntable cases slump by a wall, she recalls how she learned to DJ from a now-deceased boyfriend while a student at Franklin K. Lane High School in Queens. Though long more than the replacement for S&P's original DJ Pamela Latoya Greene, Dee Dee remembers her audition for Salt and producer Hurby Luv Bug as though it were this afternoon: "It was early in the day, maybe one or two, May of '87. Hurby's garage in Queens. Pepa wasn't there, but Salt was there, and I just stared at her. I watched how she moved. I watched how she walked—like she was The Man. I wanted to know what it was like to be where she was."

Obviously, Spin got the gig. But before she could take it, "the big issue was my parents"—especially her mother. Patricia Roper, of West Indian descent and full brood (four girls, two boys), had *sense,* and was not about to let her sec-

ond youngest child go traipsing about the country just because somebody—named *what? Salt and Pepper?*—had a song on the radio.

"We had to bring Hurby, and Salt and Pepa, and J.P.," who co-managed with Hurby, "through the projects, to the house. J.P. was real instrumental at that point because he knew what my parents were feeling. He talked about curfew; he spoke about schooling. Then Cheryl was like, 'When we go on the road, she'll stay in my room, I'll take care of her, and I'll make sure she won't get into any trouble.' They all spoke on my behalf. And then my family had to look at that like, 'Wow, this is bigger than we thought.'

"I knew I got it when they all ganged up on my mother. My dad said, 'Let 'er go, Patsy.' And when she said yes, I was the happiest girl in the world. They said yes right in our living room, in the Pink Houses."

As we get into her Cherokee to head for She Things, Spin tosses aside the Mercedes-Benz M-Class 4×4 brochure for her new car. "Two years ago, I bought my mom and dad their first house," she notes. "They're glad they said yes."

Forty-five miles southeast of Seattle's Sea-Tac Airport, our Boeing 757 gently banks its 95-ton weight 20 degrees to the right.

As it does, the stunning sight of Mount Rainier—all 14,411 feet and 700 trillion tons of it—fills my window, overwhelming my awestruck and suddenly very tiny mind. I look at this rugged, immovable, 12-mile-wide monolith—the largest thing I have ever seen in my life—and I am suddenly more than humble. I am humiliated. I turn to the woman in the seat next to me, also taking in the scene, and the only thing I can say falls awkwardly from my lips: "Whatever made this . . . is only *tolerating* people."

Cheryl "Salt" James drinks my words in like a warm liquid. "Mmmmm," she says. "And people say they don't believe in God. But then you ask, who made all of this?"

Moved by the power of her insight, I quote her the paraphrased thoughts of the British geneticist and writer J. B. S. Haldane: "'The universe is not only queerer than we suppose, but queerer than we *can* suppose.'" I tell her of my deep love for astronomy, and talk about stars, galaxies, nebulae, quasars, black holes. "'The heavens are telling the glory of God,' I say, quoting Haydn quoting the Psalms. "The entire universe speaks to an immense Intelligence."

"But then," says Salt, testifying to the infinite complexity bound by our very cells, "what about when you realize that there are universes within us; within our own bodies?"

"It's real," says her mother, Barbara James, of her daughter's divine ponderings. "Cheryl has become very close to God. She's saved, and she passes the Word to people wherever she goes." In fact, says Barbara, it was a church play that first revealed her child's performance abilities; nine-year-old Cheryl played a rhyming witch–"I'm a horrible, horrible, horrible witch / I'll tickle your nose to make you itch."

Getting her ecclesiastical swerve on in the Kirk Franklin gospel hit "Stomp," however, represents a break with the past; a "coming out" record, not out of the closet, but out of "the world"; a public profession of faith, and an indication of where Cheryl sees herself spending the rest of her musical life. (Indeed, the title of her 2001 solo debut album, *Salt of the Earth* [Matthew 5:13], can be seen as a testament to that journey.)

Once in Seattle, we wait for the van that will take Salt-N-Spin–Pepa's been delayed at Newark International–and their dancers to rehearsal. "I want to eventually do nothing but inspirational music and gospel music," Cheryl says, looking into the alpine distance. "I don't want to 'Push It' no more, I don't want to 'Shoop' no more, I don't want to 'Gitty Up' no more. It's all fun for me right now, and I'm not bugging out. But I would like to turn the gospel circuit upside down; start doing some serious gospel rap music and really corner that. And I have to be in a position of power and influence where I can do that. That's what we've been fighting for. That's what we went through all this drama over; us just gettin' our respect in this business, and havin' to prove what we can do. That's basically what these last three years and gettin' away from Hurby has been about."

Hurby. Much as it is impossible to understand ocean tides without considering the moon's phases, one can little comprehend Salt-N-Pepa without understanding the past and present relationship of Cheryl Renée James to Herbert Ernst Azor, p.k.a. Hurby Luv Bug; producer, ex-lover, Svengali, genius, and a stack of other names women call the men that have done them wrong.

Theirs was an alliance that brought them both great fame and wealth, but at the same time reeked of financial exploitation, codependence, and emotional abuse. Hurby–once not only part of S&P's inner circle, but in truth its very epicenter–has talked little to Salt over the last few years. When he does, says Hurby, "It's a lot of animosity in her voice."

Not tonight. Curled up like a leaf in her hotel room, Salt speaks haltingly, yet bluntly, about the romance from which, though it ended nearly eight years ago, she really has yet to fully heal. "I was very much in love with Hurby," she says, her large eyes expressing sadness. "He was the first person I ever loved, and I've never loved anybody since like I loved Hurby."

They met, the legend goes, while both, along with Sandra Denton, were working part-time as TSRs (telephone service representatives) for Sears' now-demolished College Point, New York, branch, selling maintenance agreements for the stores' Kenmore appliances. It was 1985, and Doug E. Fresh and Slick Rick's "The Show" was exploding with all the subtlety of a temperamental thermonuclear device. It was just the bait that Azor, a wannabe record maker, needed. "The Show Stoppa," an Exocet missile aimed at Fresh, and S&P's 1986 debut album, *Hot, Cool & Vicious*, were performed by Cheryl and Sandy, written and produced by Hurby. Indeed, Azor worked the Salt-N-Pepa concept according to strict guidelines and applied science, controlling both their image–fun-loving homegirls out to have a good time–and their sound.

"I didn't write for girls," says Azor. "I didn't give them bullshit tracks, then hope that a pretty face would get them over. 'My Mic Sounds Nice' could have been a man saying it. I had a theory: if a girl does something half as good as a man, she's better. Like the women's basketball team. They couldn't fuck with the men's basketball team. But, because they can do it that well, they almost seem better than a men's basketball team."

Azor recalls the speech he gave them on how to build an audience: "Women will be your worst critics, but also your biggest fans. The first group of people that you gotta get are women. You can't do that by dissing 'em, and you can't do that by threatening them. If you're too pretty, you are a threat to black women as a rapper. Because rapping is boasting, right? We boast all day. So what are you going to boast about–that you look the dopest? You have a problem if women's gotta buy your shit. So you need to bring them on your side. Like Hammer, who can't get arrested, but he was very large at one time. Remember?"

I remark to Azor, who's talking to me from the Philippines, where he's looking at a group for his since-defunct label, Voodoo Magic, that he reminds me of another record mogul some years his junior. "I think you're exactly right." he says. "People often say to me, 'Puffy is you, ten years later.' But the opportunities that Puffy has, I didn't have. Wasn't nobody giving you a label deal in '86. Plus, rap was very young, so I didn't know to ask for one. I didn't know about marketing, which he mastered. I did everything I did off of feel. I appeared in everybody's video off of feel. I spoke on their records off of feel. All those things I did just out of instinct. It just felt right. There was no plan. And because of that, shit slipped away."

Shit did. But first it stunk up the place. Through Idol-makers, Hurby's parent company for managing the careers of Salt-N-Pepa, Kid 'n Play, Dana Dane, Kwamé, and numerous others, money poured in by the Hummer-load. In videos and on the pages of fanzines, Hurby and Cheryl appeared to be hip hop's golden couple, working together to create, after Russell Simmons' burgeoning Rushtown Management, hip hop's *other* dynasty. "Me and Hurby built the whole thing together," says Cheryl. "We went through a lot together. We were always together. We went to the studio together. We spent every waking moment together."

Which was wonderful, except that their relationship was a lie. "I don't think I ever *didn't* cheat on her," says Hurby. "I loved Cheryl, but I just had to have my cheeks on the side. That was just my life. You have your main squeeze, then you have other girls you fuck around with. It's like, I can't have chicken every day. You gotta taste some veal, some steak. Then, becoming popular, girls—many girls—didn't even mind doing it on the D.L. All that did was feed the flame. I didn't even have to work for it."

Hurby estimates the number of women he saw outside of his relationship with Cheryl as "fifty continuously. . . . It was fifty 'I'll-see-you-two-weeks-from-now-and-then-I-don't-hear-from-you-for-a-month.' It's a recycling thing."

Salt, on the womanizing: "I was oblivious to it for a long time, and even when I started realizing it, I ignored it. I put myself through a lot of unnecessary torture where he was concerned, and hoped for the better outcome of the situation. But it got to a point where it was so blatant and disrespectful that I had to cut it out."

Hurby remembers that point with CD-like clarity. "I went by her house one day and she said, 'Let's get married.' I said, 'What?' She goes, 'I'm serious. Let's get married. If you love me, let's get married.'"

She proposed to you?

"No. As the story continues, it wasn't a proposal. I said, 'What do you mean, *Let's get married*? I don't want to get married.' And she said, 'Well, why, if you love me? We have enough money, we're old enough. What's your reason?'

"I didn't have one. And she said, 'Okay. Get out.' That was it. That's how it ended."

"After that," says Salt, "it was just a series of break-ups and gettin' back together, and breakin' up and gettin' back together. He was playing with my head, because he knew that he could, and that's what I resented. Like he knew he didn't really want to be with me, but then he didn't want

nobody else to have me, and didn't want the industry to know that I was not his girl anymore. I mean, Hurby was even able to mess with my feelings the whole time I was pregnant, to make me think that I could be with him. So it was like, 'You're just being cruel now,' you know."

She went into a deep depression. "I was so devastated at that point that it was like a death to me. I call it 'the black hole.' I was just oblivious to everything else. I was so engulfed in my world that it was like nothing else was going on in the world to me, but Salt-N-Pepa—I was *always* dedicated to Salt-N-Pepa, fiercely—and Hurby. And I was cut off from God, spiritually. I was cut off, because I was putting Hurby before God, and being cut off from God is like being in a black hole to me."

"But," she says, smiling, "you know what got me out of it? When I had Corin," her baby girl.

It was as though a fever had broken. "I remember he called me one day and was saying some of his same old spiel. I was like, 'Man, if you *ever* think that you can play me again . . .' It was so real, and it was so strong, and it was so 'Baby, I am *over* you,' that he never mentioned it or tried to play with my heart again. Which he couldn't.

Somethin' about havin' a baby, man. Hurby was probably what I thought could fill my *hole*, or whatever. But he kept falling short of doing that. And then, when Corin came, it was just all about her! And I have not been the same since. I am just as in love with my kid as I was from day one. She is my *joy*."

"**A**aaah! Puh-*shiiit!*"

In a small Seattle rehearsal studio, a boombox crackles. Salt's doing leg stretches. Spin flips through a copy of *Ebony*, sucking her thumb up to the joint—as she often does when she's very relaxed.

Pepa is nowhere to be found, her flight delayed seven hours by a nearby plane catching fire on the ground. Dancers Kim Holmes, Teresa LéBron, Lisette Bustamante, and Lani Tuyor in line, the group goes through their hits: "Push It," "Whatta Man," a grunge version of "None of Your Business," the Grammy-nominated "Champagne," "Shoop." Tuyor, with the thickest, most *mmm!* calves I've ever seen on a woman of her height and build, is the most impressive, dancing with a modulated abandon, startling speed and precision, and the "big moves" for which star choreographers like Omar Lopez (S&P, Janet Jackson), overseeing the set, look. But it's a rehearsal. By the time they all hit the stage, you'll little be able to tell any difference in ability or skill.

Ironically, despite the oft criticisms of S&P as a soft, "pop" act, it may be this determinedness to *really put on a show* that strongly links them to the original masters of in-your-face, sweat-drenched hip hop performance: Grandmaster Flash & the Furious Five, Fantastic Freaks, Cold Crush Brothers, Busy Bee. (In fact, S&P's name, and even their trademark "My mic sounds nice, check one!" both come from Fantastic Freaks routines. Hurby was a *major* fan.) Meanwhile, an evidently endless procession of other, much "harder" rappers sour the art of live hip hop, furtively caressing their dicks in shows that no one but their dicks appreciate.

Gerald Scott, who with Darryll Brooks and Carol Kirkendall form CD Enterprises (CDE), S&P's management company, calls these ogres "taco/popcorn acts." "That's what you go get when they come on," he explains. In a genre where "management" often means your boy and his beeper, CDE is an anomaly; its partners are veterans of promoting national tours for Parliament-Funkadelic, Gap Band, and Cameo. CDE has also saturated S&P with the non-hip hop extracurriculars that have kept the group's star bright—the Victoria's Secret and Cover Girl commercials; the Baby-Cal and Stand Up Harlem PSAs, and a $15 million label deal.

"One thing that we learned as promoters a long time ago," says Gerald, "is that very seldom do black kids go to see the act. They go to be a part of the party. They're just as much a part of the show as the act itself and, if the act isn't able to involve them in the party, then they aren't interested. Salt-N-Pepa involved them in the party from the very beginning."

Simultaneously, says Carol, starting in the early 1980s, a cabal of agents, promoters, and labels exploited the genre's early growth spurts, and essentially ruined live hip hop, by putting *any* act, no matter how unprepared, on the road. "So all of a sudden," says Kirkendall, "you have in different shows, in different venues, in different parts of the country, ten, twelve brand-new baby acts that have never even been in rehearsal, but have been thrown out on a stage with a DAT. They're only one song strong, but they have to get out and do twenty, thirty minutes because they're getting absurd money. The audience thinks they stink, and is left bored, angry, and tired."

Which, somehow, when she finally arrives, Pepa is not. The Big Kahuna steps into the room—black leather fisherman's hat, oversized shades, bra-less, nipples aglow—and immediately the energy in the room palpably goes up. (Even Salt later admits: "I was kind of muddling through my rehearsal. But when she came, it was like"—she makes an explosion sound—"it's not really what she brings, or what I bring. It's magic *together.*")

Enid Denton, Pepa's mother, speaking in her amiable Jamaican brogue, is accustomed to the whirlwind. "When she was about six years old, she'd always take a broomstick, which would be her mike. And the singing . . . you don't even know what she's singing, but she's singing. She always want to be in the limelight. Everybody always say, 'Mrs. Denton, you have a star here.'"

Twenty-some years later, Pepa's still moving a mile a minute, bouncing off the walls, as though that six-year-old were high off of Kool-Aid, Krispy Kremes, and Sugar Frosted Flakes, every five seconds sputtering a ludicrous laugh. One second, the broad-shouldered beauty is practicing "Gitty Up," with the dancers, playing horsey in a laughing circle of women. "Huh-huh-huh!" The next, she's executing a Michael Jackson–style kick to riotous applause. "Huh-huh-huh!" Then she's sticking her face close to the spinning floor fan. "Uhhhhhhhhhhhhhhhhhh," she drones, listening to the feedback. To no one in particular, she asks, "Ever do that as a kid? Uhhhhhhhhhhhhh." Then as Dee Dee aggressively writhes to "None of Your Business" on her hands and knees, Pep creeps over and sneakily sticks a microphone up in between the startled Dee Dee's crack. "Huh-huh-huh!"

Whatta manifestation. Who could forget this feisty Jamaican at Woodstock 2? "Yo, fellas . . . I want you to take your right hand and put it on your head. *(They do.)* Come on! Whadda ya, virgins? *(Hand on her head.)* Not this head. *(Then her crotch.)* This head!" Pepa's not "hot." She's *cayenne*. Who *cares* about flat-assed Marilyn Monroe getting her little panties blown up over a New York City subway grate, or, for that matter, the entire cast of *Baywatch?* Give me the "Whatta Man" video, and the vision of Pep arcing her legs up from beneath the suds into a powerful V, the very poster of frothy sexuality.

But over lunch—grilled chicken and Caesar salad with some extra Caesar on the side, a plate of macho nachos with chicken (which she doesn't finish), and a Coke with four pieces of lemon—Sandra Jacqueline Theresa Denton seems more delicate and reflective, some distance from the hyperfuckable Amazon that many imagine her. The laugh is still there and frequent, but most of the makeup is not, giving her bronzed skin a soft, expressive luster.

She discusses Hollyhood, the clothing store business

so hard for her to go, 'I love you, Boo-Boo.' She will go, 'You know I love you.' She won't go like, 'I love you.'"

When you say to her, "Mom, how come you never say 'I love you,'" what does she say?

The question seems to startle her. "You know, I've never said that."

You've never asked her?

(Quietly) "Never asked her."

If you were to ask her that question, what would she do?

"She'd probably say, 'I've said I loved you!' I'm like, Mom, for real, you haven't. You always say, 'You know I love you.' Never 'I love you.' I don't know. To her, that's probably the same thing.

"I know she loves me, because I call my mother and we talk every day. I'm talking from back in school, in college, grown, whatever, I have to call my mother. Cheryl thinks it's kind of bugged. So, I know my moms loves me. I know that for a *fact*. I just think it something else she is dealing with from her past."

Was your grandmother affectionate?

"I don't want to 'Push It' no more," says Salt. "I don't want to 'Shoop' no more. I would like to start doing some serious gospel rap music... And I have to be in a position of power where I can do that."

she hopes to franchise. (It would eventually go out of business.) She chats happily about her burgeoning acting career—scripts sent for *Independence Day* and *Jerry Maguire*, small roles in *Joe's Apartment* and HBO's *First-Time Felon*, as well as S&P's own fizzled TV pilot, *On Our Own*. With Prada bag by her side, she speaks warmly of the five-bedroom house on three acres that she just recently bought from the first owner for "more than a million, but right around there."

But mostly, she talks frankly about the emotional state of her life. She acknowledges her sexual image, but says the truth is more complex.

"I had a deep, rough childhood. I was teased about a lot of stuff. I have a loving family, my mother and father loved me to death—but weren't affectionate. Both of them. Very cold. I can remember as a little child, my mom never hugged me. She would fight me if she heard me say this, but it's true. My mom will go, 'Have a nice night,' but it is

(Thinking) "Granny? No. So, maybe that's what it was. Maybe someone, her grandfather, taught her that or whatever. Maybe that's why I'm so flirtatious. Maybe that's why I'm, I don't know, clingy. I'm very clingy." Then, quietly, "My son's clingy," she says of her boy Tyran. "And he must get that from me. He clings. And we cling together."

I have a sense that your relationships with men are not easy.

"No, they're not so easy." Then she speaks forcefully. "You know what my thing is? I go out for mine. That's my problem in relationships. I will go out for that man. You know, go *all* out. See, everyone says, 'Act like you don't want them, so they want you.' I hate that game. *I want you*. Why can't I act like I want you?"

Are you in a relationship now?

"At this present moment?" She smiles, embarrassed, and covers her face for a second before answering softly, "No."

You had a very public relationship with Treach, from Naughty By Nature. (In fact, Pepa and Treach married in

1999, two years after this interview, only to divorce a year later. They share custody of their daughter, Egypt.)

"Me and Treach is a trip. I don't know. The love is there. I mean, I don't know. I've moved on."

It started in 1991, in Daytona Beach, Florida. Both groups were there for an *MTV's Spring Break* taping—Naughty's "O.P.P." was blazing the charts—and the star-crossed lovers found themselves by the bungee jump.

"I was going to bungee, and he took the mike from the man down there and said, 'All right, Miss Bungee, I know you're not going to jump backwards. If you're so bad, turn around and jump off backwards,' and I was like, 'Psssst!' I turned around, and he was like, 'Oh my gosh—she's going to jump backwards!' And I leaped backwards. And when we got off, he was like, 'You're crazy.' And when he smiled at me, it just clicked.

"The whole day, we had fun together. If you show me you can get in an amusement park and go-cart and bungee, I'm like"—Pep gets a rapturous, breathless look—"*Ohhhhhh*. Like, *wow*.

"And then, that night, I was leaving to go back home the next day, and he asked me to stay. Not, 'Stay to sleep with me,' because I went to my room. He was like, 'I have another show tomorrow. Could you just stay?' It was so sincere. Do you know what I mean? And I was like, 'Okay.' I stayed. It was just the way he did it. It was almost childlike.

"And he gave me a little peck on the mouth, and I was like, '*Oh my God.*' You can ask my stylist. I ran to her room. 'Guess what?' 'What?' 'Treach kissed me on my lips! He kissed me on my lips!' I was going crazy."

When he kissed you, what surprised you about that?

"He was gentle. He was sweet with his. Because you can't approach me like hard: 'Yo, tell me whassup? *Whassup?*' Oh, I *hate* that. Anybody who says that, I *know* that we won't go any further than this. You got to approach me like I'm a flower. You gotta be gentle with me. And he did it good."

In kind, Treach's words are surprisingly tender. "Well, actually, I always had a crush on her, back before Naughty was Naughty. I had her pictures up on my wall; Salt-N-Pepa stuff, and I had solo shots of her. So when I met her in person, that crush was still there. I was trying to play cool, laid back, 'I'm not gonna sweat this or nuttin' like that.' But after I knew what type of person that she was, the feelings clicked."

What attracted you? "It was just her . . . her eyes, I guess. Her eyes and her smile. Her eyes got like a deep, innocent, special type o' glow. And her smile, it's got the innocence of a child, but it got the maturity and the *turn-on* of a mature, beautiful woman."

The relationship changed him. "Before I fell in love with Pepa, she couldn't pay me to go to a restaurant, sit down, and eat. It was, 'I ain't sittin' nowhere. Let's get our stuff and be out. I ain't all up into this boojie shit.' Ya know what I mean? She caught a thug straight off the street, and she molded me into a lot more that what I would have been on my own."

But as for the breakup's reason, Treach, like Sandy, is imprecise. "It's a mutual thing. We both came to a agreement. It was basically not going nowhere." Do you think you guys will be together in the future? "I can't say." Do you think your current breakup is very final; in other words, different from previous breakups? "Yeah, it's a lot different from previous ones." How?

He answers with a curious, but extremely telling, analogy: "Say you gonna build something. You got this plan, you try all these different ways you got set off to build it, and to work with the people that you got workin' wit' you. You try they way. You try your way.

"So, you build and you build. It's fallin', but you repair it. It falls over here, and you repair that. Then it goes this way, and everybody is going at each other, like, 'I know what I'm doin'! You don't know what you doin'!' 'I know what I'm doin'! You don't know what *you* doin'!' *But you're still fallin' down*. It's like, both parties knew what the fuck they was doing, but in actuality, they wasn't listening to the other person, who probably had good ideas as well.

"So the building was never finished."

However, Pepa's tale is even more telling. "When I was, like, eleven, I used to go with my neighbor. When it would get dark, my parents would say, 'Come inside. It's late now.' I was like 'Okay!' and I would go from his step to my step. We were literally neighbors, next door.

"In the attic, I used to have this big board, a wooden plank, and I used to put it across from my window to his window [she laughs] and crawl—four stories up. He would be in the other window, and I'd be crawlin' over.

"*That's* how I go out for my man. From when I was little, I was going out for my man."

After two weeks of intense work prepping for the release of *Brand New*, Salt enjoys what she calls her "ultimate relaxation." "I'm in the bed, and my daughter's sitting besides me bouncin' around, watching Nickelodeon."

And when Corin's not ogling *Blues' Clues*, or vetoing mommy's fashion choices, as she did in the "Champagne" video, the two share another special bond. "I like to ride horses," says Salt. "I have a Palomino. She's a yellowy color, she has a white mane, a white tail, and her name is Coco, my daughter's nickname. My daughter loves horses. She does not play with her dolls unless they're on her horses. She has an obsession with horses, so I bought her a horse.

I'm gonna get her a little cowgirl outfit. I got myself some iguana skin boots, a belt, the hat, and a top-of-the-line Billy Cooke saddle that matches my horse.

"It's added something to my life really. It's something that I look forward to doing, something that I dream about sometimes. Once I dreamt that I was riding my horse through the clouds in the sky. I guess that just represented that I really like riding. It was a pleasant dream."

In her "very humble," once four-, now three-bedroom ("I turned one into a walk-in closet") home, far outside of New York City, Salt seems to have finally found the serenity that every woman needs. "I cannot tolerate anyone disturbing my peace, because it took me so long to get to the point where I have peace. It's more valuable than anything in my life, my sense of order and my peace."

Yet, despite her peace, and her millions, the financial stake she feels she and Pepa deserve in their work still eludes them. Hurby owns 50 percent of Salt-N-Pepa's name—down from 100 percent—and "to this day," says Salt, "Hurby gets a third of everything we make. He didn't do anything on [*Brand New*], and he still gets a third of all royalties. He's like a third person in the group." (Hurby may be only slightly less contemptuous of his lucrative association with S&P. In 1998, he created a computer-generated group called Digital Delinquents. "I don't have to take anybody's mouth," he says, naming benefits. "I don't pay them royalties, I don't do nothing. If one of 'em acts up, I just delete 'em.")

Also, like 99.99 percent of the recording artists you adore, Salt does not own her own work; it is sharecropped to her by a record company, which does own it. To that end, it's fitting that "the most extravagant thing" in Salt's home is her 48-track digital recording studio, built by her and her child's father, Gavin Wray—an up-and-coming producer, like Hurby once was, but, unlike Hurby, one whom she calls "family" and "a good father." (Salt married Wray in late 2000, the last bud to open in a flowering of S-N-P nuptials, following Pepa's to Treach and Spin's to boutique owner Mario Jones.) "I made the whole *Brand New* album here, right in my basement," she says. "Like I said, we're businesswomen. We've made mistakes, and we'll make more mistakes. But that does not mean we're not businesswomen. I feel that I'm in a position now where I can have a lot more equity in myself and in anything else I bring to a record

company. And if I'm not gettin' that, then I'm gonna start puttin' out records myself."

And sell 'em out the back of your car?

"Basically."

With any luck Salt's Lexus four-door won't end its days that way. But she's faced—and overcome—bigger obstacles before. It wasn't too long ago, staring with deepest love into the eyes of her newborn daughter, that she realized just how much hurt she'd overcome. And it wasn't much later, trying to answer the hardest thing Corin ever asked her, that she realized the answer her daughter needed was the same one that, for many years, she had been seeking herself.

"The hardest thing was, Where is God? That was the hardest thing, to make her understand where He was."

What did you tell her?

"I told her that God is everywhere. That is not enough, obviously. 'Everywhere? What does that mean?' So I told her, most important, God is inside of us, and she didn't understand 'inside of us.' Like, is it, like, a person inside of us?

"So I had to go into 'The Spirit of God is inside of us,' and then she wanted to know what a spirit was. I don't remember how I explained the spirit.

"But then I explained to her that when she feels love—I was like, 'You know how when you feel love for Mommy and you want to give Mommy a hug?' I said 'That's God.'

"'When you look at a flower and you think about how beautiful it is? That's God. And when the wind blows, and when it rains, and nature?' And I was like 'That's God. He's all around us.'"

He's all around us. He's all around us, like curly zephyr winds, noiselessly brushing past bare legs on a summer day. *He's all around us,* like the warm hugs of friends with whom one has shared and borne much. *He's all around us,* like struggle, and like pain, through which we must go, in order to become that which, ultimately, we are most meant to be. And *He's all around us,* like peace, and like joy, finally achieved, tenderly embraced, and gracefully received, like a child's simple acceptance of a deep and eternal truth.

"And I guess that satisfied her," Salt says, with all the peace and joy that her life has brought her to in this moment, "because now when you ask her, Where's God?, she says, 'He's all around us, and He's in my heart.'"

MC LYTE

Never have I ever said I was good lookin' just one bad-ass bitch from Brooklyn

Photograph by Andrew Eccles

kickin'
4 brooklyn *by Michael A. Gonzales*

Most scribes who document hip hop culture evangelize about the South Bronx as though it were some sort of urban holy land, yet they often fail to recognize the residents of other New York City boroughs. Of course, Bronx bombers like DJ Kool Herc, Grandmaster Flash, and Afrika Bambaataa have already been anointed the holy trinity of black noise, but there's always room for argument. Old-school fiends in Queens will swear that nobody rocked harder than King Charles, while their neighbors in Brooklyn still brag about Grandmaster Flowers's skills on the wheels of steel.

Brooklyn gained fame as the stomping ground of Jewish superstars like Neil Diamond, Barbra Streisand, Norman Mailer, and Woody Allen, but her chocolate neighborhoods contributed their fair share of cultural heroes, too. One can almost imagine the entire posse—from old-timers like Sonny Carson, Mandrill, Crown Heights Affair, and B. T. Express, to young'ns like Lenny Kravitz, Fab 5 Freddy, Spike Lee, Biggie Smalls, and Mos Def—rocking the block somewhere on Eastern Parkway, beat box banging Roy Ayers's dynamite rare groove "We Live in Brooklyn, Baby." But the ultimate Crooklyn block party wouldn't be complete without a heavyweight microphone controller known as MC Lyte.

Inside the strawberry cheesecake pleasure-dome of Junior's, one of downtown BK's most adored eatspots, the local patrons—thirtyish black folks, hip hop's second generation of aficionados—nod in Lyte's direction, grinning toward her as though she were royalty. No disrespect to her soul sister Latifah, but there are plenty of Brooklynites who will argue that Lyte is the true queen of rap. When a brave soul does approach her table to speak, Lyte acknowledges them with a warm smile. Unlike some hip hop matriarchs who wear their bitchiness like a gleaming tiara, Lyte has always been chill.

Although born in Queens and currently based in Cali, MC Lyte has called the gritty asphalt of Planet Brooklyn home since the days when she walked to class in East Flatbush wearing a dungaree blazer and skirt uniform. Lana Moore (as her mama christened her), attended Weusi Shule African elementary school, where youngsters were intro-

duced to the negro cool of poet Langston Hughes and practiced jujitsu instead of basketball. A funky spirit having taken possession of her soul, Little Lana was addicted to music from an early age. "To this day my mother tells the story that before I was born I danced around in her stomach whenever the Jackson 5's 'I'll Be There' came on," Lyte recalls. "That was my song."

Sharing slices of life between sips of tea, Lyte says she grew up surrounded by the sounds of Gladys Knight and Al Green. Sometimes she'd put on her mother's wig and turn up the stereo. "I'd stand in the living room singing Donna Summer or Diana Ross. There was not a song by either one of them I did not know," she recalls with a smile. "I remember the first concert my mother took me to was Rick James. I was nine years old and she covered my eyes for half the show, but at least I got to hear it."

On weekends in the summer, Lil' Lana rode the subway to Manhattan and hung with her cousins in Spanish Harlem. It was in that notorious wild-cowboy neighborhood that she got her first drop of hip hop. "My cousins listened to the Funky 4 + 1 More, the Treacherous Three, and Grandmaster Flash and the Furious Five," Lyte recalls. "They had all those records, so I know I had to be influenced by them."

After graduating from the strict African academy, she entered a period of unruly rebellion in junior high. "I was so happy to be able to wear normal clothes again I didn't know what to do," Lyte says, laughing. "But there was also a certain freedom that I kind of took advantage of. I had two sets of friends—kids I could study with and kids I could be bad with." The bad ones must have been a hell of a lot more fun. From hanging in the 'hood smoking cheeba to scribbling aerosol on the walls ("My graf tag name was LUV D," she divulges. "Then it changed to Lana D."). Lyte's so-called life was going all topsy-turvy. "But by the time I was ready to graduate from ninth grade, I was over being bad."

It was during these years that she began testing her rap skills in that infamous training ground for many professional rappers—a rowdy school lunchroom. "When I was twelve, there were a bunch of kids who would write and say their raps and I thought, 'You know, that's something I want to get into,'" Lyte recalls. "There was a guy named

Eric who used to write rhymes for me. Once I started learning the process, I applied what he taught me to my own writing. To this day I still write the way he taught me," says the creator of some of hip hop's most complex narratives. "You just write one line and there's a hyphen that separates the next line. Whereas some people just write line, line, line, line. Mine kind of runs on, you know. . . ."

Unfortunately, the damage had already been done. "I wasn't able to get into the high school of my choice," she remembers. "My grades were fine, but those notes on my report card were a bad sign. I wanted to go to school in the city, but that didn't pan out."

Lana wound up as a student at George W. Wingate High School, best known in the annals of soul-boy civilization as the site of the football field where Curtis Mayfield had his last stand before being paralyzed by a fallen light tower struck by lightning. "A lot of the kids I went to junior high with also came to Wingate," she recalls over bites of breakfast. "But I managed to stay out of trouble."

Lana kept busy going to school and holding down two jobs. Besides travel agent and brokerage firm gigs, she

but she knew better than to stand in the way of her strong-willed girl. "She would make me write a composition and give it to her on why she should let me go," Lyte recalls with a warm smile. "Every once in a while she'll get on the phone and read me one of those. But I think she understood that there was really nowhere for kids to go to have a good time."

Anything could happen anytime at hot spots like the Latin Quarter and Union Square, where even rap stars might get their ornate trunk jewelry snatched from their necks. Despite their sometimes tense atmosphere, these clubs were once Gotham's most infamous empires of sound, a creative battleground for rappers to polish their rhyme-slayer skills in front of true troopers.

"Latin Quarter was open on Tuesday and Saturdays, and we went both nights," says Lyte, swept into a reverie. "I was just a newcomer; I was like Wow, look at this! I remember seeing Public Enemy perform, then there was Fresh Prince and Jazzy Jeff, as well as Rakim. Then, when Union Square opened I went to see KRS-One one night and Salt-N-Pepa another. I lived for those days."

After a night of slinging fried taco meat, Lana would step out in straight-up homegirl couture: gold bamboo earrings, starched Gloria Vanderbilt jeans, name-plate belt, shearling coat, and Pumas with fat laces.

worked evenings at Chi Chi's, a Mexican semi-fast food joint. "My mom was a bartender at night and going to school during the day," says Lyte. "Mom would bring home her tips in a bag and I would count it for her. I really wanted to make some money on my own, so I realized if you really want something you got to go out there and work for it."

After a night of slinging fried taco meat, Lana and her older friend and coworker Jill would stomp into the ladies' room in their uniforms and emerge dipped in straight-up early '80s homegirl couture: gold bamboo earrings, starched Gloria Vanderbilt jeans, name-plate belts, shearling coats, and a dope pair of Pumas with the fat laces. Then they were off to clubs like Latin Quarter and Union Square. "I told my mother that Jill was driving, but she really wasn't." Lyte laughs. "We would be on the subway at astronomical hours of the morning. It was crazy."

Mrs. Moore wasn't crazy about Lana's club crawling,

Spending her spare hours absorbing the latest black noises created by a legion of dudes trapped in their own version of the He-man Woman Haters Club, Lyte was becoming obsessed with fever dreams of rocking the mike herself. "I remember listening to Mr. Magic's and Red Alert's hip hop shows every weekend," says Lyte. "In those days the hip hop shows only aired twice a week, so that taught you to really appreciate it, you know?"

Studying the female rappers who were out at the time—"I listened to all of them: Salt-N-Pepa, Sequence, Sha Rock from the Funky 4 + 1 More, Roxanne Shanté, the Real Roxanne"—she realized there was something she wasn't hearing, something she could bring. "Stories," she says simply. "I can tell stories." But the MC Lyte story was just beginning.

Not long after they started hanging tough, Jill introduced Lana to another Brooklynite friend named Tony. His cellar was cluttered with the tools of the DJ's trade (countless records, two turntables, microphone). The wannabe producer helped Lana construct an early version of a twisted tale called "I Cram to Understand U (Sam)," which would eventually become Lyte's first single. "I just recorded the song so I could have a tape of my stuff," she says, "but I was still excited. I started going around telling the other kids at school, 'I'm going to make a record.' No one seemed to believe me."

At 30 years old, MC Lyte still looks as youthful as the first time ever I saw her face in 1988. I was slaving my days away in the stock warehouse of the Catherine Street Homeless Shelter—a vocational school that had been converted into temporary housing for the weary women of the world. Some had been burned out of their homes, more than a few had been bounced off the walls by brutish boyfriends, others were simply sucking that glass dick and speaking in the tongue of "Scotty" as their crack children boomeranged through the halls.

After unloading trucks, stacking the inventory, and giv-

"There she go again," snickered G, his Nike'd feet resting on a desk. "Bitch always talking shit." Although we weren't sure if this Sam was the same crack-smoking boyfriend mentioned in "Cram," or simply another unfortunate brother with the same name, the track was smoother than a Mickey Dee's shamrock shake. Produced by the King of Chill, perhaps hip hop's most underrated symphonic scientist, "Paper Thin" sounded like the future with its driving pre-jungle drum patterns, a crazed guitar, and a sample of Earth, Wind & Fire's heavenly horns.

Directed by Lionel Martin himself, the majority of the "Paper Thin" clip took place underground, inside the confines of a crowded subway car. After busting her man trying to playboy-scoop two honeys at the opposite end of the car, Lyte lets loose: "When you say you love me it doesn't matter / It goes into my head as just chit chatter / You may think it's egotistical or just very free / But what you say, I take none of it seriously. . . ."

In the video, Lyte's stormy expression looked like she was about to rain down on this nigga with an intense

"I listened to all of them," Lyte says, "Salt-N-Pepa, Sequence, Funky 4 + 1 More, Roxanne Shanté, the Real Roxanne." She realized there was something she wasn't hearing. "Stories," she says. "I can tell stories."

ing out supplies (mostly diapers and sanitary napkins), me and my homeboy Grant spent the rest of the afternoon getting fried on chocolate Thai while waiting for *Video Music Box* to come on at 3:30. In the days before MTV knew hip hop existed, two creative gents from Brooklyn named Ralph McDaniels and Lionel Martin produced a televised rap showcase that quickly became a 'hood-rat favorite. Featuring studio interviews, taped remotes from swinging parties, and the latest in low-budget rap videos, the hour-long program was a part of our daily ritual.

These were the days before people dared to put the words *hip hop* and *diva* in the same sentence, those ancient '80s when only a few braggadocious broads dared to cross the gender lines. Already familiar with Lyte's voice from the rock-hard single "Cram," me and G watched in wonder as the video for "Paper Thin" premiered that smoky afternoon. "Hit the road, Sam, and don't you come back no more," Lyte was saying with a none-too-pleased expression on her face.

knuckle-shower. After the vid had faded from the screen, the usually rowdy G-man sat sedately for a moment, then broke out in a big grin. "See, man," he joked, grabbing his crotch. "Even the girls in Brooklyn know how to rap."

"Lyte listened to the same people we were all listening to," says her stepbrother Milk, who with his brother Gizmo, made up the infamous rap duo Audio Two. "You know, like Just-Ice, L.L. Cool J, Ultimate Force." Lana often visited them in Staten Island on the weekends. "When Lyte was in high school," he says, "I think she spent more time writing rhymes than going to class."

Developing their skills in the basement of their crib, with a little assistance from Daddy-O of the group Stetsasonic, Milk and Giz were building the raw minimalist sound that would become their trademark on the classic 12-inch "Top Billin'." Although it was pure rap kitsch—with its scratchy sound, skeletal beat, and whiny arrogant rhymes

("Milk is chillin', Giz is chillin', what more can I say? / Top Billin'!")—the song (set to a track they had originally built for Lyte) put the bros at the forefront of the developing hip hop community, an honor that did not necessarily translate into big money. "We had the label, but we weren't really in the position to be signing new artists," says Milk, laughing. "It was easier for us to work with Lyte, because she was family and she wasn't worried about how much advance she could get."

But working with kin had its advantages, too. While some females suffered the all-too-common misfortune of being dogged by producers, Lyte came to expect nothing less than maximum respect. Equipped with a set of Technics SL1200s, a 4-track recorder, and a mixer, Audio Two began working with her on a regular basis. "Lyte would come over with her rhymes and we'd try to find the right beat," says Milk, who still lives on Staten Island. "Her voice reminded me of MC Shan. She was tough, which was good, because there were no other girls rapping like that."

Fusing their basement flavor with Lyte's fierce urban folklore, "I Cram to Understand U" detailed the rise and fall of a shady dude named Sam. "I should have known the consequences right from the start / That he'd use me for my money and then break my heart / But like a fool in love, I fell for his game," raps Lyte, who by the end of the song loses her man to a crack pipe instead of another woman.

With a beat that was perfect for kids who wanted to Wop—the loose-limbed early '80s dance that could have been created by the Scarecrow from *The Wizard of Oz*—"Cram" was an immediate sensation in the hip hop netherworld. Unlike most other antidrug songs, Lyte's lyrics were far from preachy. Yet, as she wove skillfully crafted tale, Lyte evoked powerful feelings of frustration and anger. The "Cram" story line was so vivid, it had Milk and Giz's dad Nat Robinson worried. "I even asked her if the song was based on a real incident in her life," recalls the man who became a sort of stepfather to Lyte, "but she assured me it was fiction."

It was Nat Robinson who helped jump-start the careers of Lyte and Audio Two when he formed the First Priority music label. Although he had a day job building Eastern Airlines' computer database, Robinson was far from a geek. "Dad used to promote parties in the '70s," recalls Milk.

MC Lyte and K-Rock in Brooklyn.

"He was the ultimate enterpriser, so once he saw we were serious about the music he decided to invest in our futures."

With Lyte, Audio Two, and another production team known as the Alliance (fronted by King of Chill), this Brooklyn version of Berry Gordy took a page from the diligent scriptures of self-reliance preached by W. E. B. Du Bois. But Robinson may have done his job too well. His fledgling enterprise was becoming too popular. While hawking 12-inch discs from the trunk of one's car might seem somewhat romantic, the daily realities of controlling an independent label were taking their toll.

"Believe me, our relationship wasn't anything as strange as the Jacksons, but we were protective of Lyte," says Robinson. "I was by her side every step of the way. Her mom was depending on me to look out for her, but I know for her it must have gotten a little boring. While everybody else was out partying, I made sure Lyte was back in her room."

All the same, those early rappin' road trips made quite an impression on young Lyte. "I think my favorite would probably be the Heavy D–Kool Moe Dee tour. There was also me, Latifah, and Ice-T. We all stayed at the Days Inn, which would be so unacceptable today. In between shows, we would sit in the hallway and clown around with each other. These days, everyone stays in their private dressing rooms, but then it was different."

Robinson remembers the barriers he had to kick down

so his little girl could be heard. "If any promoter wanted to book Audio Two, they had to book Lyte," he says matter-of-factly. "They didn't even have to pay her, just put Lyte on the bill. We kinda leveraged her into a more hardcore environment." Years later, Nat informed Lyte that during her first performance at the Latin Quarter, where she was completely nervous, he was in the DJ booth with Red Alert. "Look how she holds the mike," mocked the popular jock. "She'll never make it." Of course, nothing could have been more wrong.

Around the same time, Sylvia Rhone of Atlantic Records began hearing about Audio Two, and in 1986 she reached out to the Brooklyn hit makers. Linking with a major label involved certain financial and creative sacrifices, but it would plug First Priority into a major distribution machine, complete with clever marketing teams, pumped-up promoters, and tireless publicists. It would also allow Lyte to quit her job as a messenger. She still has fond memories of the day she resigned her post.

"We were the first independent to be signed by a major label," says Lyte, who stayed on board at Atlantic for 13 years. At first, the former home base of Stax Records, the Rolling Stones, Aretha Franklin, Led Zeppelin, Roberta Flack, Donny Hathaway, and Cameo wasn't too excited about the prospect of putting out a girl rapper. But Nat insisted they take all his acts or none at all. Once Lyte got in the door, she set about changing people's minds in a hurry.

"Lyte was one of the first female rap stars to be on a par with men when it came to MC skills," says Rhone, who's now CEO of Elektra with an office overlooking Rockefeller Plaza. "She never let herself become a caricature, never exploited her sexuality to win over an audience. Her Brooklyn roots and her stature in the rap community there, along with her brothers Audio Two, gave her a credibility that a lot of the female rappers lacked."

"When Lyte was onstage her voice would send chills down my spine," says Robinson. "Even if she had been a stranger, I would have felt the same way." With a voice deeper than an ocean, Lyte could hold her own in the studio as well as on the stage. "Milk had a concept in his head of how I should sound," says Lyte as a pink-uniformed waitress brings our breakfast. "Up to this day he's like, 'Lyte, you're the hardest female MC.'"

Before the days of stylists and image consultants, Lyte says she just wore what was comfortable, which usually meant a sweatsuit and sneakers. But her tomboy look also made her sexually neutral to hip hop's majority male audience. "I wanted the male rappers to listen to my rhymes as opposed to looking at my body," she says. "I wanted

to be taken seriously—like, 'Don't even look at that, just listen to what I'm saying.'"

"Lyte never would have been accepted in the male arena if she was wearing the things female rappers wear today," says Nat Robinson. "Male rappers thought she was tough. Lyte always had a raw edge, so she was able to do shows with hardcore guys like KRS-One, Eric B. & Rakim, or Ice-T."

"Lyte has never played that stereotypical girl role," says Milk. "Some people might have thought she sounded like a boy, the same way I was accused of sounding like a girl. But Lyte wasn't all made up and glamorous, she was more concerned about her skills on the mic. We all considered her a great MC, not just a great *female* MC. For Lyte, it was all about the art."

But the public didn't always see it that way. Like many other strong sisters, Lyte was forced to cope with a nasty backlash when she stepped into the rap arena. While I've heard freaky tales of one rapper boy's she-male adventures, it always seems to be the female MCs who bear the brunt of gay-baiting gossip. In the final analysis, who cares where she stuck her tongue, as long as she kept it in her mouth when saying her lethal rhymes? As Professor Cornel West points out in *Race Matters,* "Black women are subject to more multilayered bombardments of racist assaults than black men in addition to the sexist assaults they receive from black men."

KRS-One had a different sort of assault in mind in 1989, when he invited Lyte to participate in the classic "Self-Destruction," an all-star rap fest that dropped more science than Einstein. Featuring Public Enemy, Red Alert, Daddy-O, Heavy D., KRS, and Miss Melodie (who's now a singer in the Brooklyn Tabernacle Choir), the track was dedicated to battling against violence in hip hop. "I was in some great company that day," Lyte recalls. "I had these rhymes written and there were all these crime statistics listed. I read it for L.L. and he was like, 'Don't nobody want to hear about any statistics.' He sat me down, then he kicked the rhyme, 'Funky fresh, dressed to impress,' then I said, 'Ready to party.' Although I wrote the rest of my rhymes, L.L. did give me a jump-start."

The record served as a wake-up call to make hip hop kids stop their detrimental behavior. "Hip hop clubs used to be such a fun environment," says Lyte. "And then before you knew it, it became snatching chains, stealing coats, stealing sneakers. It was just impossible to really have a good time because you were always in fear of someone jacking you for your stuff." All the MCs donated their services for free, with proceeds from the gold single benefiting the Urban League. "The fun part was we were just doing it because we wanted to be involved in something that may affect someone's life. Today that would be unheard of."

nside The World, a Lower East Side venue that used to feature rap music at a Sunday-night party called "Brutal," the acrid aroma of burning cocaine was strong enough to singe one's nose hairs. Though the venue has since been converted into a synagogue, in the 1980s this spot was hotter than Lucifer's inferno. In fact, the Devil himself was probably hanging out behind one of the club's massive pillars, sporting a crimson Troop jacket.

Hundreds of bodies are smashed together in the semi-darkness, smoking weed, angel dust, coolies (coke in a cigarette), woolies (crack in a joint), or just sniffing powder. MC Lyte's audio beatdown "10% Dis" booms from the club's speakers. Over a grimy street rhythm, Lyte threatens a rival that she'll "pop you in the microwave to watch your head bubble." Spilling my drink on the already disgusting floor, I overhear a thick-accented Rican *mami* squawk, "You know she be talkin' 'bout that skinny bitch

recounts, "but Hurby never did the song. Next thing we're coming from a show in Boston and Antoinette is on the radio dissing Milk."

Speculation was that Hurby and Co. were plotting some sort of surprise attack. "Milk turned to me and said, 'You got to dis her for us,'" Lyte remembers. "They thought people would hate on them if they dissed a girl." As soon as they got back to New York they headed straight for the studio and recorded "10% Dis." Though her first take was accidentally erased, and Lyte had to do it over again, the final result was lethally effective.

Lyte and Antoinette's only face-to-face meeting on the same stage took place at The World. Unlike today's flesh-and-blood rap wars, nothing really happened beyond a bit of reckless eyeballing. But the crowd was screaming so loud they seemed to have lost their collective minds. "It wasn't presented as a battle," Lyte recalls. "Still, it was obvious that the crowd was in my favor."

In the months that followed, the battle raged on. When Antoinette dropped "Lights Out," the queen of Brook-

Lyte's tomboy look made her sexually neutral to hip hop's majority male audience. "I wanted male rappers to listen to my rhymes as opposed to looking at my body," she says. "I wanted to be taken seriously."

Antoinette." Flicking a Newport ash, homegirl rubs her reddening nose. "Fuck that," she says. "Lyte just letting her know what time it is."

In those days most female rappers began their career making dis records. But the Lyte vs. Antoinette battle was different. These women sounded truly pissed. The whole thing began with a rumor.

"It wasn't my idea that she try to dis Lyte," recalls Hurby "Luv Bug" Azor, the producer responsible for Salt-N-Pepa as well as Antoinette, who called herself The Gangstress. "I had nothing to do with it."

Not surprisingly, Lyte's recollection of events is somewhat different. "Audio Two had contacted Hurby about doing an answer record to their own song 'Top Billin'," she says. Understanding the commercial value of a little rivalry, they agreed to give him the backing track to their underground smash and he was to line up an artist to do the new song. "The song was going to be called 'Stop Illin'," Lyte

lyn snapped back with a one-two combination on her second album *Eyes on This*. First up was the feisty "Shut the Eff Up! (Hoe)." Opening with the voice of the head bitch in charge, Millie Jackson—"I've been too nice, too long. It's definitely time to get nasty"—Lyte's song threw words like bricks. On the same album, Parrish Smith (from EPMD) produced "Slave 2 the Rhythm," which seemed to hearken back to that night at The World. "Don't turn your back 'cause this mike will be in your ass," she said. "I don't dis you for the money / I dis you for the fun." It wasn't long before Antoinette disappeared completely from the scene. Nobody ever said the rap game was easy. But over the years the battles took a toll on everyone.

Street speculation about Lyte's own sexuality resurfaced with Roxanne Shanté's wicked 1992 release, "Big Mama," in which she referred to Lyte as a "bull dagger." For her part Lyte maintains that "others took it more seriously than the people being talked about." The whole controversy took an unexpected turn in 1993 with the release of "I Got a Man," a successful duet with her old friend Positive K. Then Lyte dropped "Ruffneck," her biggest hit ever, and the first gold single ever by a solo female hip hop artist. "I need a man that don't snitch like a bitch / Shed tears or switch," rapped Lyte in what Rhone called her "ode to the boys in the 'hood."

Besides a handful of guest appearances—with Common on his blaxploitation funk album *Like Water for Chocolate*, with Bob Marley on a remix of "Jammin'" for the *Chant Down Babylon* album, and on Will Smith's *Wild Wild West* soundtrack—Lyte has kept a low musical profile since the release of her slept-on sixth disc, *Seven and Seven* (1998). That record was her last for Atlantic/Elektra, the label she'd been associated with since her 1988 debut, *Lyte as a Rock*. "I wish I was able to put out *Seven and Seven* again, because there were some hot songs on there," says Lyte with a trace of bitterness in her voice. "There was this great track that the Neptunes [the duo behind smash

could speak in complete sentences, MC Lyte's longevity has surpassed even the expectations of her kindest fans. As Rhone says, "MC Lyte paved the way for females to fire off rhymes straight from their hearts." It's no secret that she has served as an inspirational beacon for a generation of strong sisters like Eve, Rah Digga, and Sonja Blade.

"Anything Lyte touches, she touches with dignity and grace," says Public Enemy's master lyricist Chuck D. "She could hang out with the guys. She gave a woman's point of view. Shit, she's the bomb. Lyte has a distinctive voice. Boom, she sounded ruff, rugged, and raw! Some chicks have to smoke a million blunts to get that voice. Lyte is the ultimate MC, with the voice, style, and the ability to cut a rhyme and make it hurt. She's been slept on by male journalists, mainly white boys. She represents a different constituency. Lyte is a hall-of-famer."

It wasn't just skills but lyrical content that set this MC apart. Like a hip hop Zora Neale Hurston, Lyte was enticed by the poetic purity of regular people. Rather than bragging about designer possessions or the number of sexual

"Anything Lyte touches, she touches with dignity and grace," says Chuck D of Public Enemy. "She's the ultimate MC, with the voice, style, and the ability to cut a rhyme and make it hurt. Lyte is a hall-of-famer."

hits by Jay-Z, Mystikal, and Noreaga] had produced, but it was never released as a single."

The year 1998 proved to be one of the most disappointing of Lyte's career. With the multitalented Missy Elliott (who did a guest spot on *Seven and Seven*) becoming her label's newest priority, Lyte was feeling lost in the sauce of poor promotion and corporate neglect. "What we should've done was: I put out a record one year, Missy puts out one the next year," Lyte reasons. "But our records were coming out at the same time, which meant I really had no one focusing on my project. So, after thirteen years, I told them I wasn't happy and I wanted to leave the label." Elektra CEO Sylvia Rhone called to ask if she was sure. "But at that point," Lyte says, "I was positive." Following in the footsteps of former label-mate Yo Yo, the Los Angeles legend who'd left Elektra two years before, Lyte decided it was time to bounce.

An independent woman years before Destiny's Child

positions she could flip—not that there's anything wrong with that—Lyte was an acute social observer. Though not as flamboyant as her contemporary Slick Rick, MC Lyte shared his ability to move outside of herself and gaze on the problems of the world through multiple perspectives.

Within her brilliant composition "Eyes Are the Soul," Lyte speaks from three different points of view. In one verse, she's an AIDS patient, in another she's a crackhead who robs and kills his mother, and last she's a teenage girl who gets pregnant and has an abortion. It's a virtuoso performance, at once sensitive and hardcore. As NYU professor Tricia Rose wrote in her 1994 study *Black Noise*, Lyte has always managed to sustain "an uncomfortable balance between brutal cynicism and honest vulnerability."

In recent years, MC Lyte began pursuing an alternative career as an actress. "Because I saw television before I heard my first rap record, I would say that I've always wanted to be in front of the camera," Lyte confesses.

"Before VCRs came out, I used to tape shows like *Diff'rent Strokes* and *Facts of Life* and rehearse the lines later. I used to fantasize that I was Tootie on *The Facts of Life*. That was a dream I had put on the back burner, though. It wasn't until after accomplishing the hip hop thing and making videos that I start building my belief system."

After she began studying the Stanislavsky acting technique with teacher Sheila Gray in New York, homegirl left for the West. Since settling amid the thick smog and plastic pretense of Los Angeles, Lyte has appeared on the television shows *Moesha, In the House, For Your Love,* and *New York Undercover.* She's tried hosting an Internet radio show on siriusradio.com, even lent her voice to the interactive Diva Starz doll. (Described by Mattel press release as: "The only interactive, electronic fashion dolls that interact intelligently with girls and share their same interests—fashions, malls, parties, pets, telling jokes, sports, the latest trends, and self-discovery.")

But her current return to New York is not just about nostalgia. As we finish our breakfast, Lyte reveals that she's quietly begun work on an album for Will Smith's new Overbrook label. "He sees the potential," she says of the man she used to watch rocking the Latin Quarter. "It's a beautiful thing." Call it one veteran recognizing another.

How MC Lyte will fit into the iced-out hip hop environment of the new millennium is anybody's guess, but she exudes confidence. "I certainly believe that I earned my stripes," she says. "And people recognize the stripes and now it's time for me to wipe the dust off and come back shining."

Come to think of it, there's never been a better time to be a woman in the rap game. Maybe the world is more ready than ever for what Lyte's always had to offer. "I think I speak for generations of women who aren't afraid to take responsibility," she states. "Who identify with strength and courage and independence. And hopefully I've sparked a whole lot of women to be able to speak for themselves and stand for what it is they believe in."

Before exiting the air-conditioned comfort of Junior's for the warmth of an Indian summer day, she wants to make one thing perfectly clear: "Although I have more than hip hop on my mind these days, it will always be a part of me." It's good to know that wherever Lyte may land, Brooklyn will always be in the house.

QUEEN LATIFAH

Since he was with his boys he

tried to break fly I punched

him dead in his eye and said

"Who you calling a bitch?"

Photograph by Nitin Vadukul

the
last
good
witch
by Kierna Mayo

I n 1978, an eight-year-old precocious and verbally gifted browngirl from Newark, New Jersey, decided—like many of her northeastern peers—to bestow an Arabic name upon herself. "Latifah," she whispered over and over again. She liked the ring of it, the flow, the way it sounded to her young ears. She liked the meaning—beautiful, sensitive, and kind—it reminded her of, well, her. The Queen would come later. Back then Dana Owens was just a Black American Princess from a loving two-parent home. A bright pupil on her way to Saint Anne's parochial school. She would go on to play power forward for her high school's state champion basketball team, rap in the girls' bathroom (and sometimes in a fly crew called Ladies Fresh), and star as Dorothy in a student production of *The Wiz*.

Today that little girl is a grown woman but her passions are the same. She still balls, still rhymes, and next year, if all goes as planned, she'll play Glinda the Good Witch in a TV remake of *The Wiz* (tentatively titled *The O.Z.*). Can't you just see La smiling benificently, waving her wand over Brandy's ruby slippers, sending her and Busta the cowardly lion off to see Little Richard the (true) wizard? How appropriate that Queen Latifah be cast as hip hop's Good Witch. She has been a sweet sorcerer of sorts, conjuring up a unique kind of magic that's propelled her career from the 'hood to Hollywood and back. After 30 years of living, Latifah knows about a woman's spells, about hard work, and when necessary, about hopping on that broom (in her case, a motorcycle) to escape the madness.

Latifah's introduction to the world via egocentric, boastful hip hop was only right—she needed a forum that would allow her to (excuse this) grab her dick. She was as powerful as any man. And the fact that she was *heard* is a testament to the real things she was talking about. Like most other women in hip hop she has consistently resisted titles like "feminist," but unlike many female MCs she works damn hard on feminism's behalf. She has never shied away from women's issues, and she has never let the presence or absence of a man determine her fate. "If he doesn't exist," she wrote in her memoir, *Ladies First*, "if I don't get my king, I also know I can be myself. A man does not make you a queen. And a man cannot complete you."

In 1989, when Latifah dropped her first album *All Hail the Queen* on Tommy Boy Records, she was seriously claiming a new space for women in hip hop. Sure, female visibility in the genre was on the come up—Salt-N-Pepa were selling more units than the industry ever believed women were capable of, MC Lyte was gaining mad street credibility with classic joints like "10% Dis," and earlier rhyming girls like the infamous Roxanne Shanté had already made their marks by dissing each other—but none of them had the balls to challenge male supremacy. "Evil That Men Do" boasted the type of confrontational title we'd be hard-pressed to find on a contemporary female rap record. And "Ladies First," *All Hail*'s breakout single featuring the sweetheart Brit Monie Love, was straight-up revolutionary. "I'ma mess around and flip the scene into reverse," La promised, and the song did become the genesis of big things for women in hip hop. According to Monica Lynch, the Tommy Boy executive who put Latifah on, the song "signaled the empowerment of a new breed of female MCs."

"Ladies First" was the trigger finger firing off the first round of discussions about what was happening to the *other* half of the hip hop nation and how we actually saw our own world. (Years later, the song was included in the Rock & Roll Hall of Fame's "500 Songs that Changed Rock & Roll.") Although the lyrics were cowritten by Latifah's friend Apache, who's very male and ironically—or maybe not—would later pen the classic "Gangsta Bitch," it was the first song to openly address sexism in hip hop. It would not be the last.

As young Latifah and Monie hopped around in their low-budget video, feeding off each other with a special magic, subtle feminist themes were tossed out into the rap universe, inevitably boomeranging back years later in potent incarnations like Lauryn Hill.

"She's the first Lauryn Hill in a way," seconds Mark the 45 King, *All Hail*'s legendary producer, referring not only to La's lyrical content, but also her music. "She was singing the hooks, all types of hooks—reggae hooks at that. Nobody else was doing that." Latifah had met the 45 King at a New Jersey house party. "I was a DJ for a long time, and she was one of the kids I was DJing for," he recalls. "I had a bunch of microphones and they used to come over my house and write rhymes and everything. Latifah can light up the room. She's very energetic, very smart, a quick learner. She's real nice, okay, but she'll kick somebody's ass, too."

Her debut also featured male guest producers and performers like De La Soul, KRS-One, and Daddy-O. The album's ultimate significance, however, had nothing to do with its production and everything to do with what it started. It was intriguing for young women to witness a

fah striking a regal stance in her riding boots, blazer, and towering head gear beside a red, black, and green map of Africa—said it all: *hip hop will forevermore deal with gender as well as race*. Suddenly all the real East Coast *mamís*—those of us who had bus-stopped to "Rapper's Delight," wopped to Slick Rick, and later became "Earths" behind Rakim—began the murmur that would become real talk. There was much to discuss. "Women have been integral to rap since its formative years—a claim that can't be made for the other dominant postwar pop music form, rock 'n' roll," posits Laura Jamison in *The VIBE History of Hip Hop*. Though Queen Latifah was in the tradition of other empowered hip hop foremothers like the Funk Four's beat-boxing gem Sha Rock, hip hop's massive corporate rise of the late '80s gave her a far more prominent forum than the rhyming women before her. Ultimately, timing would be a big part of why Latifah's work had such social impact. She would be talked about, her ideas would be considered—now there were even female "hip hop journalists" debating and documenting the female perspective.

In 1989 when she dropped her first album *All Hail the Queen,* Latifah was seriously claiming a new space for women in hip hop. No other female in the genre had the balls to challenge male supremacy.

chick so strong and outspoken enjoying so much adoration and respect from men. La appeared to be one of those girls who could chill around the guys all day and still be herself. Even as young Dana, she seemed to understand the secret powers of being "Princess of the Posse," and once she entered the rap world she became exactly that among several crews, starting with Mark the 45 King and his camp, then the powerful Afro-conscious Native Tongues, and eventually the thuggish, ruggish Naughty by Nature. That femme-confidence—the new macho—was her one consistent theme, and it was leaving an impression on everybody.

"I think she changed the path for women in hip hop," says her business partner of 12 years, Sha Kim Compere. "There's a lot of female rap artists, like Eve, for example, that's not taking any shorts from any male rappers, and that's always been Latifah's vision. You can't call a woman a bitch in a record without thinking about Latifah."

All Hail the Queen's unforgettable cover art—with Lati-

But as time wore on and the girl became a woman, Latifah's real life behind the music would have its low points. The lowest of these, the most radical and life-changing, was the sudden loss of her only sibling, Lancelot Hasaan "Winky" Owens. Her big brother died in a motorcycle accident on April 26, 1992, at age 23. On a bike she gave him. As a result of this tragedy, there are two Latifahs: one that existed before Winky's death, and the one that came after. To know her is to respect the difference. Just a year after the accident, she discussed how the experience shaped her in Lucy Kaylin's December 1993 VIBE article "It's Not So Easy Being Queen":

As kids, she and Winky had a lot of fun together, playing in the park on weekends, getting taken out for Chinese food and karate movies on Thursdays, once smearing their mother's brand-new yellow-and-white bathroom with their father's black shoe polish for fun. Winky grew up to be a cop in East Orange, tipping off Latifah on which cops were trouble, which ones were being investigated by Internal Affairs; she in turn would tell her round-the-way boys (Naughty By Nature's Treach et al.) whom to avoid. Latifah describes her brother as "cool, a comedian, a straight-up joker. He was dope. I was kind of tomboyish, as you can probably tell, so we rode together, us and a whole posse of guys and girls from the Newark area." Now, she wears Winky's bike key on a gold chain around her neck.

She wipes her eyes. "You just don't expect anything to happen to your family," Latifah says. "People come and go, records come and go, but your family is the thing that's supposed to be there always. So it's just the worst thing that could happen. Sometimes I'm okay, most of the time I'm functioning, but I walk around with this every day. And I keep going regardless, 'cause I don't have no choice. My religion tells me that to commit suicide is a mortal sin, basically, so that was never even a consideration." She ponders for a minute. "It's hard to believe in God when you feel, like, so disrespected, but you have to. If I don't, I'll become a very hostile person. Death gives you a real fuck-it attitude: fuck it, fuck you, fuck everybody."

some say, is one of the main reasons that led Tommy Boy to drop her from the label in 1993. "I think she was really disappointed about the split initially," says Latifah's placid, protective mother, Rita Owens, a high school art teacher who is also the art director of Latifah's newly founded record label Flavor Unit, which has its headquarters in Jersey City. "It's not like they were saying, 'We no longer want you,' but they seemed to indicate that maybe they couldn't deal with the changes that she was going through."

It's been suggested by people close to the situation that Latifah's unwillingness to listen to feedback and criticism about the album created subtle tensions between her and Tommy Boy. Latifah herself says, "It was kind of like, forget it, I'ma do my thing. This album's got a lot of heart in it, it's real personal to me. It was a way for me to get out some of the stuff that was on my mind, on my heart." She is unapologetic about the less-than-predictable directions her instincts take her. "I have different sides of myself, different styles," she says, a little indignant. "If I feel like flippin' on some reggae shit, I'ma flip it. 'Cause I can do that. If I wanna flip some hardcore

From human beatbox to talk-show host, Burger King employee to entertainment executive, Latifah's versatility allows her to reconcile the types of extremes many of us could only imagine.

As time passed, the tragedy receded, but, because of the strength and confidence Queen Latifah exudes, most people didn't realize just how destroyed Dana Owens was. "She wasn't well emotionally, physically, or spiritually," says her close friend Kika Martin, a former Safari Sister, Latifah's one-time dancers. "You could see it in her appearance, in her face. We'd drive, talk a lot about death and Winky, and in the middle of the night, she'd just break down and cry. This happened a lot."

Right around the time Winky died, Latifah started thinking about her third album. So it wasn't a big surprise to see her wandering even further from All Hail's optimistic street focus once she hit the studio. A multi-culti compilation full of moody reflection—including a haunting track about life in the 'hood with a bluesy hook sung by Latifah to perfection; a jazz instrumental she produced, in memory of her brother; and an aggressive rap song entitled "U.N.I.T.Y. (Who You Calling a Bitch?)"—her album Black Reign is the darkest, most ambitious, and least classifiable of the three. The lack of focus,

shit, I'ma flip it. If it's gonna be some laid-back folk shit then I can do that, too. I'm versatile."

From human beat box to talk-show host, Burger King employee to entertainment executive, it is Latifah's versatility that allows her to reconcile the types of extremes many of us could only imagine. "I have lived in housing projects and in fine homes. I have hung out with drug dealers and with presidents. I have had to clean bathrooms for a living and I have had my own maid. I've sold millions of records and have won a Grammy. I've made movies that have bombed. I've had to bury my big brother, Winky. And I've also wanted to die myself. I've felt low and I've felt on top of the world," she writes in the intro to Ladies First. "Through it all, though, I never forget who I am . . . A queen is a queen when riding high, and when clouded in disgrace, shame, or sorrow, she has dignity. Being a queen has very little to do with exterior things. It is a state of mind."

Remember, Queen Latifah is also a registered trademark. For a woman whose career began as a rapper, her overall celebrity is enormous. Too many contemporary female rap artists (and quite a few of their male counterparts) appear content to bask in the reflected shine of high-end European fashion designers, unaware that they are giving away the valuable commodity of their own ghetto glory. But the primary brand name Latifah chooses to big up is her own—and not just by way of her rap lyrics. A brand is not a small thing and you can see hers everywhere, large. On the cover of her book, a *New York Times* bestseller, the words *Queen Latifah* are printed bigger and bolder than any other text. And the QL logo with the crown will be there in the corner of your television screen for as long as her nationally syndicated talk show remains on the air.

The powerful handle Dana Owens chose for herself is now recognized in millions of American households. She laughs loud and speaks in that familiar, slang-tinged kind of way, and we welcome her into our living rooms. Most of what she offers us has to do with the intangibles of life—love, respect, self-esteem—not the flossy, glossy things that today's hip hop culture emphasizes and that so many young people covet. At eighteen, with a sense of self many adult women (and men) still seek, she spoke of the "Queen L-A-T-I-F-A-H in command."

In the decade plus since that first song, "Wrath of My Madness," Latifah's seasoned ability to communicate with and oftentimes speak for the hip hop nation—and distinct but related groups like teens, women, and black people—has become a salable quality. Queen Latifah knows this. When she puts her stamp on a thing, it is instantly given credibility in many spheres. That is why major brands like Reebok, Lane Bryant, and Absolut (though in one campaign they misspelled her name) are seeking her endorsement. Her delicate craftsmanship of the "Latifah way" is a product of the hugely complex realities of her life. All that she has seen and survived in three decades combines to make her the force she is today. The beauty of it, however, is that for Latifah, accessing the part of herself that is so likeable, believable, and intelligent comes without effort. "Me, I'm one of them types of people, I never really got caught up in all the hype," she says, though these days it's easier to

land an interview with Hillary Clinton. "Once the lights go down and everything is done, I go back to being La."

"I think her whole success is funny," says Sha Kim. "Everything that Latifah has accomplished, it's like we kind of backed into it. I don't even think Latifah set out to be the role model or the success that she's been. Her edge is that she's always done what made her happy, not what everyone else expected. This is someone who doesn't take herself too seriously. She's like, If it happens it happens, but I'm not going out there to be a so-called star. Latifah's not an image. It is Dana Owens. That's who she is, the way she lives her life."

And that way is to be in touch with God and the God within. "At least I try to give God time and that makes my life a little more peaceful," she says. "It doesn't make it easier all the time but I know my judgment is better than if I'm wylin' out and running around partying too hard. I don't think as clearly 'cause I'm not on point spiritually. The more on point spiritually I am, the more things can happen for me. It's a balance of being close to God in a devil's world."

The first part of the branding of Queen Latifah, therefore, begins with the woman herself. What people want that Latifah possesses are not six-minute abs or the sweet promises of sex that new-school video chicks sell by the bushel. No, the reason why she's still viable—even though she hasn't had a hit record in eight years—is an internal fire that burns through even the most flame-retardant self-doubt. Is there ever a moment we don't believe that La truly *likes* herself?

This is why the girl became one of the first rappers to have a successful sitcom (Khadijah still turns up on *Living Single* reruns), and so far the only rapper to have her own talk show. In 1999 she told *TV Guide* that *The Queen Latifah Show* was going to be Oprah meets Rosie meets Chris Rock. It didn't exactly work out that way. But after two seasons she proved Rosie O'Donnell was right to recommend her for the gig. La was a capable host, and her guests opened up to her like an old friend. But after two years she has decided not to come back for another season. No matter—the Queen Latifah franchise stands strong. It is a name that nets recording contracts, movie deals, TV shows, and even the occasional executive producer credit.

America likes brands, hip hop *loves* brands, and if there

ass simple common box. I've never been that artist so I've always had to fight from the inside out to do my thing."

As her talk show phase winds down, Latifah's returning to the studio at Flavor Unit headquarters, working on an album she's thinking about calling *To Thine Self Be True*. "I've never really been one of those artists where people picked my singles and told me what to wear and how I should do this," she says. "I've always been the director, basically, of this movie. If I'm not driving it, not feeling it, if I'm not behind it to say yay and nay, then what is the purpose of me doing it? Just to get a check? I can get a bigger check, I feel, if my heart is in it. Because I'm going to be more passionate about what I'm doing. This year is going to be the bomb."

What resonates about Latifah among homegirls, aside from her always fabulous, flexible natural hair, is that even in her most extraordinary of moments, Latifah (like Chaka/Whitney/Oprah) is every woman—or at least seems to be down for every woman. "She represented black women power," Treach observed on VH1's

In a season of stilettos, Latifah mostly rocks flats, and when she doesn't have to wear makeup she simply doesn't. Her plain, Ivory Girl beauty is not uncommon among black women, though the way she revels in it is.

is any poetic justice at all in the entertainment game, it is the ability of this rap chick to flip her name into something larger than herself. The Queen Latifah brand may have had an unconscious birth but it certainly has the breath of life now. Queen Latifah the rapper has had only one gold record in her career, but Queen Latifah the enterprise is an earning machine that can outmatch most rappers with multi-platinum sales. Some observers have said that she's "transcended" hip hop. Better yet—she's reworked its definition and expanded its reach. Surely one of the most defining qualities of Queen Latifah is her business acumen. Only male peers like L. L. Cool J, Will Smith, and perhaps Ice Cube have been as effective in packaging and selling themselves to America. "For me right now I don't feel boundaries and I don't see boundaries," she says, like everybody should be able to do what she does. And maybe they should. "All my career I've really fought against people trying to make me do what everyone else does. Y'know, put me in that corny-

Behind the Music. "That's why all the ladies were behind her whether they were rap fans or not."

In a season of stilettos Latifah mostly rocks flats, and when she doesn't have to wear makeup she simply doesn't. Her rather plain, Ivory Girl beauty is not uncommon among black women, though the way the Queen embraces and revels in it is. "I've always been a person who cuts my own mold," she once declared to the world on CNN. "Just because some rappers choose to sell sex—I'm a big woman and I'm not going to embarrass myself by pulling my gut out. I can be sexy and sensual in my own way… besides, I think big chicks rule."

Latifah has always been a "big chick" living in our bulimic world, but she's managed to de-emphasize her weight simply by refusing to harbor too many hang-ups. Her M.O.: walk confident, and that's how people will see you. If La has ever been a weight-obsessed yo-yo dieter, that's certainly not the face she wore. Like Oprah, her weight has fluctuated a bit before our eyes, but unlike

Oprah, she ain't dealing with it with you, thanks. It's pretty remarkable that even as a Hollywood success story, La passed on the lipo and breast augmentation so many other female celebs absolutely *must* have. Ask a woman you love would she "fix" something on her body if she had the loot to do so and see what answer you get. Understandably, Latifah admits to disliking her love handles. "But I'm not ready to chop 'em off either," she told VIBE. "I'm not going to get liposuction or some shit. I love myself just the way I am." In her memoir she even makes light of having "no ass"—now please, *all* black girls know that's a big deal. But again, Latifah likes Latifah.

Which may be why she has absolutely no rivalry with other female MCs. "A lot of queens came along while I was away from my throne for a moment," she told MTV while promoting her 1998 album, *Order in the Court,* which was, by SoundScan standards, a major flop. "It's all good. I don't knock anybody, but I'm holding my spot. The thing about me is that I've always done my own thing. So in my mind, I'm not in competition with any other female rappers out there. No other female rapper can make Latifah records, just like I can't make Foxy records, I can't make Kim records, I can't make Missy records. They're individuals and I'm an individual. But this is what I do. I'll assert myself in my own way, and I'll hold my throne like I always do."

It's true what feminist thinker Susan Sontag wrote in the introduction to the photography book, *Women:* "A man can always be seen. Women are looked at." And in the realm of the urban music video, where appearance is absolutely fucking everything, female MCs are being looked at by everyone. Men rate them with fuckability score cards while women count their fat rolls, scrutinize their hair, nails, footwear, and everything in between. The pressure is on. A lot of sisters rhyming in today's market (read: Foxy, Kim, Trina, Eve) have given up on being seen and given in to being looked at. Some women find new levels of success based purely on how they look, and conversely, some dope female MCs can't sell a single record for the same reason.

Latifah is not immune to the b.s. afflicting women in show business, she just seems to rise above it, regally unscarred. Like other female MCs, she too has been the subject of rumors that she is a lesbian. For the most part, she's refused to dignify such intrusive questions. And if she does give a damn what inquiring minds think, that didn't stop

her from joining Melissa Etheridge, Garth Brooks, the Pet Shop Boys, k.d. lang, and George Michael last year at Equality Rocks, a benefit concert in support of gay and lesbian human rights. Nor did it prevent her from portraying Cleo, a complex, compelling lesbian character in F. Gary Gray's 1996 film *Set It Off.* Around that time, she spoke to VIBE's Danyel Smith about the subject she had avoided for so long.

It's significant that the females who get the most respect in hip hop's primarily male domain are relentlessly dogged by rumors that they are lesbians. Whether these rumors are true or not, the message is evident: a female can't be tough or strong or clear or exceptionally skillful at hip hop unless she has sacrificed the thing that makes her a real girl.

Queen Latifah's face is luminous. Even under the slight shade of a blue baseball cap, her butterscotch skin radiates. She leans back in a chair, massively self-possessed, hair in a ponytail, body in nylon sweats. I've asked her about her mom (love of La's life), her high school years (she was a B student; went to the state basketball championships), the scar on her forehead (tripped over a phone cord when she was eight), but not whether or not she's gay, which is what some people say about her, about MC Lyte, about so many tough-girl MCs that you get caught between being pissed off at the stereotype (like you can't be a take-next-to-no-bullshit kind of girl and be straight?) and hoping it's true because—why not? And how dope would that be?

It's a question Latifah "shrugged off" in Essence *three years ago, and I wanted to know the answer for all the wrong— arrogant in my straightness, carefree in my obscurity—reasons. The fact that Latifah's sexuality is not the rest of the world's business does enter my mind, even though it's still reeling from the sight of Latifah-as-Cleo kissing a woman's tan, fishnetted thigh in* Set It Off. *Queen Latifah describes Cleo, her character, as a "straight-up dyke."*

"A lesbian woman in film," Gray muses. "I thought it was realistic, and something we shouldn't hide from. Al Pacino's played gay roles, Sharon Stone kisses women—and they're on the covers of Movieline *and* Newsweek. *But if black people do it, we've degraded ourselves, hurt the race. People can't seem to accept the fact that these people are entertainers. Latifah is different from Cleo; Cleo is different from Khadijah; Khadijah is different from Dana. White stars don't get persecuted for it. Why should we?"*

Latifah knows there are people who question her own sexuality. And she's unshaken in her commitment to the role of Cleo. "I'm an actor," she says. "That means I've got to play that role and convince you I'm that person. I've done that in this movie. The gay issue was not without stress. But I don't think anyone can stress me as much as I stressed over it myself."

In Set It Off, *Latifah's character is clearly tongue-kissing and loving her girl (the first print I saw, they were getting* down; *in the second print, one of two keenly directed, sensual scenes had been clipped back). The other characters in the movie, with the exception of the slimy janitorial bossman (who gets his comeuppance), treat Cleo's sexuality with barely the shrug one might feel for a peanut butter and collard greens sandwich—different, yeah. But, different strokes . . . Though Cleo's girl, Ursula, is strangely silent, their relationship— sexual, playful, and resonant with everyday emotion—is the most sophisticated treatment of a lesbian couple in this era of African-American film.*

Latifah is effusive, if not relaxed, when speaking on the controversial subject. "It's normal to me and my family," she says of homosexuality. "Everybody wants to act like they don't know anybody gay, but they do. First, they've got somebody in their family, probably, so don't even trip like it don't exist. Second, this is Cleo's character. She is straight-up gay. I knew what was in that script before I took the job. That's why it was even more of a challenge to me. It was a brave move."

She wants you to know that if you can't distinguish the actress from the role, that's your problem. "I'm not going to even answer the question. I'm going to let you wonder, think whatever you want to think." Latifah leans up over the recorder, tilts her hat back on her head. "I don't really care about what you all think personally of me. I know who I am. I'm not confused about myself. Never."

Though she said she wasn't going to answer the question, she does before I ask it. "I'm not a dyke," she says. "That's what Cleo is. Men's drawers, the whole nine—she's selling herself that way. Not me. I did my job. And I fear not. I fear not. I've prayed on this," she says, as if she's talking about one of the most important decisions of her life. "I've talked to God on this. I talked to my father about it. I talked to my mother. And as long as my family supports my decision, what do I care?"

Black History Month 2001: Bill Maher takes *Politically Incorrect* to Howard University. Sitting beneath giant portraits of Frederick Douglass, Malcolm X, and Martin Luther King Jr. are Bill and his guests: Martin Luther King III, Charles Barkley, John Salley, and Queen Latifah, who gets by far the loudest response from the pumped-up audience.

When the subject of Supreme Court Justice Clarence Thomas comes up, Barkley defends him, King rebukes him, and then Latifah jumps in. "I don't feel Clarence Thomas," she remarks, nodding toward MLK III. "I'm more proud of all of those white Americans and other people who marched along with his father in the Sixties than I am of Clarence Thomas. When it comes to him it's not even a black or white thing. It's gone beyond that, it comes back to do I agree with you or do I disagree with you? Are you with me or against me? And a lot of the stuff that he votes for, it just doesn't align up with what I'm feeling. I don't feel it represents our people at all."

Though she rarely addresses politics so directly, it seems like Latifah's had it up to here. She's on a roll now, chopping the air with her hands. "It's common sense. Anyone black who votes against affirmative action makes no sense to me. What that says is that you are totally…" Barkley tries to protest in Thomas's defense but Latifah isn't having it. "Hold up, Charles—I do a talk show. I deal with racist people *constantly.* You gotta understand there's a major part of this country that is *not* as sophisticated, they're not loving, they don't accept everyone. They still think like it's forty years ago, fifty years ago. And so when you have people like that in a position of power, who block you from getting not just a job in the NBA as a player but that GM job, that management job— when you have people who are like that, you can't just knock down all the legislation that was put in place to protect us from people like that. You just can't get rid of it. And now we've gotten rid of it. There's a lot of kids that are not gonna make it because of that."

Then Bill Maher quotes Chuck D stating that if you're a black person in the media, your job is to present your people in the most positive manner possible. "To me," says the host, "that sounds like a definition of propaganda."

Once again she jumps in with both feet. "I think what Chuck meant more so was this: You have most of the media, which is probably 90 percent controlled by white folks, they give their interpretation of who we are as black people, and all too often you've seen negative images of us. I think it's all about balance—we don't have that balance. We have the best to the worst of white folks, and that's cool, because now you can be honest with yourselves. Whereas, if we only see negative, negative, negative, we know as black people that's not who we are. We're more dynamic than that. I think our media should be more honest."

Latifah's passionate righteousness has always gone beyond Afrocentric head wraps. "I had a need to be socially conscious," she once said. "I feel a connection to African people throughout the world and I also had feelings toward females and how we should be treated." But from jump, Queen Latifah established herself as something rather all-American. She self-censored, curs-

Queen Latifah is positive from a place deep inside her. Her goodness is real but not absolute. As a black, urban youngster coming up in the Reagan '80s, her life reflected alternating realities. She did well in school, but she partied even better. She sexed and loved. And La always had good peoples. Her mother, Rita, is an amazing woman who early on taught her kids a simple wisdom: "You're in the projects but you are not of the projects." Yet if you ask has La ever been down with drug dealers and 'round-the-way niggas, the answer is yes. Thank goodness. That's part of how you get a Queen Latifah.

Designations of "positive" or "negative" were forced onto rappers in the early '90s as the media took an interest in hip hop (around the same time the term "gangsta rap" gained currency). These labels meant that hip hop artists concerned with their image might hesitate to share the real complexities of their lives. The truth is that even the most "positive" artist gets down with her share of things that are a bit "antiestablishment." (Even squeaky-clean Will Smith does the occasional 70 in a 55 zone.) Hip hop needs to break

"I do a talk show. I deal with racist people constantly," she said on *Politically Incorrect*. "There's a major part of this country that is not as sophisticated, they're not loving, they still think like it's 40, 50 years ago."

ing only rarely and always concealing that more flagrant side of herself of which she believed (at the time) neither her public nor her mother would approve.

Though there exists a buried Latifah lyric to refute each and every charge of her having been a goodie-goodie, overall, her image was just that. And this impression of wholesomeness has followed her throughout her career. When Latifah caught charges for marijuana and gun possession back in 1996, people were aghast. How could such things happen to such a nice girl?

Is it really too much to believe that some good girls smoke a little weed? Or that a woman who had recently been car-jacked would be strapped? It's not that the Queen is representing something she is not, but how can she ever represent all that she is? Latifah can't show us some parts for real reasons. As she says in "Just Another Day" from the *Black Reign* album, "Latifah's on vacation, I'm just plain old Dana today."

rules sometimes. And sometimes rules need to be broken.

The very act of being a female MC, particularly in 1989, was a rule-breaker of sorts. Besides, just being "positive" was never enough to guarantee that anybody was a half-decent MC. But for most of the public at large, rappers are still either all good or all bad.

The clever braggadocio found in La's classic music, and even more in other areas of her still-blossoming artistic and *business* career, is about a simple concept introduced by Aretha Franklin—respect. "I think that everyone feels the same way about Latifah," says my 24-year-old friend Breeze. "Everyone just respects her."

People vibe off of Latifah because, ultimately, we believe her. For all of us looking from the outside, the "Latifah way" (the woman's seemingly patented way of life) is achingly admirable. Latifah's got like a Martha Stewart thing going; she does a bunch of stuff *good*. And still, how she rolls—her character—is perhaps her most prominent feature. To describe Queen Latifah, does one start with the details of how she looks, a song's specifics or a role she's performed? No, we start with what she feels like. We end with why we feel her.

It's almost Valentine's Day, 2001. The full force of anxiety is like a reservoir of anticipation pressing hard and fast on female souls thinking about some man, somewhere—pressing like millions of gallons of dingy water against a dam. A 30-year-old single woman has a lot to deal with come yet another Valentine's Day—good love prospect or not. We are neither our mamas nor our daughters. We are not imprisoned and no, we are not free. A generation of black girls have lived (and loved) through moments and memories like Mary and Method Man, who sang to each other, in 1996, "You're all I need to get by." But those who really understood ghetto love know deep in our hearts that "You're All I Need"—for all of Mary's passion and for all of Meth's power—is still just a beautiful, glorious lie.

Of course the song per se is not what's untrue (baby if

plastic tied across my chair. It read: RAPE-FREE ZONE. I said to myself, "I know I'm here to see Queen Latifah. But *what* is she doing again?" And then I looked up.

There was a circular sea of red. Red lights, women in red, women with red boas. Slowly, I began to focus. Seated in fold-up chairs around the center stage were all of these amazing, progressive celebrity women: Jane Fonda, Phoebe Snow, Brooke Shields, Glenn Close, Marisa Tomei, Claire Danes, Gloria Steinem, Gloria Reuben, Rosie Perez, even Oprah Winfrey! And there she was among them, Queen Latifah, in the deepest of reds, in slacks (of course) and matching high-heeled boots. Her boa lay across her wide-open lap. I fixated on her from way up high and realized exactly what V-Day was all about. *The Vagina Monologues.* Sure, V for Valentine, but more important, V for vagina, V for ending the violence against women, V for an eventual victory. *Of course* the Queen is here.

"When I turned thirteen, my classmates would no longer play with me," began the testimony of the young Kenyan woman onstage before thousands of onlookers. "I was called

Queen Latifah the rapper has had only one gold record, but Queen Latifah the enterprise is an earning machine that can outdo most multiplatinum hitmakers. She hasn't "transcended" hip hop, just expanded its reach.

there were ever a "wedding song," that is undoubtedly it). But the perfect, even exchange of verses represents the fanciful notion that somehow in love, in life, and (L☺L) in hip hop, there is a fair back-and-forth between the sexes. And that notion is a farce. Not in life, not in love, and certainly *not* in hip hop has anything for women been fair. We know this. Ain't nobody playing the victim.

All alone on a pretty brutal February night, I made my way on the number 3 train to New York City's famed Madison Square Garden to witness the first official "V-Day Gala Celebration." Since I'd been just about living in a cave for a season, I entered the Garden utterly clueless. V-Day? *Valentine's?* Late again, I picked up my ticket from the "Will Call" window and rode those unending escalators up to my level. There was a smiling woman giving out free boxes of Tampax, which I grabbed, naturally. The performance was in progress and I was hastily ushered to my seat, but when I got ready to plop down, I noticed a red banner of

the 'girl with the three legs'—I was different because I wasn't 'clean' like them. It is believed that without cutting the clitoris, women will not know how to control themselves. I am one of the 130 million women who has undergone genital mutilation." So went the moving personal tales told that night at the Garden, punctuated with celebrity monologues, by turns serious, funny, and demanding. (Rosie Perez's vagina is "angry," also "curious," and "it needs to talk.") And you know the "Vulva Choir" did their thing.

On and on it went. Woman after woman lighting up the stage with drama and theatrics. Women from organizations with names like the Revolutionary Association of the Women of Afghanistan (RAWA), Equality Now, and What Girls Know. Women from Planned Parenthood, Stop Rape (who shared the detail that 78 women are raped in the United States every hour), and Feminist.com. Until finally, at the evening's very end, when there was hardly any climaxing left to be done, when the entire stadium had endured more pain and more pleasure than any of us could have imagined for one night, she stood. Her voice rose distinctively over the thick banter and silenced us all, and in an instant Latifah was in command.

"Love the woman from infinity to infinity!" she belted. "This is a rape-free zone! This is a rape-free zone!" Then she broke into the Grammy-winning classic "U.N.I.T.Y." and the crowd went berserk. When Latifah first recorded this song she was morphing into a butterfly, coming out of the cocoon of despair that followed her brother's death. "U.N.I.T.Y." was a song everyone listened to and everyone *heard* and it was happening again that night. The Queen was manifesting. There was enough power and euphoria in the air to carry Latifah through till morning had she so chosen. But she left us with a moment—a rare, part-black, part-woman, part-hip hop moment—that made her significance crystal clear. "Throw your hands up!" the Queen directed the mostly white, middle-class female audience. And they did. But it was witnessing Oprah going crazy, shouting at the top of her lungs, *"Who you callin' a bitch?"* and throwing up *her* hands that made it all register.

Talk about arriving. Imagine, there we were: me and Oprah, two black girls reveling and rappin' about the woman thing to the beat of Queen Latifah. Calling the vagina a heart. And ultimately knowing what one little rapper girl has insisted from the beginning—we are all queens.

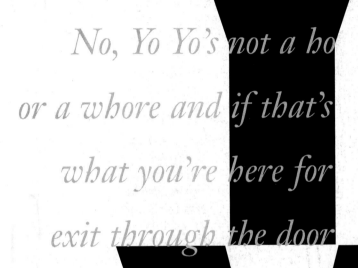

No, Yo Yo's not a ho
or a whore and if that's
what you're here for
exit through the door

YoYo

Photograph by Sue Kwon

not
for play
by Michael A. Gonzales

"**F**uck you, Ice Cube!" howled the boisterous audience inside Harlem's venerable Apollo Theater. Infamous for raining jovial hostility upon any unfortunate soul who was foolish enough to overstay his or her welcome, Apollo crowds don't need an excuse to boo. So when L.A.'s toughest G stepped onto New York's toughest stage and invited everybody to scream on him, Cube's self-deprecating appeal went over like a drive-by shotgun blast.

Since breaking with the glorious gangsta crew Niggaz With Attitude (N.W.A) and recording much of his stunning 1990 solo joint _AmeriKKKa's Most Wanted_ with Strong Island beatmasters the Bomb Squad (who even convinced the West Coast player to cut his scary Jheri curls), Ice Cube had become the first bicoastal bro to be down by law all over the map. When he flipped back his hoody to show off a fresh baldie, The New York hardrocks went berserk. Still, he was only communicating with half the hip hop nation.

As the audience shook its collective booty to the thundering rhythms exploding from the overhead speakers, Cube's sound segued from East Coast swagger to the West Coast bounce of "It's a Man's World." "Women, they're good for nothing," he rapped with a scowl. "No maybe one thing—to serve needs to my ding-a-ling." Then, just as the Apollo seemed ready to blast off, an 18-year-old beauty with Nubian braids and tight jeans jumped onstage to put a lyrical foot in his ass. "First of all let me tell you my name—it's Yo Yo," she snapped, then proceeded to trade barbs with the rapper responsible for misogynist gems like "One Less Bitch." If Yo Yo felt the least bit intimidated, she was certainly hiding it well. This bad sista wasn't hard, but she was hardcore.

Cube huffed and puffed, but Yo Yo refused to fall down. When he told her to "take a piece of the pole and be happy," she shot back with a crack about his "three-inch killer." It was a performance to remember. Indeed, that low-rider ditty damn near caused a riot in the chocolate city of Harlem.

Yo Yo challenged Ice Cube with a gusto not seen on Planet Rap since MC Lyte popped shit to Positive K on the knock-out punch "I'm Not Havin' It." And Yo Yo was facing stiffer competition. Eleven years later, she's still in awe of that blissful night. "That was one of the biggest thrills

of my life, because the energy between me and Cube was intense," she recalls. "I would press his buttons by getting all in his face, which was something he hated, but I knew if I pushed hard he would push harder." Folks in the Apollo apparently thought they got their money's worth. "It was so crazy, people started throwing money onstage—and I'm not talking about change," she adds with a grin. "Da Lench Mob [Cube's four-man spin-off group] was snatching these dollars off the stage and I was like, 'Y'all better leave my money alone. Those are _my_ tips.'"

Released on Ice Cube's platinum debut, "It's a Man's World" was the song that introduced the former Yolanda Whitaker to the world. "I was so nervous in front of the mike," Yo Yo recalls of her first sessions with Cube and producer Sir Jinx. "I had rapped in the school cafeteria, but this was different. I put so much power into the first few verses that Cube finally had to tell me, 'Just calm down and let's do it again.' I did so many takes I thought they were going to kick me out of the studio." Sir Jinx, who went to school with Yolanda, remembers it pretty much the same way: "Yo Yo is a perfectionist," he says. "She's a real artist who wants to do things her way. That's why we didn't get along." Though she and Jinx would "fight all the time," Yo Yo knew this was a moment she'd been preparing for most of her life. She wasn't about to let a creative squabble get in the way of finishing her song. "Luckily," she says, "I finally got it."

Before she started making butts bounce in tattered seats, Yo Yo was just another L.A. girl surviving in the bang-bang 'hood. Immortalized on countless rap discs, and in films like Dennis Hopper's _Colors_, South Central's gang situation has long been out of control. Like modern-day gunslingers invading the Wild Wild West, blue-clothed Crips and crimson-clad Bloods began their savage reign in the late '60s, often fighting over "territories" that neither set actually owned. When drugs became the name of the game—first weed and heroin, then, in the '80s, crack—the money, weapons, and brutality escalated.

Even now, law-abiding civilians still get caught up in the madness of midday gunshots, drugged antics at dusk, and midnight sirens shattering the darkness. Yet behind this image of fear and loathing, a community of working-class families manages to prosper. "Of course we had gangs, but

I never lived the life a lot of people in South Central live," says Yo Yo, who relocated from the small-town atmosphere of Carson, California, to 106th and Figueroa when she was in seventh grade. "My mom raised five kids and believe me, she had a firm grip on us," Yo Yo says emphatically. "In my house, school was a must."

While her truck driver pops was on the road, it was moms (Denise Wilson) who was holding down the fort. "I wrote a song called 'Mama Don't Take No Mess' about my mother," Yo Yo says with a laugh. ("The type of moms to whup you in the store if she hasta," she rapped on 1991's *Boyz N the Hood* soundtrack. "Just to let you know, you're the child, she's the master.") But it wasn't all about tough love. "My mother has always been a serious motivator," Yo Yo recalls. "She was the kind of person who would take me and other neighborhood kids on camping trips." When Mrs. Wilson took a squad of youngsters to Big Bear Mountain, half the kids had never seen snow before. "We had a ball," says Yo Yo, aglow.

Never known for being the shy girl on the block, Yo Yo

Hanging tougher than leather with Boobi, Baby T, and Diamond D (who later changed her name to Nic Nac), Yo Yo and her novice sidekicks liked to think of themselves as South Central's answer to Run-DMC. "We did a bunch of talent shows and *Star Search* nights at school," says Yo Yo, chuckling. "Everyone knew who we were." Encouraged by open-minded teachers, the girls wrote message raps like "Dope Man," about a girl who gets involved in a bad situation, as well as songs that poked fun at the playboys chilling in the school's quad. "Ha ha, you're busted, the game's on you," they mocked during lunch period.

"We had this routine that everyone in school knew by heart," says Yo Yo. Dipped in '80s fly-girl gear, they would come onstage rapping their theme song: "We're the Def City Girls / Def, def . . . the Def City Girls / Devastating, fascinating cold MCs / Make you wanna get up and move your feet / Never bite rhymes. . . ." She says her mom dropped a few friends when they didn't show up to see her perform.

One dude who did happen to catch Yo Yo in action was

"I didn't really know what a feminist was," Yo Yo says with a laugh. "I just tried to stand my ground and be myself. I wanted to be that voice for women to come back and say, 'We're not your bitch.'"

became one of the most popular students at Washington High School. "I lived in a Blood neighborhood and I went to a Crip school, but that wasn't a problem," she says. "I just never had that kind of mentality." Instead of gangbanging, Yo Yo chose to become a cheerleader, volleyball player, drama club member, yearbook contributor, and drill team captain. "Out of all the kids in my house, I was possibly the laziest," she confesses. "So I got involved in all these after-school programs as a way to avoid housework."

In between all the pom-pom waving and parade marching, she also managed to excel in English class, where she first caught the writing bug. "When I was younger, I thought I wanted to be a journalist," recalls Yo Yo (who went on to pen an advice column for VIBE called "Yo, Yo Yo"). "I would write stories, essays, and speeches." Citing her English teacher Miss White as an early mentor, Yolanda was soon scribbling lyrics for two schoolyard rap crews, the Roxanne Twins and the Def City Girls.

T-Bone, a member of Da Lench Mob. He was impressed enough to alert his homie Cube, who'd recently stepped off from N.W.A and was looking for new talent for his Street Knowledge production company. When Cube ran into Yo Yo at a swap-meet, she busted a rhyme for him off the head, and her hip hop destiny was sealed.

"I'd never dealt with a girl rapper before," Cube told the *L.A. Times* before her debut album came out. "But she was good enough to make me decide to give it a try. I liked her delivery, which is the most important thing in rap. Plus she wrote her own raps—good raps. And she had this 'I don't give a damn' attitude. She wasn't acting like a groupie, saying 'Oh, Ice Cube this' or 'Ice Cube that.' If she had acted like that I wouldn't have nothing to do with her."

There was another key question to be answered: Would Yo Yo's mother have anything to do with *him*? "All those guys lived in my neighborhood, so Cube called me and said he was coming over," Yo Yo says in a voice like Mexican jumping beans. "It was so funny, because we were standing on the porch and my mom came outside. 'Now, you're not going to be calling my daughter no bitches,'" she recalls. "At that time most of Cube's rhymes were about 'A Bitch Iz a Bitch.' But where I was coming from I wasn't going to be anybody's bitch. I tried to have some morals." Whatever Cube said was good enough to meet with Mrs. Wilson's approval. Yo Yo quit her job at a local Mickey Dee's, and hip hop's Bonnie and Clyde (as they'd later call themselves) joined forces.

Before long the whole posse—Cube, his Bay Area cousin Del Tha Funkee Homosapien, new signee Kam, and Da Lench Mob—was spending every spare moment doing preproduction on Yo Yo's historic first album. "She pretty much set it off for females rapping on the West Coast," says Del, a future solo success who wrote a few lyrics for Yo Yo during that time—but don't ask him which ones. "I damn near forgot," he says. "When she spit them, you couldn't tell I wrote them for her." He attributes this to Yo Yo's skill as well as her charm. "She was a dope rapper who could be rough," he says, "but she wasn't a knucklehead. She was always this very down-to-earth person."

That's not what Kam noticed the first time he met Yo Yo. "I'm a real dude, so I was looking at the body and the face," says the young rapper who was down with Cube's Street Knowledge camp. "She was attractive on that angle, so I was wondering, did Cube get with her just because of that or did she really get down?" But it didn't take long for Yo Yo to make Kam a believer. "Yo Yo was West Coast raw. I liked her style, her little hoarse raspy voice, her energy. She had a lot of stage presence, a lot of personality. She wasn't a female trying to sound like the males. She kept it feminine and still kept it street."

"Nobody did *nothing* with Yo Yo," says ace producer Sir Jinx. "Nothing sexual. It was straight-up hip hop. And that's how I like to get down. None of that, 'This is my girl and I'm doing her beat.' Nah. You gotta be nice for me to even claim you." Jinx was impressed by Yo Yo's dedication. "I'm talking about coming to the studio real ugly, hair all messed up," he says. "She was there, every day. And rolling with like ten girls."

Such were the beginnings of the famous IBWC, or Intelligent Black Women's Coalition. Though Yo Yo sometimes rapped about them as if they were a posse of gangsta chicks, in real life the IBWC was mostly about female togetherness. Jinx says that Cube encouraged Yo Yo (who became friends with Tupac, and harbored aspirations to rap about the thug life herself) to show that softer side of herself, embracing themes that other women could relate to instead of just mirroring his own hardcore persona. "That type of

consciousness didn't exist out here at that time," says Jinx. "That's why it was so dope. She definitely brought out the 'Girl don't be no fool,' and 'Stand up for your rights as a black woman,' and 'Don't let a man hold you down!'—that kind of situation."

These qualities were all aspects of Yo Yo's personality to begin with, but Yo Yo gives her MC mentor much credit for bringing them out. "Cube guided me from a raw talent to being an artist," says Yo Yo, tenderly. "I would take our rehearsal tapes home and listen to myself. We would sit down and listen to beats together. Even when we were on the *AmeriKKKa's Most Wanted* tour, we would listen to beats on the bus. Cube was always asking me, 'You like this? You want to use this?'"

Before going into the studio to record her debut, Cube decided that Yo Yo should pay her dues on the road—as the only woman on tour with a gang of niggas. "We had our battles every now and then," she confesses. "One guy who called himself J.D. the Gangsta would get drunk and just start talking shit. Then Jinx and I would argue over what music to listen to, so once he just threw my tape outta the window. I wanted my security to whip his ass, but it never came to that." Not long after it was decided that Yo Yo should have her own bus. "They had started calling me 'cock blocker,' because I would talk shit to the groupies going up to their rooms after a show. It used to get on my nerves."

Back in the heart of the 'hood a few months later, recording began on *Make Way for the Motherlode*, whose title Cube dreamed up. And sometimes he had to make way for Yo Yo's mother in the studio. "She and my aunt came to lend their support," says Yo Yo. "They were always so cool." But having family present didn't stop Yo Yo from getting down. With a noisy backdrop reminiscent of the Bomb Squad's chaotic black-noise tapestries, her first single, "Stompin' to Tha '90s," was a ferocious opening statement.

Transplanted Virginia rhyme-monger the Lady of Rage (who had not yet gotten down with Death Row) still remembers the first time she heard the song. "I was impressed because me being from the East Coast, I just looked at West Coast MCs like, well, they don't really have the skills of an East Coast MC," she admits. "Then when Yo Yo came out, I was like, Wow. She had this little girly thing about herself, the confidence to say, 'I can really do this and hang with the big boys and I still got my femininity and I'm cute and I'm spitting these hard rhymes.' I was like, hmm, I think I got to step up a little bit!"

"I totally think Yo Yo set it off for females on the West Coast," says Poetess, a rapper and on-air personality on L.A.'s 100.3 the Beat. She says it was not only Yo Yo's sound but her image that was important: "She represented the style of females here—just the whole look and the whole attitude, the way we dressed back then, with the braids and the basket weave, the biker shorts, the hair bobs and the crimps, the whole L.A. thing. She will always be known in my opinion as the original queen of West Coast rap."

With Yo Yo on board, Cube was ready to launch his newly formed production company, Street Knowledge. Inking a deal with East-West Records (whose CEO, Sylvia Rhone, helped steer the careers of MC Lyte, Björk, and Missy Elliott), these rough rhyme slingers had found a home. With a roster that included Del, Da Lench Mob, and Kam, the partnership produced some of the coolest young guns from the West, with Yo Yo playing a starring role.

"Her introduction to the music world through Ice Cube really set the table for her success," said Rhone after the deal was in place. "Her delivery, her lyrics, and her production have really placed her as one of the premier female rap artists." That all-important street cred combined with Rhone's marketing strategy allowed Yo Yo to break out of the rap underground and onto the pop charts.

Utilizing a James Brown backbeat and killer horns, *Make Way*'s biggest single, "You Can't Play With My Yo Yo" was a bold declaration of sass and bad-ass attitude. The song's messages, however, were somewhat mixed: one minute Yo Yo was screaming "I'm not a ho, yo," and a few beats later not only was baby girl stealing your man, but she even had the nerve to leave lipstick on his collar.

But Yo Yo made no apologies, and the booming track was a smash from skating rinks and dance floors to the *Billboard* charts. "Me and Cube wrote that song together," says Yo Yo. "We were sitting in his mom's house, because at the time Cube was still living at home. He was in the bedroom, I was in the living room, but we were both writing. I'd add a part, then he would add something to it. The excitement and energy was unreal. We were both jumping around, just crazy creative." The album reached No. 5 on the R&B chart and sold 400,000 copies, a huge number for the time. "Back then female rappers generally didn't go gold," recalls one label staffer.

Yo Yo's album had its fair share of party jams, but this young sister had a lot more on her mind than just shaking her behind. Having grown up seeing girls around her con-

Yo Yo and Ice Cube in a Los Angeles studio.

fused by their budding sexuality, Yo Yo felt a social responsibility to educate and serve as a role model. Living in an age where most entertainers shrug when asked about the influence their music has on the black community, Yo Yo was advising those who graduated "from Barbie dolls straight to sex" to use protection in her song "Put a Lid on It."

While the bumping track was funkier than a pot of chitlins, Yo Yo was more concerned with the song's message. "To me, teen pregnancy was a big issue," she says. "One of the reasons I started my organization the Intelligent Black Woman's Coalition was to educate girls. We would have meetings and I would make them show their report cards and encourage them to stay in school. For me, education has always been the key to success."

With her IBWC girls, Yo Yo visited schools and homeless shelters, and raised money for the defense fund of Black Panther Geronimo Pratt. "They used to do a lot of stuff like buy uniforms for the neighborhood teens and fund-raisers for different organizations in the community," says Poetess. "I attended one of the IBWC meetings at her aunt's house. There were a few other sisters there from the 'hood, and we sat around sharing our life experiences and supporting one another. We laughed, we cried. It was a really nice bonding experience."

"A lot of women are disrespected because they tolerate it," says Yo Yo. And with songs like "Girl Don't Get Played," in which she advises women to hold their drooling dawgs on a short leash, as well as the radical "Sisterland"—which borrows the rousing "Hey sister, soul sister!" chorus from LaBelle's 1975 "Lady Marmalade"—critics were quick to proclaim Yo Yo a feminist, a description that stuck to her after the release of 1993's *Black Pearl*. "I didn't really know what a feminist was," she says with a laugh. "I just said what I believed in and tried to stand my ground. I was just being me."

"When I first started, when I used to perform at school events and stuff, my rap was more anti-drugs, things that were uplifting that I could perform in schools and talent shows. When Cube approached me, that was the time that 'Bitch Iz a Bitch' was out and all those different songs and I used to hate all of that. It was a male-dominated field where, it seemed to me, guys could say anything they want and get away with it. And me? I wanted to have a voice and be that voice for the women to come back and say, We're not your bitch."

The winter of 2001 was no joke out east. Three solid months of snow and freezing temperatures were a drastic transition for a woman and her five-year-old daughter coming from the land of sunshine and palm trees to New Jersey. "I'm still trying to get used to this weather," Yo Yo jokes on the eve of yet another storm.

But she's always been willing to make sacrifices to pursue her dreams. And she's excited about being a first-year drama student at the Lee Strasberg School of Acting. Famous for its Method technique, the school is known worldwide as the training ground for serious actors from mumbling Marlon Brando to screaming Al Pacino.

While she's best known for her recurring role as Key Lo Lo on the TV comedy series *Martin*, Yo Yo has also had dramatic cameos in *Boyz N the Hood* and *Menace II Society*. Still, these were a far cry from her school audition—Nora's tragic monologue from Henrik Ibsen's *A Doll's House*. "Most of the small acting roles I've had have come from riding the coattails of my music," she says frankly. "I wanted to be in a place where I could be trained by theater teachers who take the craft seriously."

Although Yo Yo once had nothing but love for hip hop, showbiz has a way of trying to eat its young. "A lot of people, myself included, just jumped into the music industry headfirst," says Yo Yo. "You're so eager, but no one really teaches you about publishing or the many other aspects.

Of course, you eventually learn, but when you go from writing rhymes in your spare time to being a professional, you must be educated. With my acting career, I didn't want to make the same mistakes."

Her moment of clarity came when she and MC Lyte collaborated on the song "One for the Cuties" for Yo Yo's 1996 album *Total Control*. "Lyte and I spent a lot of time talking about our disappointments and the bullshit we had to deal with," she recalls. "Even in terms of being marketed, I never felt they knew what to do with me. I was a heavier girl, so I wasn't the image of sex appeal that they were used to."

Yo Yo doesn't blame the head of her label—"Sylvia has always been a woman to admire and love," she says—but does question whether her management was looking out for her. Her career was steered by Pat Charbonnet, the woman who helped take Cube from relative obscurity to a bankable Hollywood contender. "Pat became my manager simply because she was Cube's manager," Yo Yo recalls with a sour tone. "The less said about our relationship, the better. She was good for Cube, but as far as his outside projects go, her focus wasn't really there."

Yo Yo relied on the professional support of Street Knowledge Productions, but things started going wrong when she began working on her sophomore project *Black Pearl*. "Cube and Sylvia had a major disagreement over the direction of Street Knowledge," she remembers. "Something had happened with Lench Mob, and Cube thought that Sylvia was penalizing Street Knowledge. I was stressed out, because I was caught in the middle having to make an album."

Cube and Yo Yo would record the gangsta anthem "Bonnie and Clyde Theme," but soon outside producers were brought on board. "Cube had been the captain of the ship, so with him gone it was difficult," Yo Yo admits. "Sylvia did the best that she could do. She tried to make the situation work for me, but some of the people working with her had no idea what to do with me. Sometimes I felt as though I was defending myself."

Many tracks on *Black Pearl* advanced a strong pro-woman agenda, and the album's title was dedicated to her sister. "Darker women in our society have always been played down like they aren't beautiful," says Yo Yo. "My sister used to get teased for being dark and I know it did something to her self-esteem. My mother called her Black Pearl, so that's what I called the record."

From day one, Yo Yo had dabbled in rough-edged street tales like "Macktress" and "Girl's Got a Gun." But she insists she was never a gangsta chick. "That label had been put on us," she says today. "Where I came from some rappers had more court dates than show appearances, but I wasn't one of them."

That didn't stop the media from pigeonholing her that way. "People started seeing Yo Yo as a gangsta rapper and I was like, 'Wait a minute!' I hate to sound naïve about it, but in the beginning, it was never part of my image. I was surrounded by it, but it was never me. It's like if you're cooking and someone steps into the room and thinks, Oh, it smells good in here and you'll be like, I don't smell anything! It's cuz you're surrounded by it and don't notice it. I was just trying to grow and learn more. That's when it came to the 'keep it real' phase in hip hop. It seemed like half the rappers out were criminals! Seriously! Half of them had committed crimes, which made me ask myself, Do I want to be a part of this? I have plans for my future, I want to do more in the entertainment field. I thought what was so fun about music is it's of the mind, so it was all creativity for me. But with the 'keep it real' phase, people would be asking me, 'Yo Yo, do you really keep a gat in your purse?' Then to go out and see little kids saying your raps. It really affected me."

Living in L.A., Yo Yo had become all too familiar with the gangsta reality. Her first album was dedicated to high-school buddy Davian Banks, who was killed in a drive-by shooting. And her fifth and final album, *Ebony*, included "Iz It Still All Good?" a song inspired by the death of her buddy Tupac Shakur. "Pac was one of my best friends," she says. "I knew him from when we used to sit up hitting on a table and rapping. I admired him because he was a soldier, and he was such a conscious rapper. He was a young black man growing and aware of his surroundings and he could put it in a rap and have it make so much sense, and make you feel like, 'Oh, God.' And at the same time, I knew he wanted to grow, I knew he wanted to be somebody. I knew

he wanted to do something with his life. Every time I hear his music now, I always think, 'Damn, Pac, damn.'"

Unfortunately, few people ever heard her tribute to Tupac because Yo Yo's fifth disc, *Ebony*, was never officially released. Rashad Smith from Tumbling Dice Productions was overseeing the project, but on this occasion he rolled craps. "Rashad was like the sampling king," Yo Yo recalls, "but with my record some of the samples hadn't been cleared." After discs were pressed and packaging was completely printed, Elektra got word that Cheryl Lynn wouldn't give permission for a major sample from her signature song "To Be Real."

Although she's not bitter, Yo Yo was more than frustrated by the experience. "I was on the road doing promotional tours, radio interviews, and all kinds of freebies, but because only a single was released I never saw any money. It was like a pimp/ho thing. Who needs fame without the money?" With her contract expiring, Yo Yo saw no other option but to bizounce. "We had come to the end of our rope."

Though she's working on a new album (tentatively titled *Sacrifices*) with old friends like DJ Battlecat and Keith Crouch, Yo Yo's focus is now on her acting. "My understanding of the music world has made being creative a struggle," she says with just a tinge of regret. Unlike those aging hip hop dudes who keep trying to hang in the game when they are clearly played, hip hop women tend to be more realistic, and Yo Yo is no exception. "There are a lot of people still trying to make it happen, but I've never been like that," she says. "I love rap, but personally as an artist I feel I have to do something else," she says as the snow starts to fall. "My mission is not to talk about my coochie or how bad my ass is or the tricks I can play on men. I feel there has to be more."

TLC

*I ain't never
been no silly
bitch waiting
to get rich
from a nigga's
bank account*

three the hard way

by Mimi Valdés

At 4 P.M. on a chilly afternoon in February 1996, a limo pulls up to the plush 57th Street headquarters of Arista Records, right down the block from Tiffany & Co. Inside the vehicle are the pop trio TLC, rolling 14 females deep. Their crew, hand-picked from the 'hood in Atlanta, are no strangers to robbing and stealing.

Most are friends TLC's Left Eye met at the rehab center where the rambunctious rapper spent time after burning down the house of her boyfriend, NFL All-Star Andre Rison. Left Eye and her posse had driven to New York from Georgia in a pair of Toyota Landcruisers while T-Boz and Chilli arrived by plane. They'd met up at the Four Seasons Hotel, parked the cars, and packed into one limo like a scene out of a circus.

They enter the building calmly to avoid arousing suspicion. This is TLC's first visit to Arista, the parent company of their Atlanta-based label, LaFace. Arista president Clive Davis is expecting them. They called him on the way over to ask if they could stop by and say hello. Davis is an industry legend with crazy clout but he has no idea what TLC is capable of.

Everyone's quiet as the women squeeze into an elevator. A receptionist greets them warmly as they make their way to Davis's corner office. They're told that he's finishing up a meeting, but they go ahead and bumrush anyway. Puff Daddy and one of his Bad Boy Records employees are inside playing new tracks for Davis. The girls stand in the doorway, wearing their best screw-faces. The men don't understand what's happening at first. Davis, who's on the phone, asks if they can wait outside for five minutes. One of the hard-knock chicks snatches the phone and tells the man, "TLC needs to talk to you, you gotta listen." Meanwhile the girls inform Puffy that his meeting is over and he's got to go. He gathers his things, walks out, and dials up LaFace cofounder L.A. Reid, telling him his girls have gone crazy. Somebody gets alarmed enough to call the cops. Besides the phone chick, TLC has two girls guarding the inside door so no one can come in and two more at Davis's side so he can't leave.

For several weeks now, the members of TLC have been preparing to go to court after filing for bankruptcy in July 1995. As one of the first acts signed to LaFace, they helped establish the label, paving the way for subsequent stars like Toni Braxton, Usher, and OutKast. TLC felt they deserved a bigger share of the money they made for LaFace. "No one cares if you're starving in this business," T-Boz wrote in her 1999 book, *Thoughts*. "You look at some record company's assistant who has a house and drives a Mercedes, and you know my family and I are sitting there, the lights are off, the phone's disconnected." Their first album, *Oooooooohhh... on the TLC Tip*, had sold over three million copies, and their current release, *CrazySexyCool*, was looking like it might top 10 million. At the time, Left Eye says their contract earned them only about 7 points out of a possible hundred. Since each point was equal to 8 cents, they got maybe 56 cents for each album sold, which had to be split three ways. After paying back recoupable expenses like recording costs, promotion, travel, and videos, Left Eye says each member was making about $50,000 a year after taxes. (Arista sent a statement that the company does not comment on its artists' contracts.) TLC's attempts to renegotiate had been derailed by finger-pointing between LaFace and Arista. Rison kept telling Left Eye (who was still his boo despite the house fire) to pay Davis a visit and get to the bottom of the mess. So Left Eye called T-Boz and Chilli, they got pumped up about it, and left for New York the next day.

The conversation with Davis goes on for over an hour. The girls take turns going off on the man who signed Aretha Franklin, Carlos Santana, and Whitney Houston. Chilli starts crying about how she can't go anywhere without someone recognizing her, yet she can't afford to buy a house. According to T-Boz Davis tells them things like he doesn't even know if they'll sell a million on their next album. In the middle of the meeting the cops show up, but no charges are pressed. Left Eye's girls are escorted out to the reception area while TLC finishes the meeting.

Addressing the incident for the first time, Davis issued this statement: "TLC did come to my office fully expecting difficulty in getting my attention regarding their dispute with LaFace Records, our joint-venture partner. They perhaps were surprised that I welcomed them and invited them in. I totally rejected any Arista security being present or needed. The group voiced their complaints about their contract and I told them they had to take them up with [LaFace executives] L.A. and Babyface. I did urge them to recognize the key roles that both L.A. and Babyface played in their career both creatively and professionally. I spent about an hour and a half with them with me talking about two-thirds of the time patiently trying to give them the best advice I could."

Not everything gets resolved, but at least they've let the label honcho know that this girl group means business. On their way out of the building, the amount of TLC memorabilia on the record company walls astounds them. For whatever reason, they still haven't received their own platinum album plaques, so they start grabbing everything TLC in sight, filling their arms with award plaques, posters, and CDs. "They left my office without any incident," Davis stated. "I later heard they did take a photo of themselves and a platinum plaque off the conference room wall."

"It was at a point where we had nothing to lose," recalls Chilli. "I would never do that again, but back then it was like, *shoot,* when you work hard you should have something to show for it and we didn't. If it wasn't for us being so mad, I don't see how I coulda sat there and not laughed. Now it's hilarious." Laughable or not, the stunt paid serious dividends; a few months later, TLC renegotiated the deal for their third album to the tune of $16 million, more than double the label's original offer. After which time, according to Davis's statement, "they came to my Grammy party the following February and greeted me with a hug and a kiss."

Arista had fairly light office security before TLC's little visit. Perhaps Davis had assumed that if Puffy's Bad Boy crew had never run up in his office, he had nothing to fear from TLC. But if anyone ever wondered whether the trio's hardcore edge was just a marketing gimmick, this outrageous episode should prove that these girls are anything but soft.

It took balls to orchestrate the Arista caper, and this attribute is just one of many reasons why TLC has connected with so many fans. The take-no-shit attitude reflected in their music and videos from day one is a very real reflection of these women's personalities. The concept for TLC may have been the idea of their former manager Perri "Pebbles" McKissack, but it's the chemistry between Tionne Watkins, Lisa Lopes, and Rozonda Thomas that makes TLC an explosive, unpredictable phenomenon. With more than 28 million records sold worldwide, five Grammys, four American Music Awards, four MTV Music Video Awards, and six Soul Train Awards, they are the biggest-selling female group of all time, surpassing even the Supremes.

TLC caused controversy just being themselves. Traditional R&B women wore tight, sexy outfits and wouldn't

dream of letting a rapper hit a few bars, much less the chorus of their debut single. But TLC sported the baggiest Day-Glo clothes with condoms of all sizes pinned on as accessories. The sight of them strutting around in the video "Ain't 2 Proud 2 Beg" with Left Eye rapping lines like "I need it in the morning or the middle of the night" was scandalous in 1992. Although they were all around 19 years old, their short stature, romper-room wardrobe, and off-the-wall energy made it seem like they weren't quite old enough to be singing about sex.

But TLC's success was based on more than just shock value. Making their own creative decisions about the group's image, T-Boz, Left Eye, and Chilli came up with a look, sound, and spirit that young fans gravitated to automatically. "The trio damn near led a grass-roots womanist revolution, banji-girl style," Joan Morgan wrote in VIBE's November 1994 issue. They seemed familiar, like the fiercely independent girls you might have grown up with but never dreamed you'd see on TV. If some girls weren't comfortable with wearing baggy hip hop gear or carrying their own condoms, TLC gave them permission.

The group's formation marked the start of something new and exciting musically as well. Bell Biv DeVoe might have coined the phrase "hip hop smoothed out on an R&B tip with a pop feel appeal to it," but the beautiful ladies of TLC took that idea and made it freakier, funkier, and more fun to watch. By the time they came out, there were countless male groups copying the new jack swing sound created in 1988 by production master Teddy Riley and his group Guy. It was only a matter of time before a female group tried the winning formula.

T-Boz and Left Eye met while auditioning for a new R&B girl group called 2nd Nature. They clicked immediately, and later ran into Pebbles outside of Xscape, a popular Atlanta hair salon. The R&B singer was married to L.A. Reid, and at the same time was looking to put together a female act. T-Boz, Left Eye, and a third girl went to dinner with Pebbles; she decided to sign them, and christened them TLC on the spot. However, the original C in the group, Crystal Jones, wasn't exactly star material. Although the group had been her idea, they decided she had to go. "She let us kick her out of the group," says T-Boz, whose deep singing voice came to anchor the group's sound. "Me? I would have been like, Ho, you trippin'." Chilli took her place and was given her nickname by Left Eye the night the girls met. She had been a dancer for the local R&B duo called Damien Dame before Pebbles brought her on board. "It was so magical," says Left Eye of the new mix. "We honestly believed we were gonna be superstars. We lived it before it actually happened."

With the group's lineup in place, they started recording an album. They worked with producers like Babyface, Marley Marl, and Jermaine Dupri, but it was a 22-year-old kid named Dallas Austin who really carved out a distinctive musical style for them. TLC became the barely established producer's claim to fame, getting him work with superstars like Michael Jackson and Madonna. "I credit Dallas all day long because he created a sound that matched my voice," says T-Boz. "I knew him from Jellybeans [a local roller-skating rink where he used to hang out], and he'd worked with Doug E. Fresh, ABC, and I was like, 'He should be our producer.'" Austin produced "Ain't 2 Proud 2 Beg" (using the Average White Band sample made famous on Rakim's "Microphone Fiend") followed by "What About Your Friends" and "Hat 2 the Back"—three of the four singles released from TLC's debut album. Judging by their success, it soon became clear that T-Boz had been right.

THE T...

Although she is in fact the Cool part of the *CrazySexyCool* triumvirate, the personality of Tionne Watkins (born April 26, 1970) can best be described as whatever. She didn't care when she got kicked out of four high schools ("For me, it all seemed to stem from my anger at my dad; the feelings of abandonment and being unloved were not something I knew how to deal with"). Or when she and Left Eye asked the original C in the group to step ("We wouldn't have made it with her"). Or when she wore baggy gear in a sea of scantily dressed R&B hotties ("I was boyish; high heels and shaking my rump wasn't gonna work"). Born with a nonchalant attitude and a sultry singing voice, she's thankful to have a job where she can wake up when she wants, be her own boss (like her nickname implies), and mostly just have fun.

The Des Moines, Iowa, native, who moved to Atlanta with her single mother at nine years old, was diagnosed with sickle-cell anemia as a baby. The disease, which primarily affects people of African descent, attacks the red blood cells and often lands sufferers in the hospital. Doctors recommended that she stay away from stress, exhaustion, and dancing, but T-Boz refused to give up her dream of becoming an entertainer. Before joining TLC, the high school dropout attended beauty school, specialized in nails, and worked odd jobs in beauty supply stores and salons. Those positions were more interesting than, say, the two-week stint at McDonald's that ended when they asked her to wash the windows. That was just way too much.

T-Boz loves to laugh. Her sentences are littered with smiles, giggles, or deep-throated cackles. Watching her go bowling in Los Angeles with friends, it's clear that she is a girl who's constantly got jokes. Almost every other word out her mouth is some country grammar, especially when talking to her husband, gangsta rapper Mack 10. They met on the video set of "Unpretty" and he took to her playful, ghetto personality. "It was never no mushy, hey baby kind of date," he says. "It was like she was my homegirl so I wanted to do something fun." By their third day of hanging out nonstop, he told her he knew she could be his wife. They married in a mob-themed ceremony in August 2000 (the wedding cake was shaped like a machine gun) and now have a baby daughter, Chase Anela (Hawaiian for "angel").

"You know I be kicking big head's ass in a whole bunch of games," says Tionne, sitting on Mack's lap at the bowling alley. "Air hockey, fuzz ball . . ." It's this same silly persona that's responsible for the wacky dances in most of the TLC videos, an important aspect of the group's success. The first album's videos were like one big extra-fun party you wished you'd been invited to, complete with dances that few people outside Atlanta had ever seen: big crews of friends battling it out with moves in front of graffiti-painted walls. Tionne choreographed much of the early stuff, including the elbow-going-up move in "What About Your Friends" and the bend-down-and-jump-up "Creep" dance (which she originally made up to Mack 10's song "Fo Life"). All the girls could dance, as the Band-Aids on their shoes symbolized, and this shared talent brought them closer together. "Lisa made up this dance called the old man," says T-Boz. "Chilli would be like, 'My baby god-daughter did this dance.' We would get moves from *Fat Albert* cartoons. When you have a whole bunch of people onstage doing it, it don't look so stupid."

Tionne was also responsible for much of the group's early fashion sense. "We made it okay to dress baggy and be respected as a woman and still be feminine," she says. In the days before TLC could afford a stylist, she would go shopping for the group and convinced the others to follow her lead. "I wasn't wearing baggy clothes when I came down from Philly," says Left Eye, "and Chilli didn't own a pair of jeans when we met her."

In November 1994, TLC unveiled their new album, *CrazySexyCool*, along with a new look. "We had moved up into an area where guys wanted us and more women wanted to be like us," says Left Eye. The first single off the album, "Creep," coined a term for sneaking around to cheat on your mate. The sexy video by fashion photographer Matthew Rolston was actually the third one shot for the song. During one meeting, Left Eye pointed to a television playing Rolston's steamy Salt-N-Pepa clip, screaming, "We're supposed to compete with that!?" Sure enough, Rolston was soon brought on board. "We had these cool silk pajamas custom-made and everyone wanted a pair," says

Tionne. They called on Rolston again to direct their second single, "Red Light Special," and got even sexier with a strip poker session with a whole mess of beefy guys. However, it was the video for "Waterfalls," directed by F. Gary Gray, that pushed them over the edge. Winning three trophies at the 1995 *MTV Video Music Awards* was a feat no one expected. "We had a vision for the video, but it was going to cost a lot of money," says Chilli. "My idea was the water images; I got that from *The Abyss.* Lisa came up with the coming from space into the water, Tionne with the story lines. We begged L.A., because back then you didn't pay $900,000 for a video, not if you were black." But for TLC, the visual statement was almost as important as the music.

Despite all the trends TLC started, the hairstyles, the fashion, the girl power lyrics, Tionne insists they were unintentional. "I don't live for other people, I live for me," she says. "I ain't into feminism, that black power stuff and all that, whatever." Tionne's main concerns are her immediate family, close friends, and living a relaxed life where she blossoms creatively. She's recorded songs on her own–"Touch Myself" *(Fled),* "Wanna Take Me Back" *(DJ Clue Presents: Backstage Mixtape),* "My Getaway" *(Rugrats in Paris),* and "Tight 2 Def" with Mack 10 for his last album, *Paper Route.* She's tried acting, most notably in the movie *Belly.* She even published a collection of poems called *Thoughts.* In her poem "I Wanna Be Free" she writes, "I should sing because I'm happy / Sing because I'm free / But somehow I feel like / This business has made / A slave of me."

Now that she's discovered the creative and financial joys of songwriting, performing may take a backseat. "That's loot. I'm like, 'Oh my God, why didn't I try this before?'" says Tionne, who cowrote TLC's No. 1 hit "Unpretty" with Austin. Knowing that her bank account is straight is more important to her than fame and all the drama that comes with it. "If it makes more sense for me to be behind the scenes, then that's what I'm gonna do," says Tionne, who divides time between homes in L.A. and Atlanta. "I'm not hoggish, I'm not camera-happy." There's also the issue of her health. "I like performing, but if the record company ain't giving up the money, I ain't gonna bust my butt and be the one going to the hospital getting hooked up to wires

and needles," says this spokesperson for the Sickle Cell Disease Association of America. "If I can't get a check like the one when I sit and write a song, I'm not doing it. I love my fans but I ain't gonna die for them."

And though it cost TLC during their bankruptcy trial, she says she doesn't regret the time they went crazy with Arista's American Express card and charged $250,000. They were in L.A. for the '96 American Music Awards, roughly a month before the so-called Clive incident. "Arista was treating us bad, pissing us off, so we were like, you know what? Everybody deserves a gift," Tionne says. They were staying at the Four Seasons and decided to take their crew shopping in the hotel's gift shop. "We just charged stuff to our room," she recalls. "We told the people who'd been down with us for years to get clothes, jewelry, anything. 'Treat yourself. It's your day, boo. Girl, get this diamond ring, it looks lovely on you. And here's some earrings and a necklace to match.' I still got some cute little earrings from that day. Arista didn't find out until we were already back in Atlanta. They'll never put their credit cards down again for us," Tionne says with a laugh. But it's cool.

TO THE L . . .

Left Eye may be a little Crazy, but brilliant people often are. Born on May 27, 1971, Lisa Lopes started walking at seven months, taught herself to play the piano at age five, and mastered a multitude of hobbies (sewing, fashion design, graffiti-style airbrushing, creative writing, music) during her teenage years. The oldest of three kids, she flourished creatively even though her home life in Philadelphia was anything but stable. Lisa's military father used to beat her mom. She ran away from home several times, and alcohol became a comforting friend. At 19 she followed her then-boyfriend to Atlanta to be in a group that didn't work out. But as luck would have it, within a year she was on TV in the "Ain't 2 Proud 2 Beg" video wearing a condom over her left eye.

The rubbers were Lisa's idea. Never one to hesitate, she grabbed some condoms off her dresser before the video shoot and told the girls to pin them on their clothes. "I was like, if people ask you what it's for, say safe sex," recalls Left Eye. "I don't know what I was thinking. We just didn't care. Our attitude was so optimistic, so full of energy. We never stepped outside of ourselves to look at ourselves. We were in our own wonderland."

Lisa's spur-of-the-moment idea worked. At first glance, the whole group might have seemed like a trendy package put together by label execs and focus groups, but TLC didn't do anything that didn't represent them. "You don't have to sit and try to think of everything for TLC," says L.A. Reid. "They have their own ideas, their own thoughts on what they want TLC to be." He's adamant about the group receiving due credit. "I want them to be thought of as true creative forces," he told VIBE in '94, "to be as important to music as artists like Prince."

While promoting *Oooooooohhh . . . on the TLC Tip*, Lisa came up with the concept for the second album, *Crazy-SexyCool*, which eventually sold 11 million copies. The phrase was supposed to represent all the personalities of a female, like a TLC take on Chaka Khan's "I'm Every Woman." But problems within the group started when they went back to the studio. "It was always a struggle with me and somebody when it had to do with the creative aspect," says Left Eye, who'd written or cowritten eight songs on the first album and was planning to contribute at least as much on the second one. "The first album nobody cared," she says. "After we blew up and it became a situation where you can definitely make money, everybody wanted a piece of the pie."

Austin (who was now coexecutive producer) and Lopes began to butt heads. The only time he wanted her in the studio was to write her rap, not to help build the actual song.

She distanced herself from the project, and tried to hire producers for the songs she wrote, but the separation was causing stress within the group. Meanwhile Left Eye was going through major drama in her tumultuous relationship with Rison. There were reports of a real fight outside a supermarket in Atlanta with blows thrown and a handgun fired. Although she didn't seem to be down with the team, she managed to cowrite four songs for the album. "But when the fire thing happened," says Lisa, "it was like, Oh yeah, she's really off on her own."

The torching of Rison's house in June 1994 got covered by all the major networks, from CNN to MTV. Rumors of infidelity, domestic abuse, and alcoholism ran wild. Maybe she didn't *mean* to burn down the $2 million mansion, but damn! The TLC camp didn't know what to think of the situation at first. All the publicity was drawing attention to the impending release of *CrazySexyCool*, but "Pebbles was trying to sell us for like $100,000," says Lisa. "Tionne was cool, Chilli was worried, like, 'If you do anything else we're gonna have to ex you.'" They eventually decided to make light of the controversy, posing on the cover of VIBE in fireman's gear. There was no denying that the buzz helped spark *CrazySexyCool*'s mega-sales.

But Lisa's quick to credit the music, and not just the fire press, for the album's success. "It's our best album," she says. "The production, the way the vocals sound, the material was much better, the imaging, the videos were the bomb, we were polished."

On her day in court, instead of facing up to 20 years in jail, Left Eye got five years' probation, a $10,000 fine, and three months in alcohol rehab. At first the prying media attention upset Lisa. "It seemed like a personal thing, like you guys are personally attacking me," she says. "But I learned that if you don't give these guys a good story, they're gonna write one anyway. These guys have jobs, they've got to feed their families, so they got to turn in their stories, and I want to help." Lisa adds with a gleam in her eye, "I want *my* story to be good."

Left Eye's innate understanding of the music business led her to develop her own groups. First she signed the teenage rap duo Illegal and then the young girl group Blaque to her production company, Left Eye Productions. Now that her life is less hectic (her off-again on-again relationship with Rison notwithstanding), she's itchin' to apply her industry know-how to a solo career.

"Five years ago, I couldn't bear to live another twenty-five years," Left Eye says, reclining on the couch in her home studio in Atlanta. Now she's always talking about becoming a better person and improving the lives of others. "I wanna do a cooking show teaching kids how to eat healthy," she says. She practices yoga and reads up on different religions, as well as astrology and numerology. "Most of us live a very miserable and unhappy life and it doesn't have to be that way," she says, sounding like a born-again preacher who's seen the light. She sometimes visits a healing center in Honduras for people with terminal illnesses. Lisa isn't really sick, but she says the peaceful setting and the beautiful tropical environment revitalize her.

There's a lot more to Left Eye than TLC's fans know. Her character on MTV's series *The Cut* didn't do her justice. The songs she's done with Lil' Kim, Method Man, Donnell Jones, and N'Sync only offered a glimpse. But she hopes her solo album will prove she's more than an eight-bar rapper. With collaborators like the alternative artist Esthero and producers like Salaam Remi and Rockwilder, the album, titled *Supernova*, shows a diversity and depth that may surprise people who only know her work with TLC. "I've grown a lot," says Lisa. "Even when I deal with the record company, I don't care if I do have a problem, it's all smiles on my face." Looks as though she won't be taking hostages any time soon.

just to be down with TLC, and she adapted to baggy gear when she hadn't ever owned a pair of jeans. Although her performance in the film *Hav Plenty* was impressive, the stage is where she really shines. When she got invited onstage at a '99 Goodie Mob concert in Chattanooga, she danced it up so hard she stole the show. Chilli feeds off a crowd's energy, and she wouldn't do anything to jeopardize her relationship with TLC's fans. "It's the touring I love, being on that stage in front of all those people," she says. "That's where I feel the most comfortable, dancing, doing my thing."

While Tionne gave attitude and Lisa exuded energy, Chilli was always making love to the camera. Her innocent beauty and sweet, angelic voice made her seem approachable, the one guys were most likely to have a crush on. As the one true southern belle of the group—complete with gracious ladylike manners and the ability to cook her ass off—flirting came naturally. Even Prince was rumored to be smitten. Unfortunately for him, her heart belonged to someone else.

After a day of meetings to finalize the deal for her upcoming solo project (said to be in the spirit of TLC's first album), Chilli and Dallas Austin are getting ready to check out of

They were staying at the Four Seasons, and decided to take their crew shopping at the hotel gift shop. "We just charged stuff to our rooms," said T-Boz. "It's your day, boo. Get this diamond ring. It looks lovely on you."

TO THE C.

Chilli just can't help being Sexy. From the day she was born—February 27, 1971—her looks have made Rozonda Thomas the center of attention. That reddish brown skin and long ebony hair made her stand out from all the other black girls in her neighborhood.

Growing up in Atlanta, Rozonda longed to know the father who'd abandoned her mom before she was born. In fact, she didn't meet him until after the success of *CrazySexyCool* when the producers of Sally Jesse Raphael's talk show tracked him down. The reunion was captured on home video and Chilli later appeared on TV to share her feelings about the whole emotional experience.

But then, she's always been comfortable in front of an audience. As a child, Rozonda found comfort in performing, almost as if the attention satisfied some deep-seated need. Remember, she was willing to let people call her Chilli

their room at the W Hotel in New York. They have been romantically involved on and off since before the start of TLC. It wasn't until the birth of their son Tron (her first, his second) in 1997 that their relationship was publicly recognized. Fans might've known if they caught the picture of Austin pinned to the teddy bear Chilli was holding in the "Baby Baby Baby" video or the jacket she wore in "Hat 2 Da Back" with the words *D's Shit* embroidered on the chest pocket. TLC has experienced none of the jealous drama that can result when a group member gets involved with a "Svengali producer." Tionne's friendship with Austin was more like they were siblings, and his struggles with Lisa were creative conflicts unrelated to Chilli's relationship.

TLC simply had other problems to worry about. Despite their enormous success, the group wasn't able to capitalize beyond touring and record sales. "Think about it, you've never seen them on no commercials," says Austin. "No endorsement deals like Pepsi or Coca-Cola. It's funny, 'cause TLC is big pop underground in a way," says Austin. Chilli (who did do an ad for Coach by herself) blames their lack of endorsements on all the negative media. "Lisa took on this whole mentality when she burned down the house that bad press is good," says Rozonda.

"It's crazy to be the biggest-selling female group and have no merchandise when everywhere I go I see N'Sync lip gloss," adds Tionne. "Lisa thinks controversy made us popular, and it did, but it took away other stuff, too."

Of course, Left Eye vehemently disagrees. "No endorsements have nothing to do with the press, that's our fault," she insists. "We have a reputation for canceling, showing up late, and taking a long time to do whatever when we get there. These companies don't care about what kind of press I have; all they care about is making money."

Either way the negative publicity didn't end with the fire. When the group filed for bankruptcy in June '95, many people wondered what was preventing these girls from handling their business properly. They had already been through two new managers (former Island Records president Hiriam Hicks and former NBA player Norman Nixon) before settling on Bill Diggins. "It was just the three of us trying to get away from everybody, not knowing who was what," Chilli recalls, alluding to a series of shady deals. "It was crazy. I mean, when it rains it pours, and it was storming."

They'd already fired their former manager Pebbles, who had become a born-again Christian with her own church. But when TLC cut their new deal for the third album, she wanted money for ownership of their name. "We had to pay $2.5 million to be like good-bye," says Chilli. "She wanted three, but we were like, *Look now.*" Still the group was willing to make a one-time payment in order to escape the publishing and production contracts she'd tied them up in. "People thought we got all this money when we recorded *Fanmail*, but we had to pay to be free from her," says Chilli, who still holds a grudge against Pebbles. "She's never tried to reach out to me, but I won't talk to her," she says. "A lot of the accusations she made, implying that I slept with L.A., really hurt me. It's crazy just how insecure she was. But at this point, it's no sweat. I'm totally over it."

THREE'S A CHARM?

The distinctive personalities that made TLC threatened to pull the group apart by the time they released *Fanmail* in February '99. Before they even started, Austin declared that he wouldn't touch the project unless he could be executive producer again, this time for a whopping fee of $4.2 million. Austin's negotiations with LaFace dragged on for ten months, and Lisa—who'd come up with the *Fanmail* con-cept while they were promoting *CrazySexyCool*—was sick of waiting.

One day an antsy Left Eye decided to play a TLC demo tape from one of her producers during a guest DJ spot on Atlanta's V103 FM. Not only did she not tell T-Boz and Chilli, but their voices weren't even on the song. (It's almost eerie how Debra Killings, the singer who demos all of TLC's songs, can make her voice sound exactly like both of them.) "I'm thinking, Debra's the TLC sound so no one's gonna know," Left Eye says. "It wasn't even a big issue for me but I can see how Chilli and Tionne would get upset." It was April Fool's so they called the radio station and played it off as if it were a joke.

Drama continued when it came time to finalize the album title. At the last minute, Lisa wanted to change it to *fantasy.com.* They held a meeting at T-Boz's house and Left Eye brought along some of her girls who'd accompanied them during the Clive incident. "Before it was just the three of us when ideas would come up," says Chilli. "Now there's fifteen other people saying the idea's incredible, implying that we were jealous if we didn't like it." It wasn't just the name that bothered them; Left Eye had an idea to do something on the Internet where TLC would look as though they were naked, but really weren't. "I was like, hold up," Tionne recalls. "You can do that with yo'self when you come out, but don't expect me to be with you on this, exploiting my body."

Then came their second VIBE cover story, in May 1999. After the interview was over, Lisa called writer Anthony DeCurtis to add a few things: "I've graduated from this era," she declared. "I cannot stand one hundred percent behind this TLC project and the music that is supposed to represent me. This will be my last interview until I can speak freely about the truth and present myself on my solo project." She now says she did it because she thought their interview had been dry and boring. No one wanted to talk about all the internal problems that Lisa believed would make for better reading. "It turned into this big mess," says Left Eye, "but then we always sell a lot of records."

Critics loved *Fanmail.* The sound was futuristic but with vintage TLC attitude. "No Scrubs" even inspired an answer record, "No Pigeons" by Sporty Thieves, marking the first time male rappers responded to a females' taunt instead of the other way around. Unfortunately, Hype Williams's video for "No Scrubs"—an old term for sorry-ass guys that jumped right back into popular vernacular—looked similar to Michael and Janet Jackson's "Scream." And with the exception of one part at the end of the video where they're backing their butts into the camera, there wasn't much TLC silliness going on. T-Boz and Left Eye had their makeup done in a style reminiscent of Gwen Stefani in No Doubt's video for the song "New." The Japanimation thing was cute, but didn't seem like anything fans could really copy. The "No Scrubs" video was beautiful in an antiseptic sort of way, but all the single shots of the girls had fans wondering how true those breakup rumors really were.

All the little styling elements that defined TLC were slowly disappearing. "The image was terrible," says Left Eye. "Our stylist, Julie Mijares, was taking direction from us but we had three different ideas. I was willing to wear tight clothes, Chilli was totally against it, and Tionne didn't care." The lack of a coherent image left only the music to get excited about, but for some fans, even that was debatable.

Though Lisa thought the *Fanmail* singles were great, she saw the overall album (which sold over six million copies) as a rip-off of Britain's drum and bass movement. "For someone who's never heard that sound, it might be great," she says, "but for the pioneers who created that sound, the underground, that's some bullshit." Both Tionne and Chilli say they love *Fanmail* and feel they could still be working long after its release if Left Eye wasn't so displeased with the project. "We didn't know if she was going to show up for things. It became really stressful for us, especially for Tionne and her sickle cell," says Chilli. "I feel like she killed our chemistry."

Next came Left Eye's idea for The Challenge. During an interview, Left Eye proposed that TLC each do solo albums, package them together as The Challenge, release three singles, and have the winner determined by their chart position in *Billboard*. T-Boz and Chilli were not amused. "They were saying things like I was evil," says Left Eye, "and I'm like, What are you talking about? I came up with an idea that I thought we could all benefit from. Everybody loves a big fight. We got three records left in our deal and if we do The Challenge, we'd be out of our LaFace contract." (Arista refused to confirm the contractual details.) The plan did have a certain maniacal brilliance to it. "They wanna talk about me? Fine," she reasoned, "we should make money off it. We could keep talking shit about each other in the press until the record comes out and I guarantee everybody is gonna buy it for thirty dollars, just to see what the hell we do."

Tensions only escalated while they prepared to go on tour. After adding up how much money they'd make after expenses, touring didn't seem like the most financially sound move. Tionne and Chilli didn't want to disappoint fans by canceling, but Lisa disagreed. "Why should we bust our ass and get on the road for three months," she argued, "when we're probably not going to make any money?"

She decided to write the girls letters to express her frustration. "Her friend brought in this letter as they were getting dressed to go onstage in Minneapolis," says Austin, "It was very discouraging, like, 'Y'all don't got your shit straight, I ain't about to do this.'" Dallas got pissed. "I took a Sharpie," he says, "and wrote a letter that said, 'Fuck you. We don't give a damn. We don't like you anyway.' I put a flower on the envelope and left it in her room."

They haven't spoken since the end of their tour in March 2000—which, according to Left Eye, lost half a million dollars. None of the members of TLC can say whether there will ever be another album, but they haven't officially agreed to break up, either. "Even when we were really, really close, whenever we broke we didn't speak," says Lisa, untroubled by the silence. "We just went off and took a break into our own little worlds." Perhaps their maturing personalities, and a whole lot of money, will be enough to rekindle the old flame. Or maybe they were just one of those things that were too perfect—and too explosive—to last long.

L.A. Reid, for one, doesn't see it that way. "I guarantee that we will release a TLC album in December 2001, even if I have to do it on December 25," says Reid from his New York office. "The minute Beyonce started saying Destiny's Child was the biggest girl group, it was like Tionne on line one, Chilli on line two, Lisa on line three. They wanted to release a statement but I said the best thing to do was release an album. They asked if I would write them a big check and I said, 'Yeah, of course.'"

"It could be cool," says Chilli, considering the possibilities. "Or it could be crazy, like when New Edition tried to get back together." And if that's the case, let's hope TLC leaves its fans with our memories instead.

MARY

Who do you think you are? Baby one day you'll be a star... I'm just tryin' to get mine I don't have the time to knock the hustle for real!

Photograph by Spicer

very mary *by Emil Wilbekin*

Every man, woman, and child inside Radio City Music Hall is singing in unison. *You are everything,* they roar, eyes locked on the statuesque woman strutting across the stage, *and everything is you.* Mary J. Blige looks surprised by the sheer volume of the worshipful voices booming back at her from every corner of this flossy Manhattan venue. The red velvet seats are all empty; everybody in this totally mixed audience is up and on their feet.

Like a homegirl Statue of Liberty, Mary's brought them all together—the loving couples who left the kids with a sitter, the ghetto girls dressed in their favorite Mary incarnation, the homeboys who went nuts when Method Man showed up to bust a few rhymes, professional women, gay men, suburban teens, showbiz execs, and lots of not-so-jaded press and celebrities. Tonight they really do lift every voice and sing (along with Mary) and the sound is so loud and powerful that for a moment she can barely hear her own voice.

But make no mistake, Mary is the microphone controller tonight. She raises the steel to her lips and lets that trademark alto cut through the din. "You are everything and everything is *youuuuu,*" she replies, pimp-strolling along the front of the stage to greet her ecstatic fans. There are no precious air kisses or mosh pit high-fives. As always, Mary keeps it real, bending over to give her fans a straight-up pound—the kind usually reserved for black male bonding—a loud hand-slap followed by a quick finger snap.

Behold the sublime juxtaposition that makes 31-year-old Mary Jane Blige the undisputed Queen of Hip Hop Soul. It's all about the dichotomy. She can stand front and center, wearing a Dolce & Gabbana rhinestone-studded bikini top with matching belt and choker and white stretch pants, delivering a ballad as pretty as you please, then turn around and slap the audience's hands like they're old friends from the projects in Yonkers.

Sexy but never smutty, strong but always sensitive, Mary J. Blige is the yin and the yang of urban music, empress of the post–hip hop landscape of modern rhythm and blues. You know the rhythm; you heard it in 1992 on a jam called "Real Love." Honey was singing over the drumbeat from Audio Two's "Top Billin'" with a "Go Brooklyn" chant thrown in for good measure. As for the blues, they just seemed to come naturally. "I grew up on old R&B and soul," she once explained. "Then as I got older I got into the block

parties. That's why my voice when I sing is almost like a rapper, on the beat."

While Mary is heralded as the finest soul-singing sister in the game, she has a proven ability to hold her own with the fellas. From her round-the-way romantic remix of "Reminisce" with Pete Rock and C.L. Smooth to party anthems with B.I.G. like "One More Chance," Mary has always been able to rock with the best. Just check the resumé: There's the Grammy-winning "You're All I Need" with Method Man, "Sexy" and "Can't Knock the Hustle" with Jay-Z, "Love Is All We Need" with Nas, the "Dolly My Baby" remix with Supercat, "Let's Get Free" with dead prez, "The Message" with Dr. Dre, "911" with Wyclef Jean, and "Back 2 Life (2001)" with Jadakiss of the LOX, a group from Mary's old neighborhood that she helped get a record deal. Year in and year out, Mary's vocal punch and larger-than-life attitude carry as much, if not more weight than her masculine partners.

Sure we love the hard exterior, but we can hear in her voice that there's much more going on. Deep inside, Mary is spiritual, sensual, and vulnerable. She sings songs about some of life's most painful experiences with deep feeling and conviction. The sound physically emerges from her—bare, honest, heavy, and raw. Emotionally and sonically her voice hits you like a Mack truck.

"Mary's strength as an artist is the pure pain that comes out of her vocals," says Kenneth "Babyface" Edmonds, who produced "Not Gon' Cry" from the massive 1995 soundtrack for *Waiting to Exhale.* "It's the emotion. She has *it* unlike anyone else."

I first encountered that voice in my cramped office at a brand-new urban music and culture magazine founded by Quincy Jones (we were just starting to call it VIBE). One spring afternoon in 1992, Lisa Cambridge, the publicist for Uptown Records, stopped by to give me a preview of "the hottest" new female singer—some girl from Yonkers who was singing R&B, but over hip hop beats. Uptown was an imprint founded by Andre Harrell, the half of former rap duo Dr. Jeckyll and Mr. Hyde who had signed Harlem's own production prodigy Teddy Riley and the supergroup Guy, unleashing a dynamic new sound called new jack swing. Plugged into the MCA power structure, Uptown was already the home of Jodeci, a quartet of tattooed choirboys from North Carolina, as well as the overweight lover (and eventual label head) Heavy D. Mary was going to be Uptown's urban torch singer.

"She's got fiery red hair," the publicist said. "She has to be in the first issue of VIBE." Yeah, her and every other urban artist, I thought to myself. Then Lisa dropped a black cassette into my boombox, and as the Play button clicked, my relationship with Mary J. Blige began.

Rising above the intoxicating bass and drums of "Reminisce" came the sound of an old friend and confidante. I honestly felt like I knew this voice as soon as it emerged from the speakers. There was something familiar in the way Mary enunciated her words, idiosyncrasies of phrasing that reminded me of the vivacious black women I had grown up with in Cincinnati, Ohio. Real black women who were loud, funny, and said exactly what was on their mind—soul sisters.

At the same time, Mary's voice was refreshing. It had a youthful rawness, even a touch of masculinity that distinguished it from the reigning pop divas of the day—women like Whitney Houston, Janet Jackson, and Mariah Carey, who would all, in due time, fall under the influence of Mary's uncut funk. At this moment in musical history, R&B was going through growing pains. Traditional standards as sung by Luther Vandross and Patti LaBelle were not speaking to the hip hop generation. Then came Mary—and an unknown young producer named Sean "Puffy" Combs—blending churchified vocals with block-rocking beats that were, as A Tribe Called Quest put it, "Dedicated to the Art of Moving Butts." Though nobody (least of all Mary herself) knew it at the time, the 21-year-old ingenue was also paving the way for as-yet-unimagined stars like Faith Evans, Kelly Price, Jennifer Lopez, and the late, great Aaliyah.

"Fierce!" I declared after my first listen to rough cuts of "Real Love" and "You Remind Me." Mary's brand-new debut album, *What's the 411?* was indeed covered in the very first issue of VIBE, September 1992. And in the years since then, she has been featured on the magazine's cover more often than any other artist. The magazine's readers can't seem to get enough of her—there's just something about Mary.

Who would have thought that a black girl from the 'hood could go from making a karaoke demo tape at a shopping mall to selling 20 million albums and seeing her face everywhere, from French fashion layouts to boxes of Dark 'N Lovely hair color? It was no easy feat for a high school dropout from a single-parent home. Mary could have been

just another sad statistic, but instead she's become a survivor who inspires women all around the world. Through her music, she's shared the highs and lows and lessons learned with her fans. And since that first day in my office, VIBE has been there with her, every step of the way.

I first met Mary J. Blige, the woman, over lunch with Andre Harrell, Lisa Cambridge, and fellow VIBE editor Scott Poulson-Bryant. As Andre held court talking about his plans to expand the new jack swing movement, Mary sat silently behind her menu. "Andre, can I order the shrimp scampi?" was the most memorable thing she said during the entire meeting. But I couldn't stop looking at Mary, her red mane piled high in a ghetto-girl bouffant. I still felt like I knew her from someplace—high school? Another life?

By this time I was hearing her voice at every party I went to. Her 1992 remix album—with homegirl damn-near battling future rap royalty like Notorious B.I.G., Craig Mack, and Grand Puba—was blasting off in the clubs. Meanwhile tales of her unpredictable behavior were becoming a staple of industry gossip. I didn't really get to know her, though, until I landed the assignment to write a cover story on her for VIBE's February 1995 issue:

This is the new and improved Mary J. Blige. Gone are the temper tantrums, waves of depression, and stank attitude. It's been two years since her double-platinum debut and a year since her full-length remix album blew up the spot. Mary is 24 years old now, she's in love (with K-Ci Hailey from Jodeci) and she's ready to move on. No more playing the banji-bitch role. The new album is called My Life, *and the title of the first single, "Be Happy," tells you all you need to know.*

"On this album I wanted to feel younger," Mary says of My Life. *She says some of the tracks remind her of her jazz musician father (who taught her to harmonize, but left when she was four) or of being seven years old, singing at the House of Prayer Pentecostal Church—in short, times when she was happy. "We used to go to church all night," Mary recalls. "Everybody would be real good to us. I miss that."*

This round-the-way girl from the projects of Yonkers, New York, sparked the world with her distinctive brand of new jack swing. With a little help from Puffy, she fashioned herself as a seductive soul siren who was hard and feminine at the same time. The secret of Mary's success may lie in this ability to effort-

sound system. Her black Lincoln Town Car drops Mary and Taureen, her 308-pound bodyguard, at the offices of Double XXposure, a black-owned public relations firm where Ms. Blige has just finished a 24-week artist development course.

Playing Professor Higgins to Mary's Eliza Doolittle, Angelo Ellerbee, the company's president, coached her on interviewing techniques, personal finance, etiquette, and diction. "When her first record came out, I knew she wasn't prepared," says Ellerbee. "I would hear all the stories and say, 'Why do all you people talk about this girl and you won't deal with it? Tell her!' When I met her, I said, 'I am the person who dogged you. I did it because kids love you and you gotta be a role model.'" Mary credits Angelo's "tough love" for helping to turn her around. "He gave me a totally new kind of light. There was a time when I wouldn't read nothin'," says the eleventh-grade dropout (who eventually got her GED). Ellerbee had her digesting books like Zora Neale Hurston's Their Eyes Were Watching God *and Donald S. Passman's* All You Need to Know About the Music Business.

Today she's returned to Double XXposure for a Flair *mag-*

"You'll never survive being weak as a woman in this business," she told me, "Because it's dominated by men. That's how people like Aretha Franklin lasted—they wasn't having it." And neither was Mary.

lessly combine opposites. It's more than just singing "that smoove shit" over a breakbeat or getting shout-outs from dope MCs on an R&B album. The Queen of Hip Hop Soul *has to be somebody who can sum up all the joy, pain, and love in a song that a whole generation understands.*

Two years ago, though, she didn't seem ready to be the voice of a nation. Everybody's heard about Mary doing shows—and not just onstage. The stories of tardiness, cancellations, and general lack of professionalism are endless. Mary was eight hours late for one photo shoot, and threw a fit and walked out of at least one other. Then there was the show in London where she was so out of it the crowd booed her off the stage. All of this may sound like fabulous diva drama, but for a young artist, it's more like plain ol' bad attitude. But nobody ever said overnight success would be easy.

It's a new day for Mary. Just back from shooting the "Be Happy" video in the Arizona desert, she's rolling through midtown Manhattan traffic with Method Man pumping on the

azine photo shoot; Mary just seems to feel comfortable here. Angelo taught her how to deal with people, but she also learned how to deal with herself. "You can't pay attention to the negative," she says. "Or it never goes away. Every time I go to Angelo's, I feel free. So I learned to be like that every day.

"I definitely feel like I came a long way from where I was before," she continues, "because I was a savage. And when I say I was a savage, trust me." (Some details she won't discuss, like the scar under her left eye.) The thing that changed her, she says, was "wanting to learn, wanting to be somebody. Just knowing what my gift is and wanting to carry that out. I was afraid to let people see my real feelings."

The car pulls up to the Top Line Nails Salon. The stylist is sure nobody will recognize Mary here—this is where she takes her clients Salt-N-Pepa. Tiffany, a young Korean manicurist, soaks Mary's feet in sudsy water and then starts to clip and peel off the false nails. This is very Mary. In classic black-girl fashion, she's as comfortable showing off onstage as she is picking from fake "designer" nails glued onto big emery boards. "I don't have to be a glamour girl everywhere," she says, then realizes that the manicurist has put six-inch curls of acrylic on her fingers. "Wait a minute," she gasps. "I'm not tryin' to do the claw!"

"No, no, no, we cut down," Tiffany assures her, asking what color polish she wants. Mary digs into her purse and pulls out a bottle of Chanel fingernail polish, still in the box with the $18 price tag on the back. It's Rouge Noir Vamp. She says, "My favorite color."

If you want to understand a woman, look at her fingernails. Mary's are long, kinda curled over, and painted a deep, sexy color with a sultry French name. All this allure begs the question of who Mary's trying to romance. New songs like "You Bring Me Joy," "I Never Wanna Live Without You," and "I'm the Only Woman" certainly sound as if they were written by a woman in love. And Mary says she is. "K-Ci is my friend, and I love him dearly," she says, showing a gold "friendship ring" with a good-sized rock on her left ring finger. "He makes me feel good. He makes me feel like he's there. It's like, you know, talkin' to one of my girlfriends. We just be sittin' around, talkin'. We share things like maybe old people that is 60 and married and shit." She laughs. "It's real, man."

Nail mission accomplished, Mary and company pile back into the limo to grab some jerk chicken and return to the hotel before taping an MTV special later tonight. The radio plays "Ladies Night" by Kool & the Gang. Mary hangs her hands out the car window so her polish can dry. As the black Lincoln zooms toward the highway, nails in the wind, the DJ mixes in a sample of a voice repeating "I'm the ultimate." It's the perfect soundtrack for a fresh-dipped diva on the move.

Ghetto fabulousness aside, Mary was clearly serious about handling hers even back then. "You'll never survive, being weak as a woman in this business," she told me, "because it's dominated by men. That's how people like Aretha Franklin lasted—and they're still around. They wasn't havin' it, you know?" And neither was Mary.

What I didn't know then was how much pain she was in. Mary has since described the album *My Life* as a "cry for help." And it soon became clear that Mary was going through changes—even as her star was shining brighter than ever. Her relationship with K-Ci had been the source of

much heartache, and she parted ways with Uptown and Puff Daddy before the release of the album *Share My World*. It was a difficult moment, one that dream hampton captured in a sensitive piece called "Real Love," which marked Mary's second appearance on VIBE's cover, in April 1997:

Guarded and vulnerable, Mary has always, albeit unwittingly, seemed to beg for our protection. There was the sudden explosion that followed the definitive debut album What's the 411? The awkward dance with new fame. The visible panty lines at the Soul Train *Awards*. There was the intense love affair with Jodeci's K-Ci Hailey (and the Uptown MTV Unplugged *performance of "I Don't Want to Do Anything,"* in which she and K-Ci exchanged verses with true passion, Mary's tears glistening behind her shades). There was the perfect My Life in 1994, an open, painful letter to K-Ci. And there was her departure from Puff, the brother figure who gave her wings and guided her through her first albums by setting the tone and providing the themes. Now there is the fear—though it may not be Mary's—that her third album will not fly without him.

Though it happened relatively quietly (compared to the attention given Puff's every other move over the past two years), the split has had resounding repercussions for both of their careers. Nobody quite knows why they went their separate ways, but whatever differences existed couldn't be resolved, not for a single song. Mary split from Uptown Entertainment in 1995 when Andre Harrell left the company for Motown. Her new deal with Uptown's parent company, MCA, granted her virtual autonomy for Share My World.

For his part, Puff realizes what he's lost in Mary. "No one has sounded as perfect for the music I produce as Mary," he says. "My tracks were totally made for her, and she was made for my tracks."

Mary was his prize. And they were indeed perfect for one another. Where Puff was all exhibition, Mary was reserved and slightly cagey. They both believed that style was created on hot Wednesday nights, on the 125th Street strip where ghetto trends like Catholic-figure gold charms and one-leg-up sweats were improvised. And, of course, they were both born stars.

"What made Mary a star was she really didn't give a fuck, 'cause she'd been through so much," says Puff from his car phone.

voices in rap, 'cause they're antimelodic. Mary also has that kind of recognizability, but she's a singer."

When Mary is called a hip hop singer, it has to do with her music memory as much as her sensibility and posture. The songs she covers, or in some cases samples, are ones she and her older sister LaTonya grew up singing. It was nothing if not completely courageous to cover Aretha ("Natural Woman") and Chaka Khan ("Sweet Thing"). On Share My World, she covers "Our Love," one of Natalie Cole's greats. "I sang that song at a talent show when I was seven years old," she says.

"There's so much I learned about Mary from working with her," Shocklee says. "She's extremely intelligent, real quick, has a nearly photographic memory. And she knows and loves black music. She knows everybody and not just their hits. She knows their off songs. She's like a DJ. There aren't that many producers who know what she knows."

In 1999, she delivered a triumphant album called simply Mary and the theme this time was self-love. Musically, the record was her most mature effort to date, incorporat-

"No one has sounded as perfect for the music I produce as Mary," said Puff after they parted ways. "What made her a star was she really didn't give a fuck, 'cause she'd been through so much."

"She's so totally distinct." After we hang up, he calls back—he has something to add about Mary. "She's the greatest artist I've ever worked with."

"He said that about me?" Mary asks, surprised. "Puff is family; he'll always be family, even if I see him at a party and don't speak to him."

For Mary, whose collaborations with Puff have come to define what "from the streets" means, authenticity is worth its weight in links. The process of making music has to be organic for her, or it simply isn't worth it. "I write how I feel. Certain songs . . . I let my spirit get into the song, and it will write the song. It comes from here." She puts her hand to her chest and clenches her fist. "I'm not saying I can blow everybody away. It's just . . . I feel what I sing."

"Mary's tone is thick and full," says Hank Shocklee, the production genius who crafted Public Enemy's sound before going on to work with Mary. "She's almost precise tonal-wise. Like a synthesizer or sampling voice. It's easy to distinguish the

ing the sounds of Lauryn Hill and Elton John, and the voices of Aretha Franklin and, yes, K-Ci (though the former lovers sang their verses of the duet "Not Lookin'" in separate sessions). The black-and-white portrait on the CD cover made a strong visual statement as well. It displayed a powerful profile, announcing her unshakable resolve and exposing that scar she once tried to hide. Something about that photograph said, "I've been fighting for my life, and I have won." Then you flipped the CD over and on the back, Mary's mouth was open and her eyes were closed and she was singing about the fight, pouring it all out.

The whole album sounded like Mary coming to terms with who she was and starting to become who she wanted to be. As the African proverb says, in order to go forward we must first go back, and that's where Danyel Smith took Mary during the no-holds-barred discussion recounted in her third VIBE cover story, September 1999's "Hail Mary!":

Mary J. Blige grew up in Yonkers, a part of New York I've only seen in the winter. It's not pretty. In a housing project called Schlobohm Gardens, named after some long-dead local politico. (Residents call it Slow Bomb.) Her mom's name is Cora Blige. Mary says Cora always played "Misty Blue." Mary recorded the song herself for her 1998 live album. "My mother played that song every day when we were little," she says. "It brings back memories of when we didn't have a care in the world. We just played all the time."

Things did get blue, though. "In the projects," Mary says, sitting in a deserted N.Y.C. restaurant, picking at her chicken wings, sipping on her Merlot, "you're fightin' every day, fighting for your life. You're gettin' scratched up, you're scratchin' other girls—over nothin'! My mother always told me, 'Fuck people,' but I never learned to be like that. I just learned you can't please everybody."

Mary remembers the bad in Technicolor. The good things in fuzzy shades of gray. . . .

Let's talk about music. "'You Remind Me' is my baby," she says. "That's my first song ever, you know? I was living in the projects, walking around, and 'Real Love' and 'You Remind Me' were on the radio and I was, like, still in Building 5 on the third floor. It was a nightmare. I was like, Jesus, please give me some money so I can get out of here. People were like, 'You still livin' here?' I didn't have no money for a long time—1996, that's when I was getting paid for the first time."

Lewis Tucker, vice president of promotions at Universal Records, was part of the original Uptown crew. He says people at MCA, Uptown's parent company, did not believe in Mary's first album. "Mary was fifth priority," he says from his office. "I'll never forget that. Fifth behind Patti LaBelle, Stephanie Mills, Eugene Wilde, and somebody else I can't remember. Those artists were paying bills for MCA at that time. A lot of people didn't get who Mary was—a female in combat boots and a tennis skirt. They thought she should dress up."

But Harrell and Puffy wanted her to be her, which was fine with Mary J. It's all she knew how to be. "Mary was naturally Mary," says Puff. "Mary is always Mary. She just opened her mouth and sang."

Mary's ad libs come in like the tide. Soft, sure licks. When she rips, it's death. Mary and her voice are one thing. Her phrasing and her life are one thing. The occasional flatness, the odd pronunciation of this or that word, the tears onstage, the sweat,

the hoarseness, the slight awkwardness of her shows—that's her. And it's us. Learning to play the violin in public! That's real life. Mary's voice—pretty, growly, sexy, sad, emotive, often perfect—is life, too. She sings to all us folk scared to be happy. All up on love every day, afraid to touch it. All of us burnt brittle. Tentative as hummingbirds. Ferocious as beasts of prey. You remember how Mary blew it out on "My Life": "Keep your head to the sky / I don't need to tell you why." And she doesn't.

Mary sings about love and betrayal and sadness and abandonment and need and the kind of pain you only talk about through tears or clenched teeth. Mary is about the specific girl-type emotion girls think boys find accusatory. The kinds of feelings girls feel handicapped for having. Purpley tender vulnerabilities hidden behind kids and jobs and the zeal to keep shit going. Mary sings about the literal and figurative blows that make a strong girl buckle, a weak girl break. A pitiful girl addicted or dead. Keep your head to the sky, indeed.

"Not that I was addicted to drugs or anything like that," she says. And she's real clear. Real matter-of-fact. "I smoked weed, and I drank drinks—I sniffed coke. I was doing it. I was havin' fun with the shit! But when I got a little older and I started doing it again when I was twenty-two, that shit almost drove *me crazy. Now I'm accountable for what I know. And I had a crazy revelation: That shit was going to kill me. It was killing my voice. At photo shoots, people'd be wondering, 'Why she keep her glasses on?' Because I was fucked up every day, that's why!"*

Mary got past it. "By My Life," *Harrell says, "she began to believe in herself. She realized she didn't have to be afraid." But Mary says she was still having issues. "That album!* My Life—*that shit was a straight relationship-abuse album. And it was not only abusive in the way of a man; I was abusing myself with drugs and other shit. I was depressed and couldn't handle what was given to me; success. I didn't know how to handle it. . . . But now I'm living my life for what it is."*

And what a life. These days it's not unusual for Mary J. Blige to sing at the Superbowl alongside Britney Spears and N'Sync, or show up at an Elton John concert to sing "Deep inside I wish that you could see / That I'm just plain old Mary." As if. "It's crazy," she says, "a lot of white people know Mary J. Blige. I just look at it as a blessing all the way around in disguise. Because what I represent is going to bring people together."

It *is* crazy, though, because Mary has never been anybody's flavor-of-the-month. "I am straight R&B, no matter what I do, no matter what comes my way," Mary says, distancing herself from singers who make the series of subtle artistic compromises required of those seeking to "go pop." Like most R&B vocalists, her voice was trained in the House of the Lord. And Mary stays true to her cultural experience, singing music that inspires. When she goes into a vocal riff, it sounds like the witness-bearing catharsis normally heard in a Sunday afternoon gospel celebration.

"It was never a lot of money behind Mary J. Blige except for the hip hop community," she says. "You have a choice if you want to be pop or you want to be R&B. My choice was to be R&B forever." Unlike pop divas like Mariah and Whitney, who occasionally stray from the path of pop superstardom to dabble with urbanites like Ol' Dirty Bastard and Wyclef, Mary started out the same way she will end up, keeping it real.

Of course, that doesn't mean she can't be glamorous, too. Mary represents women at their most beautiful and dynamic, and the fashion industry has recognized her undeniable allure. "Mary speaks with soul and conviction," says M.A.C. president John Demsey, who signed her up as a spokesperson for the VIVA Glam line. "You watch the way she connects with women. It's all about self-help and self-love." Mary now appears with her friend Lil' Kim in ads shot by photo whiz kid David LaChapelle. "It's a blessing," Mary says, clearly excited. "People don't understand that

this isn't something that we're doing. What you put into the universe, you get back. It's karma. That's a blessing to me. To see my face in *Vogue* magazine every time you open it? The M.A.C. picture with Kim is like 'Whoa!'"

At the fall collections in Manhattan, February 2000, Mary and Kim sat in the front row at Marc Bouwer's show holding court. The fashionistas—shutters clicking, bulbs flashing—were steady buzzing around the ghetto-fabulous girlfriends in the house. Mary did look stunning with her hair in a blond-streaked surfer-chick shag and wearing Versace rhinestone-encrusted aviator sunglasses, a turquoise fur jacket, tight faded blue jeans studded with rhinestones and trimmed with fur, and high-heel snakeskin boots. Blond-beehived Lil' Kim had on a beige feather contraption, a brown fur jacket, and gold high-heeled boots—all of which made her look like an exquisite baroque porcelain doll dipped in cocoa. While Kim was fierce and fashion-conscious, Mary was classic.

"Mary's very aware of fashion," says her stylist, Misa Hylton-Brim. "It's her personality. She's the black woman with money. Her look is part accessible and part unaccessible." Her fans have seen her in every role from the Lycra pants–wearing diva in the "Reminisce" video to baseball cap and jersey–wearing round-the-way girl—complete with big gold hoop earrings—in the "Real Love" video. We've seen her with every hair color imaginable. We've seen her gain weight and lose weight. Mary is a chameleon.

But she has always been confident in her individual style. A seventh-grade teacher remembers that "Mary J. had a flair for wearing clothes and makeup." Since then, lots of women have been inspired by her eclectic mix of ghetto-girl hairstyles, high-drama makeup, and luxurious European fashions. The look is bold—purple hair, black lipstick, animal prints—and ever-changing. One day Mary's hair is a red bob. The next week, it's a blond asymmetrical with a brown stripe across the back. "You just have to constantly keep trying to see what you feel comfortable with," Mary says, forever keeping it fresh.

Because she used to do hair, it's not uncommon for MJB to jump up from a professional stylist's chair, stare into the mirror, and fix her own hair so it's just right. "Yeah, I used to do my own weaves," says Mary. "Every little piece of money I got I made sure that I went and got me some hair from 125th Street. Curly or straight. Then my own weaves. My own doobies. My own curly asymmetric. Of course, everybody copied."

Mary tries not to get salty when her hairstyles, clothing, and jewelry are imitated by other women, stylists, and fashion designers. "It's hard," she says, "because once you snatch up something like the Farrah Fawcett flips"—the hairstyle she first rocked in the spring of 2000 that was picked up by Toni Braxton, Beyoncé Knowles of Destiny's Child, Mariah Carey, *and* Jennifer Lopez—"everywhere you go, you see flips on like fifteen thousand women. Somebody's got a red flip, a blond flip. Even the hair color I went with, the cinnamon-orange-brown, I saw like twenty girls in SoHo with it yesterday," she adds with a laugh.

When girls actually duplicate Mary's whole look, her feelings might best be summed up by Biz Markie's immortal line from "The Vapors"—"Damn, it feels good to see people up on it." She takes the imitation not only as the sincerest form of flattery but as motivation. If others are going to follow, then somebody's got to lead. "I was like, okay, I can't have nothing to myself," Mary explains. "I can't have a hair color to myself. I can't have a hairstyle to myself. And I can't get mad, so I gotta keep flipping it and staying creative and coming up with new things." And that in itself can be a full-time job.

So what exactly is the Mary look? "Whatever I wanna be, whenever I wanna be it," she says, and you know it's true.

7:45 P.M.: Perform "Overjoyed" at the U.N.
8:15 P.M.: Tape a public service announcement entitled "Breaking the Silence on HIV."

In the middle of this manic day, Miss Blige makes an executive decision. At 1:15 P.M. she juggles the hectic schedule to take a moment for herself. "I gotta go get this coat—a black, shiny shearling," she says. "It's at Bergdorf-Goodman. I saw it in the window. It'll only take me a minute—I'll hurry," Mary tells her sister turned manager LaTonya. ("That's my best friend," says Mary, who shares everything with LaTonya, including the sign Capricorn. "No woman understands me like she does.") Mary grabs her monogram Gucci satchel on her way out the door.

Flash: Mary's in a limousine with her assistant cruising uptown to Bergdorf's on 58th Street and Fifth Avenue. Flash: She's breezing through the eyewear section, trying on some clear Gucci shields—a replacement pair in taupe to match her tiger-print outfit for tonight's performance. Flash: She's riding down the escalator in a vintage tan leather

"In the projects you're fighting every day for your life. 'Real Love' was on the radio and I was still in building 5 on the 3rd floor. It was a nightmare. I was like, Jesus, please give me some money so I can get out."

"Doing whatever I want without disrespecting me or going against the grain and being comfortable enough to look in a mirror and say 'I can wear this all day.' It's got to be something that when I see it, it just jumps out at me. And it's gotta be comfortable from the shoes on up—if they are heels like stilettos, they gotta be comfortable. It's got to be very Mary."

October 23, 2000 is a very Mary day—and it goes a little something like this:

> 11:00 A.M.: Sound check
> 1:00 P.M.: "Light" hair and makeup
> 2:30 P.M.: *Fox News* interview
> 4:00 P.M.: "Real" hair and makeup
> 5:00 P.M.: Arrive at the United Nations for an AIDS fund-raiser
> 7:00 P.M.: Present a check (along with M.A.C. daddy John Demsey) to the United Nations Development Program

jacket (belted with a matching leather Plein Sud scarf), brown cords with brass studs down the legs, and tan boots.

Although she never actually finds that shiny shearling—she checked every floor to no avail—Mary does snag those sunglasses. She's standing by the door in the hat section, waiting for the limo to pull around so that she can jump in—it's time to get back on schedule. Just then she spots a drab olive and orange plaid beret under a stack of the Burberry variety. "What's that," she says, grabbing *le chapeau.* "Let me see this. It's ugly, right?" Then in one fell swoop, Mary pulls the hat down low on one side, slides her new Gucci shades out of the shopping bag and onto her face, and starts shaking her head. "I think I like it. I thought that hat was ugly, but it's working," she says, regarding herself in the mirror. Suddenly she starts bobbing back and forth and snapping her fingers. "Now this is *very* Mary!"

A few hours later, homegirl is sharing the stage with U.N. Secretary General Kofi Annan, presenting a quarter-million-dollar check on behalf of M.A.C. AIDS Fund to support grass-roots programs for people living with HIV in Africa and singing that Stevie Wonder song about dreams: "And though you don't believe that they do / They do come true…" Mary's representing at this global celebrity kind of event with everyone from Danny Glover to Renaldo, the Brazilian soccer star, to African singers Angelique Kidjo and Youssou N'Dour. They're all in the house to "Break the Silence" and honor heros in the fight against AIDS, which has moved beyond being a "gay thing" to being a major threat to the lives of people around the world.

"I usually stay neutral," says Mary. "But as far as AIDS, nobody's neutral. You don't even know where it's at, so you just have to pray that it's not in your home or in your system." As with her music, Mary does not get involved in "causes" unless she feels a personal connection. But her and Kim's involvement with M.A.C. has made a huge impact, raising over $4 million for AIDS charities in one year. She's also given her time for a TV commercial for the Partnership for a Drug-Free America.

says. "That's what I really wanted to do, to see muscles in my stomach. And I got it because I really wanted it. I worked hard for it every day." Ain't nothing like the real thing.

But when she debuted her shapely new body, the rumor mill started to roll. Did Mary get liposuction and breast implants? It's no secret that her friend Lil' Kim—like so many other stars—has had a bit of body augmentation. But not Mary: "Did I get my breasts done? No, I didn't. My trainer just dropped my body fat down. My stomach was so big you couldn't even see my breasts. And that's what happens, people think they have to go get a breast job when in reality, all you have to do is pull all this off," she says, motioning to her waist and stomach. "I busted my ass for this body—like literally crying in the gym like, I hate my trainer. I really, really honest-to-God wanted it and I stuck to my guns. And every night on that stage . . ." her voice trails off and a smile appears that explains the rest.

But Mary insists she's not motivated by selfish reasons. She's just giving back all the love her public gives her—and then some. "I'm a woman that a lot of women look at for

"I know that the ghetto is always last," says Mary, remembering the people who still are where she's been. "But believe me, I am you, you are me, we are one. Just to let you know, I am not lost. I haven't lost myself."

"I am not like everybody in the music business," she says. "I mean yeah, I like money, but it is not about money all the time." These days there's nothing more valuable to this hip hop diva than peace of mind. For underneath all the multicolored hair and extravagant attire, Mary J. Blige is humble. "I finally have self-esteem," she says. "I'm happy. I'm no longer a people pleaser, dying at an early age 'cause you worry about who likes you," Mary explains. "That just don't mean nothing to me."

And she looks better, too. During Mary's four-night stand at Radio City Music Hall, she sang and danced, did three costume changes, and left no doubt that she was in the best shape of her life. "It's not me being competitive, but it's me knowing 'Okay, Mary, everybody's running around trying to sound like you. Wanting to have an album like you. Wanting to do everything like you. So what can you do to separate yourself?' And I said, 'I'm going to get in shape. Not just lose weight, I'm going to chisel myself out,'" she

strength," Mary says. "I wanted my women to walk away from the concert like 'Okay, I'm going to do that. I'm going to get my body together.' Or 'I'm going to stop drinking and smoking so much, I'm going to cut back.'"

Though Mary J. Blige hasn't quite bought the whole pop culture goddess trip, she's okay with being a role model for women of all races. Through her voice, image, femininity, and soul Mary has been able to make the world a better place to live. Like Aretha Franklin is to soul, Tina Turner is to rock, and Madonna is to dance music, Mary J. Blige is to hip hop, a muse with muscle.

"Yeah, I draw from the fact that my life is real. I'm on another level of success right now, on my way, not fully there, but on my way," Mary says. "But that doesn't change my life. I'm still flesh. I'm still breathing. I still have the exact same problems that every woman out there who strives to be independent has."

"You get nothing for free," she says, as if it's a mantra.

"Nothing sitting down. You have to work hard for everything in order for it be yours." But for a long time, no matter how much sweat Mary invested, some part of her felt that she didn't deserve what she got. Because deep inside she feels as though she *is* just plain old Mary. That knowledge used to feel like a burden, but she has turned it into a strength. "I know that the ghetto is always last," she says, remembering the people who still are where she's been. "But believe me, I am you, you are me, we are one. Just to let you know, I am not lost. I haven't lost myself."

Her next album will be called *Mary Jane: No More Drama.* "It's a little bit of everything, hip hop, rock 'n' roll, all of that," she says. The record is packed with power producers like Dr. Dre, the Neptunes, and Rockwilder, as well as guest appearances from Eve and Jadakiss. There is a track called "Rock Steady," a reinterpretation of Aretha Franklin's 1971 classic, featuring Lenny Kravitz on guitar. There's the title song, "No More Drama," produced by Jimmy Jam and Terry Lewis that uses "Nadia's Theme"—better known as the song from *The Young and the Restless.* All in all, a playful, powerful album about enjoying the beauty and bounty of life.

Like the ghetto-avenger super-girl cartoon character that opens each of her sold-out shows at Radio City, Mary is stronger than ever. "I feel like sometimes I get lost in, Is this really happening?" she says, set adrift on a memory. "I dreamt about being onstage one time. I thought it was a dream. That was a long time ago, when I was younger." She says there are still times she can't even believe how far she's come.

"But you know, I'm just thankful now," says Mary J. Blige. "Now, I believe it. Because I've put in so much work— and I still have a lot of work to put in—but now I *can* believe it. I believe it. I believe it's really happening."

LAURYN

*Showin' off your ass
'cause you're thinkin'
it's the trend girlfriend
let me break it down
for you again... don't
be a hard rock when
you really are a gem*

Photograph by Jonathan Mannion

the rationalization of lauryn hill

by Selwyn Seyfu Hinds

18 FEBRUARY 2001

Dear Lauryn,

You've been gone from us too long. I know that rings unfair, even presumptuous. Really, I do. After all, who are we to begrudge any artist removing him or herself from our draining attention in order to spend time with self and family? And Lord knows we drained enough from you in the wake of 1998's *The Miseducation of Lauryn Hill*. But you can't blame us. Your impact, your influence on our collective music psyche, was such that your absence, for even a few short years, seems painful. With *Miseducation* you created an intimacy unlike any in short-term pop music memory. You strode upon a public stage, letting your soul soar, cry, and shake with deeply personal emotion. And we shuddered along with you, not as spectators, but as participants in the cathartic dance you led. So when you left, Lauryn, when you retreated deep into your own space, when you pulled back from the media, when you disengaged from us, it did not feel like the typical down period between an artist's albums; it felt like abandonment.

In the meanwhile we get by with wispy fragments of you. Because that's all they are, even your albums, solo and group efforts, just fragments of your complex self. We all have our favorite wisps, the memories of you that have sustained us. Mine is not your music at all, but a moment. Do you remember spring of 1997? You, Wyclef, and Pras were in Haiti to put on a grand concert. That homecoming event was a key moment during the buildup to Clef's first solo effort, *The Carnival,* as well as a pit stop on what would be the last stretch of the Fugee race.

You sat by the poolside of Le Ritz Hotel, a high-post establishment in the craggy hills outside of Port au Prince, where the Fugee crew was staying. You were pregnant with Zion at the time, and the bulge of your belly distended the cotton shirt you wore. A hat shaded you from the afternoon rays of the Caribbean sun, and in your hands you gently cradled an acoustic guitar. I sat quietly nearby with reporter's tools in hand—pen, pad, tape recorder—listening to you strum the chords from "The Sweetest Thing," the Refugee Camp All-Stars song, featuring your vocals, from the *Love Jones* soundtrack.

"Did Clef write that?" I asked.

You just looked at me. Not with anger, or even annoyance. Just a touch of wry, incredulous amusement.

"No."

Then you let me know how things worked. How you would come up with the underpinning of the idea and use more developed musicians to flesh it out. And how determined you were to learn and master an instrument yourself, so you could do your own damn fleshing out, thank you. Determined. And focused.

I glimpsed steel in you that afternoon. And a year later, as I listened to your solo debut and heard that steel echoing throughout, no image burned clearer than that look in your eye on a hill in Haiti.

At first you had us fooled, Lauryn. 'Cause in the beginning things seemed more silk than steel. I well recall that black-and-white video for "Boof Baf," lead single from the Fugees' '93 debut *Blunted on Reality*. I remember the confusion that nettled my brow on observing the high-octane antics of the then bald Wyclef and the heavily bearded Pras, and you, of course, with the close-knit cap, braided tresses, powerful vocal presence, and beatific features. Some folks knew that face from your adventures in acting—*General Hospital, Sister Act 2,* etc.—but it was new to me, though I did remember catching sight of that smile dancing around MC Lyte in her 1991 video for "Poor Georgie."

Neither my confusion, nor the almost otherworldly quality of the aggressive, ragga-driven "Boof Baf," could mask the fact that the three of you made sense. Some hip hop groups seem so poorly patched together they resemble nothing so much as the bastard children of some urban Dr. Frankenstein. But you three were organic, integrated, despite surface differences. You, a smart-as-nails Jersey girl from South Orange, Valerie Hill's Columbia-educated daughter; Wyclef and Pras, Haitian boys by way of Brooklyn. But the mix worked. In later years Clef would fondly tell me the story of how you three got signed, the story of your office performance for Chris Schwartz of Ruffhouse Records. He painted quite the picture: him atop Chris's desk, doing his best Sly Stone act; Pras grooving with his usual effervescent cool; and you, singing, rhyming, performing with the assurance of a star born.

When I saw that "Boof Baf" video, I marveled at the sight of a female MC holding equal opportunity mike status within a group. There'd been male hip hop groups and female hip hop groups, male soloists and female. But with the exception of Digable Planets, maybe, the integrated archetype had not been seen since the days of Sha Rock in the Funky 4 + 1 More, and even Sha required a special setting aside. No such mandate for you. It was the silken quality of your voice and presence that helped pull together the eclectic, disparate thoughts that ran wild on *Blunted on Reality*. You were the middling anchor between Wyclef's frenzy and Pras's slow burn. Perhaps it was a foregone conclusion, albeit an unfair and premature one, that the critical public would laud you as the group's saving grace. Thus we shut the book on the Fugees' first album, pausing momentarily as we heard the 1994 remix for "Nappy Heads." The melodic sounds and straight-ahead drum programming of producer Salaam Remi were a harbinger of better things to come for the Fugees, and your strong vocal performance on the song portended the same for you as an individual.

Even so, I didn't expect the album that landed on my desk late in 1995. It was a simple TDK cassette, 90 minutes long. Someone at Columbia Records, your parent label, had scribbled the name of the album along the spine of the cassette's paper insert: *The Score*. Curious, I slipped the tape out of its case and placed it in the stereo system that serves as the heart of any music editor's office. The sound glided out of the system, almost shocking in its near perfection. The record had personality, broad narratives, and poignant musicality. And each of you sounded significantly better, although you, Lauryn, always had less of a hill to climb in most ears.

Still, the range and technique you exhibited on *The Score* were evidence of striking growth. On the one hand you could appropriate a vocal performance by a singing legend and make it your own—Roberta Flack's "Killing Me Softly"—on the other you hit the three zones of MC ability—tone, delivery, lyrical content—with a consistency that few could approach, male or female. When the folks at *The Source* magazine, my old professional home, heard your vicious battle lines from "How Many Mics" they were fit to be tied. Our favorite part was the section that ended with: "Claiming that you got a new style / Your attempts are futile / Ooh chile, you puerile."

As music editor it was my responsibility to choose the best verse of the moment for the magazine's rhyme-of-the-month column. There was no question whose verse should be featured in the February '96 issue. But you came damn close to missing it, Lauryn. All because I couldn't decipher three words in your rhyme. And I'm pretty sure "puerile" was one of 'em. So I called your crib, left a message explaining the honor involved in being awarded rhyme of the month. Waited patiently for you to call back. You didn't. I called again, left a similar message accompanied by a bit more pleading. Waited for your call. No dice. By this time we were grumbling back at the ranch. The magazine had to go to press soon; time was precious. And we couldn't go with lyrics that weren't accurate. Maybe we'd have to pick another verse, though that was the last thing anyone wanted to do. So I called yet again, and got you this time.

"Hey, Lauryn?"

"Yes?"

Went on to explain what the magazine needed, and you gave it to me. No fuss. And you know what struck me, Lauryn? How much more impressed I was than you with the whole situation. Not that you weren't grateful and genuinely pleased. But here I was thinking that I'd made some giant step for womankind in hip hop, while you acknowledged it as the matter of course that it was: you had the hottest verse at the time and you deserved the recognition.

The Score went on to capture the music stage, to the tune of 17 million records sold worldwide, an achievement largely driven by your hip hop flip of "Killing Me Softly." Between the months spanning the moment I got that tape and the album's release, *The Score* became both a personal and staff favorite. In the March '96 issue, *The Source* gave the album a rating of 4, an excellent mark just two rungs below the highest possible 5, a great mark by any standard. But oh, you guys didn't let me off that simply.

The publicist from Columbia was soon on the phone.

"Listen, I've got the Fugees on the line. They just want to talk to you about the rating, okay?"

"Well, um, sure," I replied curiously.

"Lauryn, Pras? Are you on? Okay, go ahead."

I admit it; y'all had me a touch anxious. Were you calling to thank the magazine for its support? Or to flip about the rating? Talking to an artist about a review they've received is always a nervy game. Usually I didn't bother. But you are near impossible to refuse.

"Um, hey, this is Sel."

Then y'all let me have it. Well, Pras mostly chimed in with affirmative grunts. As for you, Lauryn, you skewered me with your arguments: Yes, you were pleased *The Score* got a 4, but it really should have gotten a 4.5. Why? Leaving aside the merits of the record, a year ago, summer of '95, the magazine gave Raekwon's *Only Built 4 Cuban Linx* a 4.5 rating, in your eyes validating the entire street/criminology narrative with the hip hop faithful. And if the Fugees album was to provide a more nuanced, more intelligent alternative, it should have been placed on equal footing.

I tried to disagree and make the point of judging records separately on their own merits, but that wasn't an argument I was gonna win with you. Didn't know it then. I'm too wise to try that again.

You remember 1985, Lauryn? Damn, I sure do. Especially summertime. The crawling heat that snaked through New York's still graf-covered subways. Nighttime, weekend radio battles between Mr. Magic and DJ Red Alert, fervently witnessed by teens sitting on stoops, clustered around radios. And the urgent music leaking from passing cars or boomboxes atop the shoulders of sidewalk-strolling kids: Run-DMC, Doug E. Fresh, and Slick Rick.

Honestly, at that juncture I wasn't into female MCs; I did enjoy Roxanne Shanté's back and forth with UTFO, but that seemed almost a novelty. Hip hop in 1985 was still thoroughly male dominated, and we reveled in it.

Then came these girls from Queens doing a take-off on "The Show" by Doug E. Fresh and Slick Rick. They were engaging, personable, and just sheer fun to listen to. They came to be known as Salt-N-Pepa. That was the moment when many of hip hop's testosterone crowd etched out genuine room for women on the mic. The late '80s and early '90s would flesh out that moment with a steady stream of talented women laying their own claims—Queen Latifah, MC Lyte, Yo Yo, and my personal, one-song-having favorite, Antoinette (despite her evisceration by MC Lyte on the scalding "10% Dis").

I thought about Antoinette the first time I heard "Lost Ones," the initial underground salvo from *Miseducation*. Not because I imagined there'd be some modern-day MC Lyte waiting to take you out. Heaven forbid. But because, in contemporary hip hop parlance, Antoinette was *spitting* on "I Got An Attitude." She sounded tough, capable, steely even. And that's exactly what came

Lauryn Hill with fellow Fugees Wyclef and Pras.

to mind the first time the chest-knocking strains of "Lost Ones" exploded around me. You'd always done a marvelous job of creating an identity outside the two-poled paradigm that this increasingly commercial and sexualized hip hop industry has forced upon women MCs since those late '80s, early '90s days—hyper sex kitten or gangsta bitch, sometimes both. "Lost Ones" showed that you could still spit and be authentic and credible without falling into the clutches of either stereotype. And the underlying narrative of betrayal gave us a not-too-subtle indication of the narratives that would be in play on *Miseducation*.

Columbia sent me another tape in the spring of '98. Actually, they snuck it to me on the low. The tape had just four songs—"Ex-Factor," "To Zion," "Lost Ones," and "Doo Wop (That Thing)." I was struck by several things: your maturation as a singer and songwriter, your development as a producer, and the fact that your complex relationship with Wyclef might just have provided much of the emotional and narrative thrust of the album. I knew from whence "Ex-Factor" stemmed, and the stark honesty of the song made me squirm at its emotional nakedness ("No one's hurt me more than you / And no one ever will") while marveling at the strength and steel it took to compose, never mind its technical perfection.

You know, Lauryn, before Wyclef talked about your one-time relationship in 1999 prior to releasing his *Ecleftic* album, before you sent speculation rampant with *Miseducation*, and even before Wyclef dropped hints of a sort on "To All the Girls (I've Cheated On)" from *The Carnival*, some of us in the hip hop press knew of the relationship between you two. But we never put it out there. Maybe we had too much hope for what the Fugees represented. Maybe we loved you too much. Maybe we fancied ourselves a hip hop version of the 1960s Washington press corps, covering up the peccadilloes of our own JFK. Maybe we were bad journalists who crossed the line between subject and friendship. Know this, though: I, for one, have no regrets.

It was no surprise that *Miseducation* launched you to the top of pop music, though the heights of that success—seven million albums, five Grammys, and sundry other awards—surpassed even the rosiest expectations. Not only did you make the most incredible record of the year, you redefined the core notion of what constitutes hip hop performance. You rhymed and sang with such facility, such equal dexterity, that labels—"Is she an MC who sings? A singer who rhymes?"—were rendered useless. Some may have been surprised by your musical breadth but you always knew the potential of the hip hop form.

"I wanna bring the musicianship, the songwriting, back to hip hop," you told VIBE in 1998. "Drums gotta be banging. But I want changes. When I went to the bridge in 'Sweetest Thing,' people thought I was crazy. I said, It's a change. Remember? They used to have those in songs back in the day. There's no reason why Carlos Santana can't pick to hip hop drums, because he's a musician."

The real surprise came with *Miseducation*'s aftermath. I was dismayed by your separation from us, the demanding public that had learned to adore you. Dismayed by the moralists who tried to lambaste you as a hypocrite for touting God and morality in every breath while making no apologies for having two children prior to marriage. Dismayed by scattered reports in the press about discord and rupture between you and Rohan Marley. We all had been so tickled at the idea of you becoming a part of the legendary Marley clan, of you bearing Bob's grandchildren. And your joy was always so evident. I remember a rainy December night in Jamaica, a tribute concert for Bob in 1999. Backstage a reporter asked you about being part of the Marley legacy and your emotion flowed.

"Well, you know, since meeting Rohan and having our children, my love, admiration and respect has just intensified and grown," you said. "The more I get to know about the man, the more I just love and the more I respect. And the more it teaches me about my craft and my career, and things to do and not to do."

I prayed that the rumblings of you and Rohan splitting up were not true. You don't deserve to have your heart shredded again, even if beautiful music flowers from such pain.

And I was especially dismayed by the lawsuit leveled against you in November of 1998 by Vada Nobles, Rasheem Pugh, and twin brothers Tejumold and Johari Newton of New-Ark Entertainment, the young producers who worked on your album, charging that they were cheated out of production and songwriting credit. Lord, I know that must have punctured your very spirit. The focused woman I remember strumming guitar strings in Haiti had to have been stunned. The producer who did sterling work for Aretha Franklin and Mary J. Blige would have been dumbfounded. The artist who walked up to me at her birthday barbecue in a New Jersey park to say, "I'm looking for some young producers to do session work for my album," must have been floored by this turn of events.

So I was cheered to hear that the suit was settled in early February, though the lack of details in out-of-court settlements is always vexing to a journalist, and this one proved no different. But I was more cheered by finally talking to you two days past, after more than a year, to tell you about this book, this piece. And to solicit your participation, even though I knew you were still in a quiet, contemplative mood.

"Hey Selwyn," you said. Your voice sounded full, strong, unbent by the drama between *Miseducation* and the now. Then you listened. And gently told me that you were not ready to talk. I appreciated your honesty, Lauryn, your frankness. Even more, I appreciated the sounds of music filtering through the phone when I called that studio, the sound of your voice atop music once again, the sound of one of our greatest talents working her magic.

I know now that you will come back to us.

Yours,

Selwyn

BLACK MAGIC WOMAN *by Karen Renee Good*

There are children here in South Orange, New Jersey. Everywhere. Moist green grass underfoot and a strong sun. A humble red-brick house where many burdens have been laid down. It's hard to peer into the black Range Rover pulling up in the driveway, but you figure it's Valerie Hill behind the wheel. Her daughter, Lauryn, is in the backseat, watching over Valerie's grandson, one-year-old Zion David.

On this May afternoon in 1998—one day away from putting the final touches on her premier solo outing, *The Miseducation of Lauryn Hill*—the artist also known as L-Boogie chooses to outstretch her arms in the skies of normalcy, doing the things young mothers and geniuses do. Here comes something magic.

the wicked. When I was thought to know this, it was too painful for me. But God is the strength of my heart, and my portion forever."

Lauryn Hill comes back, settles on the steps. As conversation unfolds, freckled and Afroed childhood friends will stop by with jokes and stories—as will uncles, neighbors, a little girl with a gold name-plate necklace that spells Denesha, and another girlchild who just finished babysitting class. "Come on in!" Lauryn will yell from the steps. "You gotta meet the baby!" To these folks, Lauryn has always been a star. You *can* go home again. It's okay, even, to want to. Maybe even necessary.

"I take my music seriously," she says. "There's noth-

"If you're a man in the music business, there's girls throwing their panties at you. And you can either accept it or reject it. For women, it's very different. Men are often intimidated by you."

Lauryn teeters gracefully in baad five-inch stilettos. ("Oh, I have a shoe fetish," she'll admit later in the kitchen, coyly tilting a heel.) Locks gathered on top of her head, baby positioned on her hip, she greets with a quick "Hey," and walks into this brick house where she was raised and still lives (though she has bought her parents a roomier place five minutes away).

The front steps will do nicely, for we plan to speak easy, even if we have to sometimes shade our eyes from the shining. I pull out my Bible and Lauryn turns to Psalm 73, the one of Asaph—a Levite, musical composer and leader of David's choir. "Read this," Lauryn says, "and I'll be right back." She disappears inside only to check on Zion.

The Word follows: "But as for me, my feet were almost gone; my steps had well nigh slipped. For I was envious at the foolish, when I saw the prosperity of

ing fictional about what I'm doing. Everything I write, everything I say, is a profession. You're not going to hear me talk about what I have—and what you don't have. My role is to communicate what I experience to the greater world. To me, *Miseducation* is about me becoming aware of the things I was really naïve to. I really wasn't thinking about doing a solo album. A lot of people told me to do it.

People were trying to make you do R&B? Or stick with hip hop?

Some were like, "Girl, just sing." And then you had the people who always thought I was in the wrong crew. There was always a lot of energy for me to do something solo, but to me it was a little bit negative. It was flattering, but it was like, "Cross them cats; get rid of them." But that's not me. I'm not a jump-ship type of person.

That must have made you feel uncomfortable.

Very. But I was young and naïve. And it caused some stress in the group. I felt because I paid no attention to it, that meant other people didn't pay attention to it. Who knows what insecurities are in the minds of people because of what someone says? In my mind, I was happy because those were my boys; we grew up together, I loved them very much. But the hill looks different depending on where you're standing—if you're at the bottom or at the top, or in the middle—you know.

Everybody knew those comments wounded, that they were painful. I chose to ignore them. But it did cause some strain. I think it made [Wyclef and Pras] feel like they had to champion other agendas. Like, just in case I did jump ship, everybody else was going to be all right.

And you being the only woman . . .

Because I was one female and I was surrounded by guys, I got so much attention. We all existed in denial for a while. But when you're in denial, you're sort of stagnant. We stayed on tour for a long time. Tour is interesting because it ain't home, which means it's not reality. It's the road. Every night you play for an audience that's clapping for what you do, so you have this warped sense of self. And when I came home—not because I really wanted to but because I was forced to [by the pregnancy]—I was able to watch Wyclef and everything that went on from the outside in, and now I thank God.

What did you see?

I saw how they welcome you into Jerusalem only to crucify you. I remember seeing the publicity and the energy go from like, "You thought the girl was all that? Here's the guy who really sings." I was just like, *Whaaaat?* I said, Okay, have I been stagnant for the sake of promoting this "group collective effort"? I was so busy trying to convince the world of how strong we were as a unit.

How tough of a realization was it?

It's kinda like realizing the Easter Bunny is fictional. You go from this naïveté to like, Wow, okay. This is how it works. My energy has always been very idealistic. I've always been in this record business loving what I do, but it wasn't the world. If it didn't work for me, there were other options.

I wonder how you managed to stay grounded. You're not on no superstar thing.

I actually resent superstardom, because with that comes a lot of shit. Not because I don't want my music to travel across the world—but I'm not a superstar, I don't fit the profile. I can't come into a photo shoot and rip through clothes and holler at people. I think there are people who play that role because they think if you're actually cordial and nice and polite, that people'll walk over you. And there's a lot of truth to that. People do take kindness for weakness. Especially when you're female. So a lot of women feel like they have to overcompensate.

How much do you think you're responsible for giving to the world?

I'm very clear, especially now that I live my life for God. I love humanity, and every day that's a struggle because the devil—I mean those negative forces—they're always out there trying to give you reasons not to love humanity. It makes you say, Let me go up in my house, close my door, turn my TV on, hug my boyfriend, and hold my child.

Onstage with the Fugees you always seemed like you were holding something back.

Remember there was a lot of shared energy there. It was very important for my brothers to shine. And I think for a period of time I was almost afraid to shine. Even though we can sell 17 million records, I still have to convince people that I'm a self-contained unit. I think part of it had to do with the fact that I was with a group of guys who, for some reason, were perceived as being the breath and the life and the reason I do what I do.

Do you see each other a lot?

Right now we don't. Clef is doing *The Carnival;* Pras is doing his thing. And, you know, I assumed the domestic role for a minute, and then I went headfirst into the studio. It had to do a lot with my personal development. I learned some really incredible things about myself.

Like what?

My capacity, my threshold for pain, and my threshold for creativity. I was very blessed to have done this album by myself. I wasn't going to say, you know, Clef, come off the road and let's do this.

They're not on the album at all?

Only because it's kinda out of context. Because the album is so narrative. I think every woman goes through a relationship which is a great lesson in love. I had gone through one earlier, and it was kinda like my therapy to write about it. I made peace when I created these songs. I've revealed myself because I'm an honest musician.

There was the rumor that Wyclef and you were going out.

All of us in the group were very close. I don't have a response to that one. We were a dynamic group in the sense that we grew up together. So there will be a lot of love there.

Do you think it was hard for the public to see you as a woman?

As a real woman? Yeah. [*laughs*] I'm allowed a personal life. [*long pause*] If you're a man in the music business, there's girls throwing their panties at you. And you can either accept it or reject it, and most of the time they accept it because they've never had that much overwhelming attention in their lives. For women in the music business, it's very different. Men are often intimidated by you, or they're crazy. So it's not easy to make connections with real people.

I value the relationships that exist outside this industry. Those people, they just want my attention and my love. So when I try to save my relationships from media attention, what I'm doing is saving that dynamic.

Do you have an agenda with your music?

I want to empower; I want to inform; I want to inspire.

Inspiration is so important.

It is because there were so many things in my life that inspired me to be who I am today. That's

the motivation that inspires us to create. Zion is my inspiration.

I was not raised to be beautiful and not say it. I was not raised to have grievance and not cry out. Some people would prefer to say, "Be pretty and don't talk too much." But you gotta keep talking, or people forget about you, and your agenda. My agenda is to make sure that we're taken care of, and educated, and healthy, and happy.

And you're happy?

I'm very happy. With a foundation, with a good man and a child, and a family—and I don't have the fear of losing my job. You know how in the office space people are sometimes hesitant to be vocal 'cause they could be fired for what they say? The only person who can fire me is God.

ERY
KAH

See I picks my friends like I pick my fruit my Granny told me that when I was only a youth I don't walk around trying to be what I'm not I don't waste my time trying to get what you got

BADU

Photograph by Piper Carter

badu
& the
soul sisters *by Margeaux Watson*

In the midst of the mid-'80s hip hop explosion, when gaudy gold jewelry and clichéd slang were de rigueur, a new movement emerged, right on time. Groups like A Tribe Called Quest, De La Soul, and the Jungle Brothers—collectively known as the Native Tongues—brought a carefree blend of individualism, black pride, off-beat humor, and bohemian style that defied stereotypical notions of black masculinity as hip hop had defined them until then. Incorporating elements of jazz, reggae, and house music, their music boldly scribbled outside the lines while stretching the scope of hip hop to reflect a broader range of the black man's experience in America. In the process, it also transported hip hop beyond the inner city and into the suburbs while appealing to middle-class black and white kids alike.

Ultimately, the Native Tongues proved that the essence of hip hop is in the heart rather than the 'hood. In the process, they paved the way for such like-minded artists as OutKast, Common, The Roots, Mos Def, Talib Kweli, and Hi Tek to further diversify the sometimes complacent atmosphere of hip hop in years to come.

Similarly, Erykah Badu single-handedly injected a much needed shot of refreshing diversity into the female hip hop aesthetic with the release of her groundbreaking 1997 debut album, *Baduizm*. The 29-year-old Dallas native's delicately fragile voice evoked lofty but warranted comparisons to Billie Holiday as she sang over a lush blend of soul, jazz, and blues arrangements driven by thick, syrupy bass lines and Jeep-rocking hip hop beats. She was a singer rather than an MC, but she addressed the sort of topics usually reserved for rap lyrics and peppered her poetry with curses and the *n*-word. Her smash single "On & On," for instance, espoused the self-righteous, pro-black philosophies of the Five Percent Nation of Gods and Earths, an offshoot of the Nation of Islam that considers the black man God.

"If we were made in His image," she sang, "then call us by our names / Most intellects do not believe in God, but they fear us just the same." Till then, Five Percent teachings had only been referenced in the lyrics of such macho hip

hop artists as Rakim, Big Daddy Kane, Wu-Tang Clan, and Brand Nubian. What's more, Badu's self-described "Rasta-style flower child" chic and towering head-wraps stood out in defiant opposition to the swarm of bootylicious R&B kewpie dolls of the day.

At last female hip hop fans who identified more readily with Lisa Bonet's Denise on *The Cosby Show* than with Bernadette Stanis's Thelma on *Good Times* could really relate to a woman in hip hop. Till then, it seemed as if hip hop divas only existed in one of three categories: Butch Tomboys (Queen Latifah, MC Lyte), Ghetto-Fabulous 'Round-the-Way Girls (Roxanne Shanté, Mary J. Blige), or Raunchy Vixens (Lil' Kim, Foxy Brown).

A less confident artist might not have had the moxie to boldly go where no women in hip hop had gone before. But Badu was determined to do things her way—even back when she still answered to her "slave name," Erica Wright. Born in 1972 and raised on soul music of the '60s and '70s, Badu fell in love with the spotlight at age four when she appeared onstage with her mother, Kolleen Wright, a professional actress. By the time she was seven, Badu had already written her first song on an old piano that had been a gift from her grandmother. She cultivated her creative passions while attending Booker T. Washington High, an arts-oriented magnet school where she studied voice, dance, and art, and rapped under the name MC Apples on a local hip hop radio show.

By the time she enrolled at Louisiana's Grambling State University as a theater studies major in 1989, she'd already renamed herself Erykah Badu—*kah* represents the "inner self" and *ba-du* was inspired by the scatting pattern of great jazz vocalists. She dropped out of college and returned to Dallas in 1993. Supporting herself as a dance and drama teacher and waitressing in local coffee shops, she formed a rap duo with her cousin Robert "Free" Bradford. The pair dubbed itself Erykah Free and set about generating local buzz while opening for established hip hop acts when they passed through town.

Although the duo recorded a 19-song demo that attracted

interest from major record labels, Badu received her big break when she opened for up-and-coming soul man D'Angelo in 1994. The gig put her in touch with the corn-rowed crooner's then-manager, Kedar Massenburg, who signed Badu to his fast-rising management company and brokered her a solo deal with music giant Universal Records.

Baduizm was an immediate hit, entering the R&B charts at No. 2, the highest debut for any female artist at that time. And while Badu was praised in R&B circles for her soul-ful vocal stylings, her cinematic music videos further solidified her presence on planet hip hop. She enlisted Pete Rock, Method Man, and her boyfriend Andre "Dre" Benjamin from OutKast to costar in the self-directed clip for "Next Lifetime," which depicted Badu resisting the tempta-tion to cheat on her man in various lifetimes marked by the past (pre-colonial Africa), present (black power movement of the 1970s), and future (space-age Africa). Dre also appeared in the video for "Otherside of the Game," which addressed the mone-tary allure of the drug trade, as well as the pitfalls awaiting a wife and mother whose man is doing dirt.

Within two months of its February 1997 release, *Baduizm* was well on its way to selling more than three mil-lion copies. That summer, Badu embarked on the Smokin' Grooves Tour alongside rap acts like Cypress Hill, Foxy Brown, the Pharcyde, the Roots, the Brand New Heavies, George Clinton and the P-Funk All-Stars, and OutKast. In the middle of the outing, Badu became pregnant with Dre's baby, but that didn't stop her from finishing the tour or recording a live album that was released on November 18, 1997, the same day she gave birth to her and Dre's son, Seven Sirius Benjamin.

Erykah Badu Live! earned her a 1999 Grammy for Best R&B Album and spawned the hit single "Tyrone," a con-versational ballad about dumping a trifling live-in lover, which won the head-wrapped homegirl a second Grammy for Best Female R&B Vocal Performance. In 2000, Badu returned to the Grammy podium yet again to accept a statue for her work on the Roots's hit single, "You Got Me," which won in the category for Best Rap Performance by a Duo or Group. By then, Badu had also appeared in two films, *The Blues Brothers 2000* and 1999's art house favorite, *The Cider House Rules,* in which she portrayed a young woman whose

Macy Gray.

father gets her pregnant. But for the most part, Badu remained out of the spotlight for much of 1999 and 2000, as she took a break from the hectic pace of recording and touring to concentrate on raising her son.

"I breast-fed for two years and I've taught him all the things he's learned from the time he was in my womb till right now," she explained upon emerging from her hiatus. "Seven is three now, and as a mother, I know I'm the most important influence in these years of his life. We've been together every day of his whole life with the exception of maybe one or two weeks when I had something to do that I didn't want to subject him to. I don't miss a step. Even if I go to bed at five A.M. after coming in from the studio, I still get up to be with him cause that's me and Dre's son and we want him to have the advantages we didn't have. I don't have to do nothing but be responsible for that human's spirit and his life."

Badu's groundbreaking achievements, followed by her self-imposed recess, opened the door for others to breathe new life into traditional R&B. While Badu walked away from the 1999 Grammys with her third prize, disappointed newcomer Macy Gray, who had been nominated in two categories, went home empty-handed. But the evening was not a total loss: host Rosie O'Donnell closed the show by urging viewers to go out and purchase Gray's funky debut album, *On How Life Is.*

Apparently, folks heeded O'Donnell's call: *On How Life Is* quickly shot to the Top 10 of the *Billboard* 200 album chart. That summer, Gray opened for Latin guitar legend Carlos Santana when he toured in support of his wildly successful *Supernatural* album. By year's end, her record sales had exceeded three million. Despite Gray's seemingly meteoric rise to mainstream stardom, however, she was neither an overnight sensation nor the detached pop prodigy that the hip hop community perceived her to be.

Born Natalie McIntyre in 1970, Macy Gray took her stage name from a friend of her father's in her native Canton, Ohio, where she grew up the second of four children in a solid middle-class household that was filled with the tunes of Marvin Gaye, Aretha Franklin, and Stevie Wonder. Her mom is a schoolteacher, her dad a retired steel-factory worker and barber.

As a kid, Gray didn't speak much because she was mercilessly teased about her unusual voice, which sounds like a cross between Minnie Mouse, Daffy Duck, and James Brown. Instead, she excelled at academics, took piano lessons for seven years, and played flute in a marching band.

In high school, she became a Prince fanatic after his *Purple Rain* album came out and repainted her entire bedroom magenta. Her parents sent her packing to a midwestern boarding school on scholarship but she was expelled and ran away. Eventually, the wild thing was found sleeping in a car on the side of the road in Kansas.

After returning to her local public high school in Ohio, she fell in love with Rakim and L.L. Cool J, and started reading black writers like Angela Davis while taking in a cinematic diet of Martin Scorsese and blaxploitation flicks. "I liked Rakim 'cause I thought he was fine," Gray recalls. "But then I listened to his voice and I thought it was sexy," she adds with a sly giggle. "Plus, he had a good flow and I liked his rhymes, they just kind of floated in the air and hung like notes—you could almost see the melodies in the air.

"Hip hop was the first music I could identify with," she says emphatically. "It was the only music talking about something; like, most songs are about love, but hip hop was like black people talking to me. It put black people on a whole other level, like the first time I heard 'Rapper's Delight' and they were talking about 'Look at me and what I have. Fuck you.' Hip hop was just perfect. And it had beats so you could dance to that shit, too."

After graduating in 1988, she enrolled as a writing major at the University of Southern California's film school in Los Angeles. But instead of writing scripts and screenplays, she developed a passion for songwriting. "I got into music because I liked this dude who was a music major," she explains. "I was trying to impress his ass and make him think I was down." Gray had also become obsessed with Billie Holiday. "I liked the fact that she had style in her voice," she says. "She was real clear and wanted to make sure you heard every word she sang. She had real good diction." There were other attractions as well. "I wanted to die young and go on drugs and all that shit," she says of her fascination with Holiday, "but she must have been miserable."

She hooked up with some musician friends who worked with various singers and began writing for them. At the time, Gray had never even tried singing, much less considered doing it professionally. Then one night, when somebody didn't show up at the studio, Gray sang a song she wrote herself. A copy of that tape found its way to the leader of a local jazz band, who asked Gray to join his group.

Just a semester shy of graduation, Gray dropped out of college in 1992 and worked a series of temporary office jobs by day while singing jazz, blues, and soul standards at Hollywood hotel bars by night. Before long Atlantic Records came calling with a deal. In 1995, Gray recorded an unreleased rock album for the label but was dropped after the executive responsible for signing Gray left the company.

At the same time, Gray, then 24, met and fell in love with a black Panamanian mortgage collector from Hollis, Queens (who happened to be a Five Percenter). "We had sex the first night we met and I was pregnant six weeks later," she says. The sex was great, but the marriage—after living together for two years, and having two kids—was a disaster. She says this unfortunate episode served as inspiration for the song "Still," in which Gray candidly sings the gory details: "In my last years with him there were bruises on my face . . . / Say what you will, he does me wrong and I should be gone / I still be lovin' you, baby, and it's much too much."

After six months of marital hell, the couple separated and Gray, now pregnant with their third child, returned to Ohio, moved back in with her parents, and decided to become a teacher. Meanwhile, somebody had forwarded a copy of her unreleased rock album to Jeff Blue, vice president of Zomba Music Publishing. Blue fell in love with the record, tracked her down in Ohio, and persuaded Gray to go back to L.A. and record a demo in 1997. In her spare time, Gray also hosted We Ours, a popular after-hours open-mike night at a Hollywood coffee shop that attracted rap notables like Tricky, the Roots, Mos Def, and Black Eyed Peas.

Within months, Gray signed with Epic Records, which sent her into the studio with producer-manager Andrew Slater, who'd previously worked with the Wallflowers and

Fiona Apple. Seven months later, *On How Life Is* was finally completed. But unlike *Baduizm,* which easily found a place on black radio, Gray's raspy, smoky vocals and organ-driven grooves—which blended old-school soul, funk, R&B, and rock with a hip hop sensibility—had her label doubting whether she would get played alongside Jay-Z and Mary J. Blige on urban radio. On the other hand, Epic feared her sound was too sophisticated and soulful for pop radio, which was dominated by teenybopper sensations like Britney Spears and Christina Aguilera.

When *On How Life Is* was released on July 27, 1999, its first single, "Do Something," which contained samples of OutKast's "Git Up Git Out" and Nice & Smooth's "Funky for You," scored points with progressive hip hop heads and on college radio. That summer, Gray toured as the opening act for Gang Starr and the Roots, and appeared on a few dates with Everlast. By fall of 1999, her record was selling 20,000 copies a week.

The buzz became a thunderous roar in January 2000 when Gray received Grammy nominations for Best New

particularly the younger black audience, first saw Macy Gray, they didn't have a reference point to compare her to because she didn't sound like something they'd heard fifteen minutes ago."

Macy Gray concurs: "I think that the biggest tragedy is that the media and radio really underestimate black audiences. They seem to think that all we wanna hear is rap and R. Kelly, so that's all we get. But when you talk to your peoples and you just hanging out, everybody's listening to all kinds of shit and everybody's trying to do everything. I don't think that we're as limited as the media make it seem we are."

And there may be other sorts of limitations as well. Although it seems to have become acceptable for male rappers to brag about selling and abusing marijuana, cocaine, angel dust, and ecstasy, black folks were curiously turned off by Gray's free-spirited extremism and admitted recreational drug use—especially her penchant for psychedelics, which has drawn ready comparisons to Jimi Hendrix and Arthur Lee. "I've done a lot of shit," she says. "I never did

Badu singlehandedly injected a much needed shot of refreshing diversity into the female hip hop aesthetic. Her towering headwraps stood in defiant opposition to the swarms of bootylicious R&B kewpie dolls.

Artist and Best R&B Female Vocal Performance. Even though she didn't win—Best New Artist went to Christina Aguilera—the nominations, along with O'Donnell's endorsement, prodded pop radio programmers to take a gamble and add Gray's second single, an orchestral love ballad called "I Try," to their playlists. Audiences responded, the song went into heavy rotation on pop radio, *Saturday Night Live* booked her as a musical guest, and suddenly Gray was a bona fide pop star.

But with crossover success came the inevitable derision from the hip hop audience that had helped generate the initial buzz about Gray. "White folks in America generally have a lot more access to information and history than a lot of black folks," opines Mos Def. "They have a lot more reference points that they can attach new things to. Because they have broader social access, they tend to get an artist like Macy because they can draw the relationship between a Macy Gray and a Billie Holiday. But when black folks,

heroin, but I like shrooms and hallucinogenic drugs like that. I like being out of my mind a little bit; it's good for the soul."

Gray was publicly humiliated and stripped of some street credibility at the 2000 *MTV Video Music Awards,* where hosts Marlon and Shawn Wayans staged an unflattering spoof of the video for "I Try," depicting Gray as a hard-up ugly duckling with Afroed pubic hair. Ultimately, Gray got the last laugh: when the cameras panned out to catch her reaction in the audience, she dismissively flipped the brothers the bird.

"At first, I was real salty," Gray says about the incident. "They just dissed me and I'm sitting there trying to be cool in front of all these people—Eminem is sitting next to me, Dre is in front of me, Eve is next to him, Busta's in back of me, Lenny is next to him. But I was crackin' up when I saw it two days later at home. I thought it was hilarious."

Undaunted by the affront, Gray used her mass appeal to help expose blossoming hip hop artists on the verge of mainstream success to a wider audience by touring and collaborating on remixes with Mos Def ("I've Committed Murder," which also featured Gang Starr), Common ("Ghetto Heaven"), and the Black Eyed Peas ("Request + Line").

In 2001, "I Try" earned Gray three more Grammy nominations: Record of the Year, Song of the Year, and Best Female Pop Vocal Performance, which she won. But her award-show misadventures continued when she snagged her full-length white rabbit-tail fur coat in her seat, tugged at it unsuccessfully, then had to drop it on the floor and accept her Grammy in a T-shirt and jeans. That night, Gray attempted to redeem her hip hop credibility by opening her performance of "I Try" with an excerpted portion of her Black Eyed Peas' duet, "Request + Line."

"I was really impressed with Macy's Grammy performance," says Mos. "She could've just come out and did 'I Try,' but she freaked it and showed a real nod to her people. Macy has been real keen to make it a point that she is a hip hop fan and I gotta give her a big nod for that because she's a

on the beat of the music, as Jill's mighty voice soared to the heavens and beyond.

The moment was especially sweet for Scott, who says she felt as if she had been punched in the stomach when Badu received a Grammy for her contribution to the Roots's breakthrough hit "You Got Me" back in 1999. It was 25-year-old Scott who wrote and originally sang the hook for that song a year earlier after she returned from starring in the Canadian production of the Broadway musical *Rent*.

When the Roots album *Things Fall Apart* was released in February 1999, and Scott finally heard "You Got Me" on the radio, she was stunned to find out the band had tapped Badu to redo her vocals. Apparently their label, MCA, felt Badu's presence would boost the song's commercial appeal (which it may have done, as *Things* was the band's first album to go gold).

Rather than brood over the disappointment, Scott took it in stride and accepted the band's peace offering to go on tour with them in 1999. Night after night, she would step onstage and transform the hook of "You Got Me" into a

"I think MCs have the best flows," says Scott. "I paid attention to Slick Rick and Rakim and the stories they tell, as well as the way they tell them—real personable. Jay-Z rhymes like that. So does Mos Def."

real legitimate American pop star. I think more people are getting the idea that she's not this distant pop phenomenon that belongs to white folks."

The evening of the 2001 Grammy Awards was also a big night for Badu and rising neo-soul diva Jill Scott, who competed in the Best R&B Female Vocal Performance category. Although both women lost to R&B coquette Toni Braxton, the night belonged to Scott, who was also nominated for Best New Artist and Best R&B Album. Awards aside, the Grammy ceremony was a coming-out party of sorts for the Philly-bred spoken-word poet turned singer, who won a thunderous standing ovation after appearing with the performance art troupe Blue Man Group and Moby in a magnificent live rendition of "Natural Blues." The undisputed highlight of the show, their performance was a wild abstract visual composition in blue, white, and black with showers of silver foil shooting into the audience

stunning solo set that ended with Scott's vocal calling card. She'd sing "My name is J-I-L-L S-C-O-T-T," showcasing the range of her full, mellifluous voice as she undulated between a delicate soprano and a strong yet gentle falsetto.

Unavoidable comparisons to Badu ensued, culminating in an unplanned sound clash that erupted one night when Badu unexpectedly joined Scott during her set at New York's Bowery Ballroom. "I don't battle," says Scott, remembering that night. "I feel like if you want to battle, you gon' mess up the song—'cause everybody's trying to get their point in real quick. I did my little bit and then she wanted to do more so I chilled and listened. I win because I'm getting a chance to hear what you doing as well as listen to what I'm doing." When Badu finished performing, Scott, who says she and Badu are "cool," resumed her set, emerging as the victor to anyone keeping score. That's when Badu stage-dove into the audience in a last-ditch effort to steal back the spotlight from Scott. "I'll never forget that," recalls

Scott with a smile. "When she did that, I stopped singing and clapped, like, 'Yo, you crazy! I ain't playin' them games.'"

After the tour, Scott returned to Philly, enlisted the services of Jazzy Jeff's A Touch of Jazz production house, and began working on her solo debut album. In the late 1980s, champion turntablist Jazzy Jeff produced several hip hop hits that put Philly on the rap map, including Will "The Fresh Prince" Smith's "Girls Ain't Nothing But Trouble" and "Parents Just Don't Understand." After the duo broke up in 1993, the Fresh Prince relocated to Hollywood while Jeff moved behind the scenes to focus on producing new music.

"Nowadays it seems producers are only interested in making a beat for you, but they don't really pay attention to what you're saying," says Scott, who came up through the ranks of Philly's open-mike poetry circuit, which mingled with the local underground hip hop scene that gave rise to MCs like Bahamadia and Black Thought from the Roots. "Because Jeff's dealt in hip hop for so long," she continues, "he really knows how to listen to the words and the stories; he listened to my mind as well as my voice." The result of their inspired collaboration was *Who Is Jill Scott? Words and Sounds, Vol. 1,* a divine mix of deeply soulful songs and melodic, poetic verse set to lush musical arrangements that blend touches of hip hop, jazz, funk, R&B, gospel, and go-go, a bouncy, percussion-oriented musical gumbo that's indigenous to Washington, D.C.

Released on July 18, 2000, the album's jazzy hip hop sound drew immediate comparisons to *Baduizm.* Indeed, once Scott entered the arena, it seemed you couldn't mention her name without referencing Badu, or vice versa. "I see Erykah and Jill as bringing forth an unspoken part of hip hop," says Monie Love, commenting on the way Badu and Scott combine different genres. Still, aside from their fondness for rim shots, Scott and Badu's music represents two very different takes on the concept of fusing hip hop, soul, and jazz. "I think that Erykah Badu and her success made it much easier for the audience to comprehend somebody like Jill Scott," says Mos Def, "but Jill's thing is totally different."

Where Badu's carefully wrought songs sometimes drift into far-out imagery, Scott's lyrics are smart, witty, and refreshingly down to earth. On "Gettin' in the Way," a

Jill Scott.

mood-drenched groove about confronting a lover's persistent ex, the voluptuous, full-figured beauty sings with gospel fervor about beating her rival's ass: "Queens shouldn't swing, if you know what I mean / But I'm 'bout to take my earrings off / Get me some Vaseline."

"I think MCs have the best flows," says Scott. "That's what it's all about when you're a microphone controller—how you flow," adds the singer, who acknowledges her love of hip hop at the start of her album. "I paid attention to Slick Rick and Rakim and the stories they would tell, as well as the way they would tell them—real personable. Jay-Z rhymes like that, so does Mos Def, Talib Kweli, and Biggie—I like a good flow. So I really tried to take some of that and incorporate it into my little bit of jazz, funk, and go-go."

Through her conversational compositions, Scott comes off like a sincere friend that anyone, especially women, could relate to. "I wrote so sisters could know they're not by themselves," she says, "their intuition is real, that love sometimes stinks and will hurt and when it does, acknowledge the pain, don't front on it. If it hurts, cry, goddamnit! Or if you're in love, acknowledge the fact that you feel like you could float, that you got a smile on your face, your eyes are shining and your skin done cleared up—that's real."

"What I dig about Jill is she doesn't sing from her mind, she sings right from her heart," says Mos, who appears on a hidden track (no. 44) on Scott's album. "She doesn't over-intellectualize anything too much, she just goes with the feeling and trusts it. She's really experiencing the music and I think people have responded to her that way."

But just when everything was going well for Scott, she was stricken with sudden deafness syndrome. After an exhausting series of connecting flights from Berlin to Philadelphia, she lost 85 percent of her hearing. "Basically, my ear shut off," she recalls. "It was like somebody had hit mute and there was nothing. It was very frightening because, for one thing, it meant that I would be changing careers, and I wasn't exactly happy about that because I had just started this one. But I figured if this is the master plan, then so be it, I'm not gonna fuss about it; I'll just do something else, though I would miss singing and being onstage."

Fortunately, after several weeks of bed rest, a fully recovered Scott celebrated her clean bill of health at a sold-out, emotionally charged performance at New York's Hammerstein Ballroom in October 2000. Three-quarters of the way into that show, the audience's thunderous applause and amplified cheers reached a deafening crescendo when Jazzy Jeff and Steve McKeever, CEO of Scott's record label, Hidden Beach, snuck onstage and presented the singer with two large gold plaques commemorating the sales of her album, which received hardly any promotion at all. Perhaps the most interesting—and telling—aspect of Scott's success is that the release of her album wasn't accompanied by a flashy marketing and promotional campaign. Her buzz came the old-fashioned way, by word of mouth.

As *Who is Jill Scott?* approached sales of one million copies in the fall of 2000, Badu was preparing to unload her long-awaited second studio album, the aptly titled *Mama's Gun*. In the wake of Macy and Jill, would folks be feeling Badu the same way they did last time around? Back then, Badu and her music were received with open arms—self-righteousness and all—because her sound and personal style were so fresh and new. But could she compete with these flavorful new variations on the potent bitches' brew she had concocted?

As it turns out, yes, she could. The album's sound was owed in large part to the Soulquarians, an elite society of MCs, singers, and producers that includes Badu, Roots drummer Ahmir "?uestlove" Thompson, James Poyser, Common, D'Angelo, singer Bilal, and beatmaster Jay Dee.

Much had happened in Badu's life since we'd last heard from her. After a very public three-year romance with Dre,

which was marked by several cross-collaborations (Badu appears on OutKast's albums *Aquemini* and the smash hit *Stankonia*), the couple split up in October 1999. Broken-hearted and coping with the pressures of single motherhood, Badu encountered the inevitable backlash that befalls so many true originals. And after being criticized in the press for flaunting a crown of dreadlock extensions, Badu shaved her head bald.

But for better or worse, suffering does breed good music. Joining albums like Mary J. Blige's *My Life* and Lauryn Hill's *The Miseducation of Lauryn Hill*, *Mama's Gun* was a deeply intimate and musically adventurous album, as well as a platform for Badu to shoot back at her detractors. In ". . . & On," a semi-sequel to *Baduizm's* hit "On & On," she confronts her critics by singing from their perspective: "What good do your words do if they can't understand you? / Don't go talkin' that shit, Badu." On "Orange Moon," a tender ode to her son, Badu lovingly sang, "I'm an orange moon and I shine so bright 'cause I reflect the light of my sun." But the album's centerpiece was the stunning closing track, "Green Eyes," an excruciating ten-minute, three-part suite in which she laments her breakup with Dre. (Dre told his side of the story on OutKast's smash hit "Ms. Jackson," in which he sincerely apologizes to Badu's mother for breaking her daughter's heart: "Askin' what happened to the feelin' that her and me had / I pray so much about it, need some knee pads.")

"Bag Lady," the first single from *Mama's Gun*, which borrowed Dr. Dre's beat from "Xxplosive," seemed to allude to Badu's failed relationship with Dre as it warned sistas to let go of emotional baggage. It was nominated for three Grammy Awards in 2001. Although Badu, who presented that night, went home empty-handed, the nods signified that she was not only back on top but also sharing the spotlight with two worthy successors who had clearly benefited from her example.

The other beneficiary of these soul sisters' musical contributions is hip hop itself, which can only grow stronger as it departs from tired formula and returns to its essence—reshaping hybrid sounds and styles with reckless abandon.

Not even pop success can stand in the way of the musical morphology. Though *On How Life Is* gave Gray a taste of stardom, she's proudly pushing the envelope with her new album, *The Id*. Executive-produced by Def Jam cofounder Rick Rubin and featuring collaborations with the likes of Billy Preston, Ahmir "?uestlove" Thompson, Sunshine Anderson, and Badu, *The Id* is "a lot more extreme than my last album," Gray says. "All the elements are more to the left: It's more rock than the last album, more hip hop than the last album, and more R&B than the last album," she adds. "It's all about love and impulse and sex and oblivion."

Songs like "The World Is Yours," a trippy cover of Slick Rick's classic "Hey Young World," featuring a verse by the Ruler himself ("his watch just glittered," she recalls, "it lit up the whole room") strongly suggest that Gray—now managed by Blue Williams, who also handles OutKast and Mystikal—hopes to attract a wider black audience. However, the singer says her true objective is to expand the confines of black music rather than conform to the standards defined by black press and radio.

"Erykah, Jill, and Macy have not modified their personalities or characters in any way to communicate or express that they have great affection for hip hop culture and the hip hop aesthetic as it relates to sound," points out Mos Def. "They're not bending over backwards to show they're down. They make very wise choices about how they use hip hop, which not only gears them toward the hip hop audience, but it also makes hip hop bigger because it shows that hip hop can be utilized to effect in a lot of different climates."

"I think it's only right to use hip hop and integrate it in what we do" says Jill Scott. "Erykah, Macy and myself are all from the same generation. We grew up listening to MCs like L.L., Kurtis Blow, Run DMC and Big Daddy Kane. We were wopping, Fila-ing and Pee Wee Hermaning in different parts of the country at the same time. It's who we are and what we grew up on."

In much the same way that the Native Tongues of yesterday paved the way for the Soulquarians of today, Badu has blazed a trail for up-and-coming hip-hop-soul sisters such as Gray and Scott, not to mention Alicia Keys, whose debut album, *Songs in A Minor,* reflects the street-smart influence of urban griots such as the Notorious B.I.G. even as she cites Roberta Flack, Marvin Gaye, and Nina Simone as musical heroes. (Best of all, the classically trained Keys's piano playing is as lovely as she is.) And then there's the indomitable India Arie and the whole Black Lily crew, Sunshine Anderson, Res, sassy rap singer Jaguar, and Flo Brown, a wicked MC/poet who's performed with Common and the Roots. All these women, and others as yet unknown, will undoubtedly draw on the collective sister-soul to concoct the sounds of tomorrow.

Maybe that's what Badu was getting at when she told VIBE's Karen Renee Good that music was going through a rebirthing and she was one of the midwives. Not to say that anybody's trying to join the school of Badu. It seems the only formula is to do one's own thing and truly *feel* it. And if it's real then other people will feel it too. Easier said that done within a music biz that tends to put business before music. "You can't be an individual in this muh-fucka," says a wrathful Badu. "You have to be like this or like that, 'cause if not you gonna be picked apart and torn apart. Once you get too big, they're gonna tear you down. So you can't lose respect for your individuality no matter what anybody says."

Call her what you will: soul, r&b, hip hop, diva, Badu is, was, and will be simply Badu. "I don't believe in rules or laws—laws of music, laws of society," she says. "The laws of the universe are the only ones I go by, and that's to try to keep balance and harmony within self. When people saw Erykah Badu when I first came out, I was, like, exalted—'Oh, she's wonderful.' That's how I want to feel about myself. Perhaps I'm already there, I'm just not convinced yet."

DA

Ain't too many hos that can hang with me it's like that and as a matter of fact when it comes the Brat-tat-tat-tat I make your neck snap back

BRAT

Photograph by Marc Baptiste

wild child *by Andréa Duncan*

Driving toward downtown Atlanta on Interstate 95, motorists are greeted by an aging pink and green billboard with an image of an Afroed, sunglass-wearing mack daddy that reads "Welcome to Atlanta, the home of So So Def Recordings." The sign has a decidedly small-town quaintness, reminiscent of a time when the business of hip hop was either based in Los Angeles or New York, and the only sound coming from below the Mason Dixon line was country & western. Nowadays, this town is Hot-lanta—a thriving nexus of urban culture and home to superstars like TLC, OutKast, Goodie Mob, and most recently Ludacris. But in the early '90s, before flocks of music and sports celebrities were lured by the ATL's cheap real estate and friendly, laid-back southern hospitality, a former

delivery—capable of flipping from an effortless Snoop Dogg-like drawl to a frenetic, rapid-fire flow—Brat made hits and history by becoming the first solo female rapper to sell a million albums. And as a woman in a male-dominated industry, her unapologetic tomboy image, creative self-sufficiency (laced with undeniable sex appeal), and ability to expand her career as a writer, producer, and actress, Da Brat continues to challenge established perceptions of femininity.

Her first single, "Funkdafied," which borrowed the hypnotic, party vibe of Dr. Dre's *The Chronic*, heated up dance floors and airwaves, propelling her 1994 debut album to unprecedented heights. With gangstafied lyrics illuminated by Dupri's laid-back, West Coast funk-inspired beats, the 20-year-old shorty emerged as the Down South Bon-

Brat and Jermaine Dupri have a true creative and business partnership. "We almost share the same mind when we go into the studio," says Dupri. "It's just like Batman and Robin."

teenage dancer for Whodini named Jermaine Dupri had the Peachtree State's biggest city on lock.

After making a name for his fledging label with Kris Kross, he met a couple of preteen boys at a shopping mall who wore their pants backwards and then taught them how to rap. Dupri built himself a hip hop empire without leaving the South—signing the R&B girl group Xscape, the hard-rock harmony quartet Jagged Edge, and his latest discovery, the pint-sized rapper Lil' Bow Wow. A much-sought-after producer, Dupri solidified his reputation by churning out hits for artists like Usher, the Notorious B.I.G., 112, Mariah Carey, and Jay-Z.

But JD's empire would not be what it is today without the presence of Shawntae Popsy Harris, a.k.a. Da Brat— the Chicago native who became the yin to Dupri's yang. As an early signee to So So Def, Da Brat not only emerged as the label's brightest star, but a cornerstone of the entire operation. With her brash lyrics, an unpredictable ice-grill

nie to Dre and Snoop's Clyde. *Funkdafied,* which also contained the hits "Fa All Y'all" and "Give It 2 You" (where she warned: "Truth of the matter is / I splatter kids tryin' to dis / In a gangster's way / That's how dem fools get dealt with") earned its platinum plaque within a few months.

Da Brat appealed to female fans who had grown up listening to MC Lyte and Queen Latifah, and were hungry for another bangin' MC they could call their own. Here was a young, streetwise woman who had obviously been raised on hip hop. She was talkin' shit and takin' care of business, yet her toughness did not alienate the male audience. Female rappers like Nikki D and Boss may have put the gangsta bitch concept on the map, but Brat's skills as a lyricist raised it to new heights. If she didn't have the rhymes and attitude to back up her hardcore image, she would have been dismissed as novelty.

Since her debut, Da Brat has remained in the spotlight, defying the here-today-gone-tomorrow odds of hip hop stardom. She's appeared on tracks with everyone from Biggie—who called her the "funkdafied cutie pie"—to Missy Elliot. She has started her own Chicago-based production company, Throwin' Tantrums Entertainment. And she's expanded her career to include acting and ghostwriting hits for emerging artists like teen sensation Lil' Bow Wow.

Da Brat has become someone all too rare in hip hop: a woman who is fully in control of her destiny. She's not the token female in a crew of men, nor a studio creation. Instead, she and Jermaine Dupri have a true creative and business partnership that makes her role go beyond the honorary title of So So Def's First Lady. "We almost share the same mind when we go into the studio," says Dupri. "It's just like Batman and Robin." Not only can Brat rock the mike and shine in the spotlight, she can make hits behind the boards, and do it all on her own terms.

In the parking lot of a chi-chi Asian fondue restaurant in the equally chi-chi Atlanta enclave of Buckhead, the Jay-Z and R. Kelly jam "Guilty Until Proven Innocent" is bumping out of a silver Lincoln Navigator. When the song is over, the door to the driver's seat swings open and Da Brat emerges, still singing. "Everybody with a case gotta love that song," she says with a wink, admiring the way Jay-Z turned his own legal problems into professional triumph.

At 27, after close to a decade in this business, Brat appears ageless, still wearing the baggy jeans, baseball jerseys, cornrows and only a hint of makeup. Her hands, nose, ears, and neck sparkle with diamonds, and those trademark sunglasses hide her eyes. "I don't know what it is," she says of the shades. "I guess I'm kinda shy." These days she sports Chanel shades given to her by her friend Mariah Carey.

Brat chose this particular establishment because she likes the healthy food and because it's a good place to "break the ice." Despite her initial reserve, she warms up quickly. After being joined by her manager, her best friend, and her hairstylist, Brat assumes the role of a tour guide, excitedly explaining things about her favorite restaurant, which is built around a boat. "Look down there," she says, pointing to a small pond in the middle of the cavernous room. "There's alligators and turtles." As promised, under

Dupri and Da Brat in the lab.

a heat lamp lounges an uninterested, sleepy gator. She giggles and leads us back toward the small private room where she prefers to dine.

Over dinner, Brat commands the table like a mother hen, overseeing the bubbling pots of oil that contain shrimp, chicken, and vegetables (no gooey cheese fondue here) and knocking back glasses of port. The sweet brown beverage is typically an after-dinner wine, but Brat, in her typically nonconformist stance, drinks the syrupy elixir before, during, and after dinner, making sure everyone's glass stays full. She is friendly and approachable, chatting up the waitstaff and getting up from time to time to pose for pictures and sign autographs. And though she rarely smiles in photos, the off-camera Brat smiles easily, making her eyes sparkle behind the shades.

She has reason to celebrate. After writing Lil' Bow Wow's No. 1 hit "Bounce with Me," Brat has just received some nice checks and a flurry of offers from other new artists who want her name and pen attached to their projects. This particular evening, she is scheduled to stop by the studio to hear a teenage female rapper and determine if she will executive produce her debut. "I don't think I'll ever stop being an artist," Brat says, stirring the pot. "I like being in the spotlight too much. But I also love being behind the scenes helping new young artists. Their hunger and drive motivates me."

It's a fitting twist of fate for Brat, who was still a teenager full of hunger and drive when she got down with Dupri. Driven by her love of music, Brat had been trying to make a name for herself as a rapper since she was 14. After being in bands and church choirs in the Windy City, she joined a number of performance troupes, including a girl group called Simply Nasty, before striking out on her own under the moniker Paris Paper Doll. After performing at schools, clubs, and contests, she caught the attention of super producer Teddy Riley and New Edition's Michael Bivins, but the deals they promised never materialized. Her break finally came at age 18 in a meeting so unlikely that it seemes to have been predestined.

"I started having dreams about being down with Kris Kross and Jermaine Dupri because when I saw Kris Kross on TV I was like, Whoa, they like me!" Brat explains. "I used to wear my pants backwards just for the hell of it, and I had braids all the time." Her prophesy was fulfilled at an October 1992 Kris Kross concert in Chicago. Before the show, Ed Lover, the host of *Yo MTV Raps!* held an MC competition. "I went onstage and rapped and won the contest," says Brat. "I was supposed to win fifty dollars, and that jerk never paid me, you know what I'm saying? So I still want my fifty dollars, Ed Lover, whatever you're doing. It might not mean a lot to you, but I want my money. Okay? And when I get it I'm going to frame it 'cause that was the start of my life."

As the first-place winner, Brat got to meet the pint-sized rap stars. "We exchanged numbers," she recalls, "and they told me they'd keep in touch and tell their producer about me, and I didn't believe them." But sure enough, when Kris Kross returned to Chicago for a taping of *The Oprah Winfrey Show,* they gave Brat a call.

Dupri remembers that they were impressed with her from the beginning: "Chris called me and was like, 'JD, you gotta come see this girl rapper from Chicago,'" he says. "And I was like, 'I don't want no fuckin' girl rapper.' I said it exactly like that, and she was on the three way. They had put me on the spot 'cause she was on the phone. And when I said that, with her attitude, she snapped on me. She acted like somebody I knew. So she was talkin' shit in the phone, and I'm like, 'Yeah, whatever.'"

But Brat was not so easily discouraged. She got his number and called again, finally convincing the young producer to come see her. "Girl rappers wasn't really on my radar at all, y'know what I'm sayin'. But there was some-

thing about her attitude and the way she presented herself," Dupri says. "When I met her she had a rap ready, and there was a glow about her and something hit me."

Her first recording for So So Def was on Kris Kross's not-quite-explosive sophomore album, *Da Bomb.* While she worked on the record, the 19-year-old Brat lived in Atlanta with JD (who was only 20 himself) and his mother.

"When she stayed with me," he says, "I guess we kind of joined forces, and just like, did a lot of stuff together— started dressing alike, doing videos. Even now when we do shows, we might not even rehearse, but we don't bump into each other. We know what the other person is going to do. And we like all the same stuff. If I was a girl, I'd be just like Brat."

But after *Da Bomb* was finished, Mama Dupri pulled Brat to the side. "She was like, 'You've been down here a long time,'" Brat recalls with a smile. "'You should probably think about getting you a place.' I had never even had my own place. I was like, man, that's a great idea!"

Driving through the streets of Chicago's rough and tumble West Side there is a distinct chill in the air, even on a crisp spring day. Colorless, dilapidated buildings line a main thoroughfare called Kostner Avenue, where slit-eyed men congregate outside, speaking in code. But just around the corner stands an oasis of modest brick homes with manicured lawns, home to hardworking, blue-collar black families with ties to the South—families who moved to Chicago for a better life during World War II, and bought homes to pass on to their children. These are the folks who managed to escape the ghetto, even if it lurks right outside their doors. It is here that Shawntae Popsy Harris grew up, and Chicago is still where she calls home. In fact, her childhood room has not been disturbed since she packed her bags to go to Atlanta eight years ago.

When her mother, a Chicago transit worker, and her father split up, school-age Shawntae shuttled back and forth between her two grandmothers. It is this house off Kostner, home of her father's parents, Grandpa and Grandma Harris, that holds Brat's fondest memories. The woman Brat calls "Gran" is a twinkly-eyed spitfire who wears fly sweatsuits, nail tips, and teaches line dancing. She refuses to wear her hearing aid, makes a mean batch of moonshine, and admits to packing a gun sometimes when she goes out after dark. It was she who gave Shawntae the nickname that stuck.

"She was just spoiled, always," Gran recalls, sitting on the couch in her cozy living room. "When she didn't get what she wanted, she'd fall out and have her tantrums, on the floor kicking around. And I just started calling her

Brat." The story elicits a giggle from the sleepy Brat, sporting her usual baggy jeans, T-shirt, and a mop of braids, even when she's home for an all-too-brief weekend. When she spends time around Gran, her face softens, losing its characteristic scowl. "I didn't think she liked me; I thought she was mean," Brat says of Gran. "My granddaddy used to spoil me and Gran used to tell him he couldn't do that because there were other grandkids in the family. And I didn't understand. I wanted to be special."

Gran describes Shawntae's early childhood as one of almost suburban bliss: "She liked open spaces, she didn't want to be closed in. We used to take her to Disney World. She loved to play in the backyard and splash around in the portable pool." As Gran speaks, Brat looks at her with a wistful, almost reverential expression, and smiles. "She liked to ride those—what do you call it—Big Wheels and run around with all the kids in the neighborhood. I never worried about her because she was tough and everybody looked out for her."

who Brat calls her "sanctified" grandmother, is a devout Christian, one who attends a church that prohibits makeup, pants, open-toed shoes, and jewelry. "When I was staying with her, I used to wake up every morning to a big sign that read: 'No Boys'," she says with a sigh. "Don't get pregnant. Don't do this, don't do that."

"I hated it," says Brat, rolling her eyes. "But I'm glad for it now. Who knows what I would have been without the strict upbringing? Some of my girl cousins who didn't have that didn't turn out so good. They would run into drug dealers who started givin' them nice sneakers and stuff and then they got off into doing drugs because there was no one there to say, 'Don't do that.'"

By living in two separate universes, one of the church girl (who attended etiquette classes, no less) and another of the ghetto bad-ass, Brat developed a knack for learning to adapt to whatever situation she faced. "Because of how I grew up," she explains, "I know how to flip it. I can hang out on the corners with the homies, but I can also be a

"I used to go fight my daddy's girlfriends," she says of her childhood in Chicago. "He'd send me to fight 'em since he'd get in trouble if he hit 'em. I'd fill up a pillowcase with hairspray cans and swing."

Out of Gran's earshot, Brat will paint a different picture of the neighborhood, and how things changed as she got older. "During the week, I'd stay with my mom and her mother, who was very strict," she says. "Then I'd come here and go crazy, go hang out in the streets. I've been robbed, I've had guns put to my head." She shakes her head as if in disbelief. "I used to go fight my daddy's girlfriends," she says. "He'd send me to fight 'em since he'd get in trouble if he hit 'em. I'd fill up a pillowcase with hairspray cans and Miracle Whip jars and wrap it around my hand and swing. I used to do a lot of stuff."

Brat, who was arrested in 2000 for allegedly assaulting a woman during a dispute at an Atlanta nightclub, says she has to work to control the temper she believes she inherited from her father. "He's been in jail for getting in fights," she says. "So I try and watch my temper because I know that's in me. These streets get me in trouble."

Brat credits her Granny Polk (her mother's mother) with instilling a sense of discipline in her. This woman,

lady. And I know when to act a certain way." This ability has followed her through adulthood, as she can "flip" at any time from tomboy to vixen or from her wild, weeded-out image to a shrewd businesswoman. "Brat's really business smart. She wants to dominate the game more than it appears," says Dupri. "Publicly she'll be smokin', drinkin', but there's so much more to her."

The one thing that remained constant in any situation was Brat's love for music. "From [when I was] a little girl to high school I was always in the band," she says. "I played the trumpet, the trombone, the baritone, the tuba." But she needed a beat. "I wanted to play drums *sooooo* bad," she says, "and no one would teach me. You know, like girls don't play drums. So I just started to watch the guys, and finally I got a drum set and I got real good."

Her love of the rhythm naturally expanded into a love of hip hop, and Brat soon began writing rhymes. Though her room at Gran's house is still decorated with posters of Big Daddy Kane, L.L. Cool J, and fellow Chicagoan

R. Kelly, Brat says her true inspiration was New York rhyme buster MC Lyte: "I grew up lovin' MC Lyte! I liked Latifah and Monie Love too. But MC Lyte had the whole tomboy thing, so I was like, Oooh, that's me! Oooh! I can relate. I'm just like her!!!"

Of course, Da Brat's tomboy image has both endeared her to her fans and fueled the gossip mills. In the beginning of her career, her baggy clothes and hard rock demeanor was not just a popular look for female MCs (with the exception of the made-up, bicycle shorts–clad queens from Queens, Salt-N-Pepa), it was the *only* look. Most female rappers weren't pushing their sexuality to the forefront in the way they looked or the things they rhymed about.

Brat's sexual orientation became a topic of speculation because her tough-chick image–combined with her gangsta posturing and references to herself as "the baddest pimp in this hip hop biz"–struck many listeners as

never knew she had, and some slinky black lingerie. "That was my real panties and my real bra that I actually wore," she confesses. "I was just getting dressed, and they snapped the picture. I'm real picky, I like my bras and panties to match–be like a fresh, pretty, elegant set. But I still wear boxers, I wear them over my panties so the jeans aren't so hard on my skin." Go figure.

Then in a move that sent shockwaves through the industry, she performed on The Lady of Soul Awards *sans* her trademark braids, in a tight, cleavage-baring pantsuit and heels. "That's the most nervous I have ever been in my life," she confesses, lighting up a post-fondue cigarette. "I can't be movin' and hopping all around and bugging out being me. 'Cause I gotta worry if my titty gonna pop out, or my pants are gonna split, or my makeup's smudged. You know, nothing's wrong with all that beauty stuff, but I prefer to just get up and go."

In the year between her show-stopping Lady of Soul Awards performance and the release of her third album,

"Nothing's wrong with all that beauty stuff," says Brat, "but I prefer to just get up and go. I can't be hoppin' all around and buggin' out 'cause I gotta worry if my titty gonna pop out or my makeup's smudged."

overly masculine. While doing press for her second album, *Anuthatantrum* in 1996, she found herself constantly addressing rumors that she was gay. She has been linked romantically to NBA roughneck (and erstwhile rapper) Allen Iverson, and says she still has a special man in her life (though they're both so busy they hardly get to see each other). Yet to this day, she consistently deflects–rather than denies–these rumors. "If you even give me so much in your day to say 'Brat's gay,' you obviously thinkin' about me," she will say, "so go buy the album." It seems like fun to her, using her ambiguous sexuality to titillate the media and her fans: Brat is heavily tattooed, curses like a sailor, calls her friends "nigga" regardless of their gender, and is quick to fight, yet says she "loves to play around with makeup" and "show a little titty here and there."

Then there is the matter of her underwear. In 1999, she appeared in a Women of Hip Hop calendar showing off a glammed-up, sunglasses-free face, a set of curves her fans

Unrestricted (2000), Brat continued to vamp up her image. The video for *Unrestricted*'s first single–the oozing-with-sex "What'chu Like"–featured Brat in a see-through body suit surrounded by muscled, shirtless men or romping on the beach with R&B heartthrob Tyrese. Brat's sudden makeover, especially in the era of glamour girls (Eve, Amil, Rah Digga) and sexpots (Lil' Kim, Foxy Brown, Trina) seemed like an attempt to compete.

If her new sexy image was supposed to help sell records, it had little effect. *Unrestricted* failed to live up to Brat's prerelease predictions of three times platinum. "I thought it was the best album I've ever done," she says, shrugging. "So when things don't go the way you want, you just get more determined. I can't focus on the past, that's done. I've got so much more in me."

Brat insists her foray into diva-dom was about maturing and coming into her womanhood. She plans to continue the experiment. "I love my body," she says with a cocky smile, "and I feel like I'm older, and I got a few nice assets to show. So I'll dibble and dabble from time to time. I'm not afraid to be different, and no one is making me. I don't live to please other people."

The older, wiser Brat *does* live to make music, whether as an artist or a writer-producer. So she pours one last glass of port and prepares to head to the studio to meet her teenage would-be collaborator, who's traveled from Nebraska to meet Brat. "I heard she's got a tight flow, she's cute, and she wants to work with me, so I wanna hear her," she says, perhaps thinking of another little girl from the Midwest who came to Atlanta in pursuit of a dream. But Brat knows the rap game leaves no room for romanticizing. "I wanna see if she has potential and if we click before I make any decisions."

Brat has achieved "veteran" status in the fickle world of hip hop, and it's a title she doesn't mind wearing. Still very much in demand, she's recently recorded songs with Destiny's Child, Eve, and her idol, MC Lyte. "Aw, man, it was great working with Lyte," she says. "It's an honor to do anything with her. I didn't even talk money with her yet, and I usually don't do anything without getting some money first!" Down the road, Brat looks forward to releasing a new album and continuing to appear on the big and small screens, including her role in MTV's recent *Carmen:*

A Hip Hopera, as well as working alongside Mariah Carey in the film *Glitter.*

In the years since her incandescent debut a number of MCs have appeared to eclipse her shine, but Brat says she's never felt left behind. "I have never lost my place," she asserts. "I got my platinum, I made my mark." And though females in the rap game today have more opportunities for fast fame and fortune—landing modeling contracts, endorsement deals, movie roles—Da Brat says these perks often come at the price of losing their identity. For her part, she's managed to avoid the common syndrome of male rappers acting as puppeteers to a token female—writing their rhymes and controlling every aspect of their image.

"Girls that can't do nothin' for themselves are just tryin' to get stuff from men," says Brat, before heading off to start the evening's work. "That's not good because if they drop your ass, you don't have nothing to fall back on. I think you should be yourself, know who you are, know that you have talent, and you don't have to do anything just because someone told you to. I didn't get pressured like that." She drains her glass of port, takes a deep breath, and smiles. "Fortunately, I got with Jermaine and he was very satisfied with who I was. I was just a tomboy that wanted to rap. I had hot lyrics, and that's how I made it, off my *talent.*"

Foxy

No more waitin' to exhale we takin' deep breaths ladies take this over I be Fox so peep this love thyself with no one above thee 'cause ain't nobody gon' love me like me

Photograph by Marc Baptiste

she got
game *by Danyel Smith*

Foxy and I are naked. Almost. We've got on paper panties. We're on top of the Delano Hotel in Miami. A spa called Agua. Sun deck and low walls, pale blue with white trim. Like sitting on a solid part of the sky.

It's hot. Too close to the sun. Just had the salt rub. Getting the custom massage and the Mini Peppermint Twist. They soak Ace bandages in seaweed and hot water and peppermint essential oil. Wrap you tight from the waist down like you've broken all the bones in your lower body. Wrap you snug in a Mylar blanket (the kind of material those shiny HAPPY BIRTHDAY balloons are made from). Then you simmer in the hotness. We each end up sitting in a quarter-cup of our own minty sweat.

Foxy and I are talking about being female and just how bananas it is. Talking about truly corny feelings. Foxy, who has been linked, at one time or another, to Jay-Z, RayShawn from Junior M.A.F.I.A., Allen Iverson, Andre Rison, DMX, Master P, Nas, as well as a number of dancehall artists, and who is, as we speak, engaged to Kurupt, says that though a lot of times it is all about sex, a lot of times it isn't.

Foxy is saying, "I'm talking about love. Love. *Love.* Everybody wanna talk about why Foxy doesn't show up at a video shoot, why I'm late to my show, why I won't take my sunglasses off in an interview. 'Cause everything ain't always all right with me. Okay? You know? We have fucked-up days. You might catch me when I just hung up with my man and I'm arguing with him and this muthafucka ain't told me he loves me in a week—and I'm trippin'. I might not be all smiles on that day. I tell you this: until you've been in love with a nigga, until you've been standing on the edge of a building ready to give it all up for a nigga—I *ride* for my niggas. Until you've done all *that* shit, don't talk to me. I tell a muthafucka, look: grow titties, get a pussy, get your heart broke before you talk to me about how I'm acting." Foxy, sweet brown like the best chocolate, leans back in her lustrous cocoon, face to the heat. "Do *that* before you talk to *me* about *shit.*"

On the Delano's verandah; Foxy and I have salty breasts, peppermint butts, ginseng faces. Daisies sit in a tiny vase. Inga Marchand, a.k.a. Foxy Brown, says she has more than the blaxploitation screen diva from whom she took her name for an idol. "Roxanne Shanté!" Foxy almost screams. "For real, like hands down! She's a pioneer for the type of shit I'm doing. I swear by her. She was a bitch back in the day—for having skills. She was stepping out of limos with full-length minks. *Diamonds.* She was like, *'I'm that bitch. I'm here and these are my niggas and this is how we roll.'"*

Foxy says "ride" a lot. When she says, "I ride for my niggas," she means she will go with them wherever, whenever, for whatever. She means loyalty. And she's serious about it, like she's serious about Jay-Z, the Brooklyn rhyme mogul and founder of Roc-A-Fella Records, otherwise known as Jigga or Jayhovah.

"That's my Clyde," she says on this day in 1998. "I'm his Bonnie. You ever had a nigga that can't do no wrong in your eyes in *any* situation? That's who Jay is to me. Our shit is unconditional." Jay seems to feel pretty strongly about Foxy as well. On "Bonnie & Clyde Part II," from her 1998 album, *Chyna Doll* (Violator/Def Jam), Foxy asks Jay, "Would you die for your nigga?" And he answers, chillingly, "I'd hang high from a tree."

Foxy says Jay put her on. She met him when she was like 13 or 14 through her cousin, DJ/producer Clark Kent. "Did I think Jay was cute?" She smiles big. "I wasn't even looking at him like that. He wasn't even out yet." But then, in 1996, they voiced "Ain't No Nigga" for Def Jam's soundtrack to *The Nutty Professor.* "No one can fuck you better," went the chorus, as Jay rapped hardcore rhymes to 16-year-old Foxy, who gave as good as she got. "You know the pussy was all that," is the way she replied. "We never expected 'Ain't No Nigga' to be a hit," she says. "It was the biggest song that year."

So just how much does Jayhovah contribute to Foxy Brown? She admits she can't write without a Biggie or Jay-Z CD in the studio with her. "What made Jay love me was the verse I wrote for 'Ain't No Nigga,'" she says. "I write my songs and have always written my songs. When my schedule is hectic and I'm too busy to go to the studio, Jay collaborates with me. He catches me when I'm falling. But this is *my* nine to five. This is what *I* do."

A lot of people don't know that Inga Marchand was signed to Capitol Records as Big Shorty. Soon thereafter she changed her name to AKA and was eventually dropped from the label. Then a rapper named Red Hot Lover Tone brought her to a rising producer named Sean "Puffy" Combs, who turned her down. But the Fox was determined.

Chris Lighty, CEO of Violator Records, has managed artists like Busta Rhymes, Missy Elliott, L.L. Cool J, Mobb Deep, Nas, Capone-N-Noreaga, Maxwell, and Foxy through their most brilliant moments. Lighty says he was probably the first, aside from Jay-Z, to give Foxy a shot. "She didn't even have a real demo," he says.

As the story goes, Tone and Steve "The Commissioner" Stoute of Trackmasters Entertainment were in Chung King Studios in 1995 with L.L. Cool J. Lighty was there, too; he'd been working with L.L. for years. Tone and Foxy had known each other from around the way in Brooklyn, from when they used to hang out at Daddy-O of Stetsasonic's crib, making songs in his cramped studio. Lighty says Foxy "had been bugging me to put her on a record. And Tone had been trying to get me to sign her. We all agreed to put her on [the remix to the single "I Shot Ya"] without telling L.L."

The night before she recorded her verse, Foxy left the studio "early" because it was three in the morning and she had a big test the next day. "She was caring about school a lot at that time," says Stoute. "But she came back the next night. Myself, I was just thinking about the money."

"I was the new bitch," says Foxy. "They had me in there with L.L., Keith Murray, Prodigy, and Fat Joe. I was like, 'Y'all got me rhyming against some dope-ass MCs.'" Foxy wanted to be fly, yes, but more than that she wanted to be fierce. No favors please. Foxy was ready to write, grab the mike, spit. She didn't want to just hang in there. All she wanted was to rule. "And you know what?" she said to herself. "I can *do* this shit."

"Foxy wrote her rhyme right then," says Violator's Eric Nicks. It went a little something like this: "Four carats of ice rocks / Pussy banging like Versace . . . / I'm sexing raw-dog without protection / Disease-infested."

"Everybody ran out of the room screaming like that shit was the *bomb*," Foxy recalls of the fateful night. "I knew right then it was going to be on for me. I was a female truly rhyming with some real niggas."

Judith Marchand says she didn't know about her daughter's talent until Inga turned 16. "Only after every record company head was expressing interest in her did I become aware," says the Ill Mama, who's an elementary school teacher in Brooklyn. "Something that stays with me: I was at a studio. On the other side of the door they were playing a Foxy track. I heard them screaming. A guy ran out and said, 'She is the *50-Foot Woman*. She's going to be the Whitney Houston of rap.'" Okay, so maybe she wasn't doing the remix of "I Will Always Love You," but Foxy was still a pretty, profane, sexual girl with skills—do the math.

"It was the *craziest* bidding war," Foxy recalls. "Puffy, Russell [Simmons, chairman of Rush Communications], Sylvia [Rhone, then chairperson/CEO of Elektra Entertainment], Andre Harrell [then CEO of Motown Records]." The high school sophomore narrowed her options down to Bad Boy and Def Jam, noting that "Russell had longevity."

Spend a little time with her and you'll notice that Foxy likes to win. Just ask Eric Nicks, who worked closely with her as Violator's head of Artists and Repertoire. "She spazzes out when something's off," he says. "It's got to be the right beat, the right lyric, the right stylist. Everything has to be *win win win*, or she's not doing it."

Back when Foxy was in junior high and Kimberly Jones, a.k.a. Lil' Kim, was in high school, they were friends, living in the Clinton Hill section of Brooklyn. They used to stay on the phone with each other until six in the morning, planning how they were gonna tear shit down. *Who would get on first? Which bitch was baddest?*

"We always had a pact," Foxy says. Each agreed to help the other. Back then, both were down with Lance "Un" Rivera's Unlimited Management. "But then we kinda branched off. She went with Big, I went with Jay. She got on first, I was real happy for her. She paid her dues."

Foxy remembers one call from Kim in the wee hours of the morning. "I had to go to school the next day and she was like, 'You know AZ?'" Foxy says. "I was, 'The rapper? The one that gets with Nas?' This was like before AZ was even out. She was like, 'Yo, I got him on the other line. He wants you to rap for him.' I was real scared. She was like, 'This is Inga,' or whatever. I just started busting for him at like four in the morning. He was like, 'Yo, give me your number. Shorty is dope.'" When Foxy met AZ and Nas, they all just clicked. "It was like, 'This is how we gonna do this. It's gonna be *The Firm*.'" They ended up recording 1997's *The Firm—The Album* with production by Dr. Dre. Sold a million copies. She says Nas and AZ are her fam. She rides for them.

Right now we're all riding in a long limo eating Twizzlers and Milky Ways. Violator crew is along for the ride. All the guys' socks are brand-new, bottoms of their shoes spotless. We eat Kit Kat bars, sip 20-ounce Cokes, Tropicana from the carton. We're on our way to a restaurant, but no one's had breakfast, so we stopped at a corner store and got stuff for the trip.

In the limo, Lighty is on his StarTAC incessantly. Everything is urgent. He says that Foxy was always determined. "She trooped it out," he says. "Be in the studio with us till four or five in the morning, and then go to school." Lighty's got a tattoo of his two daughters' names. In Japanese lettering it also says, TO FAMILY GIVE LOVE. A platinum pendant dangling from his neck means the same.

"I knew who I wanted her to be musically," he says. "Foxy was reluctant to do 'Get Me Home' at first. That was too pop. We had her on more mainstream records than she wanted to be on. If you listen to Foxy's first album [*Ill Na Na*, Def Jam, 1996] and Kim's first album [*Hard Core*, Undeas/Atlantic, 1996], Kim was more underground. We took Foxy straight to the clubs. Kim had Biggie, though. There was a lot of power on that side. Fortunately, we were able to keep up."

Kim and Foxy are not really friends anymore. They maintain what could be termed a ride-or-die connection. "It didn't have to do with Kim and I personally," Foxy says. "It was the people around us." They were supposed to cut a song a few years ago called "Thelma & Louise." Even though both women had come to be accepted, and to a lesser degree respected, for their abilities to rhyme, the scene was still

Foxy says after 30 minutes of going back and forth over who said what and when, "I was talking to a dial tone." But she decided to go to the studio and record her verse anyway. Then Foxy, Un, and Lighty waited several hours for Kim. "Shorty never showed," Foxy says. "Even still," she says, sounding like an old school chum, "I have nothing but love for her."

And the love flows both ways. One of the scariest moments of Foxy's life was in July 1998 when her house got broken into and a gun was pointed to her head. "Kim was the first one concerned," Foxy says. "I appreciated that."

But it's safe to say she did not appreciate the song on Kim's 2000 album *The Notorious K.I.M.* in which she called herself "the heavyweight champ female MC," then proceeded to toss a few subtle barbs that sounded like they might have been directed at Foxy. Some months after that—and after being released from rehab for addiction to painkillers—Foxy hooked up with Capone-N-Noreaga and made a song called "Bang Bang" with a few choice lines for her girl from back in the day. "Let's be truthful, give a

Foxy knows that because she sells sex (and she will tell you that, straight out), the impulse to stigmatize her is pretty automatic. People are awaiting her fall. Something bad must happen to the "slut."

is alienating. Rapping is about constantly showing and proving, but it's also about the cypher and camaraderie. And girls, especially at the highest level, should rhyme from their own side of the room. An all-girl cypher? Maybe in the high school cafeteria, before the girls have been separated from those who are committed for life to hip hop. To be a girl in hip hop requires more defiance, more heart. More willingness to be dissed—not for wack rhymes or beats—but for being what you are.

"At the time we were supposed to record, we weren't speaking," says Foxy. "I can't remember why. Un came to me and said, 'I know you and Shorty ain't on the best of terms right now, but . . .' And at first I wasn't really with it. I told Un it's not gonna be right. The day after, Kim called me. But when you have two women who once were friends who now have bitter feelings toward each other and are getting fed bull from every angle . . . the conversation was useless."

fuck if your album push back," Foxy rapped. "When it hit the streets, bitch, it's still wack / It still sound lame, my name still reign." It was not a friendly song. There was so much tension in the air that when Kim and her crew ran into Capone and his crew on February 25, 2001, outside the studios of Hot 97 FM in lower Manhattan, guns were pulled, 21 shots exchanged, and one man was wounded. Kim reportedly fled in a limousine and Foxy was nowhere to be seen. All the same, the next day's headlines screamed KIM VS. FOXY.

Miami Beach, 1998: Foxy's eating Key lime pie, talking about the Oliver Stone film she's been reading for with Puffy. Puff is supposed to play the football hero—the role that eventually went to Jamie Foxx—and Foxy would have been his woman (she did not, ultimately, get the part). "I respect Faith," Foxy says, mentioning Biggie's widow a little out of nowhere. "When you're the wife, you needn't worry. Anyone can be a girlfriend or a baby's mama. But there's only one wife."

Foxy was, for a time, engaged to Kurupt, a label-owning, West Coast-by-way-of-Philadelphia all-star, who was down with Snoop Dogg. Her platinum engagement ring was wide and jammed with diamonds. She got the ring in 1998, but the couple never got married. Foxy said back then if it was up to Kurupt, she'd already be married. "You know what?" she added. "We really love each other, but right now, what's really important to me is focusing on my album and getting my career straight."

Her career: Foxy knows that because she sells sex (and she will tell you that, straight out), when a female is sexual the impulse to stigmatize her is pretty automatic. "Harlots or Heroines?" was the question posed in a 1997 cover story in *The Source* about Foxy and Kim. "I remember this one article a girl wrote," Foxy says. "She titled it, 'Black Girl Lost.'" Foxy hated that. "I'm *not* lost," she says. "*My* grown ass? I know what the fuck I'm doing." Foxy knows people are awaiting her fall. Something bad must happen to the "slut." The "bitch" must have her come-uppance in the end.

The Firm: AZ, Foxy Brown and Nas.

"Inga has childlike qualities and womanlike qualities," says Foxy's mom. "I've taken heat from a lot of people about her image. I've had to defend her and myself. I'm not going to let anyone take advantage of her. I will fight for her tooth and nail. I have her back. Inga is my little girl."

In Miami all the girls wear bikini tops for a bra. We go to Clevelander's, which is kinda like TGIF's. Foxy likes the shrimp with pasta and marinara sauce. Cuban guys on scooters want to take a picture with Foxy Brown. Seeing her pose with them reminds me of a scene from 1960's *Where the Boys Are*, the movie where the fast girl gets pregnant and almost dies. (And the two girls who hold out—because they understand the politics of freaking but not fucking—get the fraternity boyfriends who love them.) There's not a feeling of bad-girl-gone-worse about Foxy, though. She's the child God blesses because she's got her own—but she's still figuring out what to do with it.

"I had an interview with some magazine," she recalls, "and the guy asked, 'Where do you wanna be in a couple of years?' I was like, 'I wanna go from silver to gold to platinum.' He saw me again recently and was like, 'Foxy, you've got your platinum.' I told him I want to go back to silver. I said, 'I have everything I want, but I wish I could go back.' I was happier being a virgin to the game. I went from having to talk to teachers at lunchtime to having to talk to accountants and lawyers. And to making people watch my money."

Rolling with Foxy does feel like being at some special kind of college where you learn about beats and rhymes and money and men and celebrity and hair and makeup and clothes and shoes. Where you cultivate attitude.

"So Fine" is playing as the waitresses rush around Clevelander's restaurant—*Keep my wrist laced / Cartier with the cage face*. A little later "Big Bad Mama" comes on at the eat spot. Foxy asks, "What is it, Foxy Day up in here?"

She's got on dark gray Iceberg hot pants, a matching Band-Aid of a top. Gucci slides. Platinum Rolex. "In the beginning," Foxy says, "I was in Chanel, Prada, and Gucci all the time. But now that my mom comanages me, I'm learning to spend wisely. You can be made today and broke tomorrow. I'm not trying to be broke." With that in mind, she purchased a brownstone in Brooklyn.

Joe Sherman, Foxy's bodyguard, is six foot six inches, 340 pounds. Very nice guy. He says to me one day in the lobby of Miami's Tides Hotel, like it's a secret: "I've thought about it. If someone ever took a shot at her, would I jump in front of her and take the bullet? I've thought about it, and I would. Because I've lived. She hasn't. She *thinks* she has."

"She's supposed to be this extreme bitch," says Lighty. "But if she was a dude she would just be taken as a matter of fact. It's a double standard. We're all rude, we all wake up on the wrong side of the bed. People harp on it more because she's a female. No one says anything when Q-Tip or Meth or DMX curses someone out or is late to a video shoot. It's just accepted." He pauses. "You be sixteen and be chased by Puffy Combs and Russell Simmons and Chris Lighty—see how you handle it."

On her last album, 1998's *Chyna Doll*, Foxy remade Howard Johnson's 1982 smash "So Fine" with Next singing the hook. "If we skip Prada / You gets nada" is what she said on the song.

I ask if she could ever date a guy with no money. "A nigga that *appreciates* me, I could. The brother with no money is gonna spend time," she says. "The guy with money is gonna be like, 'I just gave you a thousand dollars to go shopping. What the fuck is you calling me for?' Then I'm sitting around with a bunch of gifts and a nigga be long gone. You ain't *got* to buy me. I have my own."

Yes, she does. But Foxy's a fast girl. A girl who looks at her lips, her teeth, her waist, her ass, her legs, her breasts and sees that they are what people, what men, have always responded to. So why not use them, as her old girlfriend Lil' Kim says, to "Get Money"? Foxy was seven years old when Janet Jackson hit with "Control" and "What Have You Done for Me Lately." Five when Madonna broke it down with "Material Girl." No wonder she's got such fabulous arrogance. No wonder she's so consumed with consuming. Foxy's the kind of girl who believes that financial independence (and the constant display thereof) might just bring about emotional independence—but grown as she is, she hasn't hit the big wall yet. The one that's tagged IT ISN'T SO.

What she does know (and what is true) is that attitude is nine-tenths of the law, that shock wins, that profanity is the new norm, that as long as you can pretend to yourself that being a girl with a guy's macho mentality is possible, you can play—and it's fun—but then you fuck around and *like* a guy. You hear something massive and embracing in his voice, feel all the things you never felt as a baby girl in his arms, and then you are—not lost—but mad at him for being stupid and sexist and human. A victim himself of

genes and environment and these wary, changing, sexual times. Mostly you're mad at your own life or whatever it is about life in general that makes you need anything from anyone at any time. So you dis dependence. Go all the fly places bad girls do. Do a remake of Gwen Guthrie's song "Ain't Nothin' Going On But the Rent."

But I have to ask her, since it is a federal law, why she isn't rapping about world peace. "To me, that's normal," she says. "I do things to keep people talking. To bring issues that the average female MC ain't raising. To talk about things average females are talking about. Not even so much about niggas. Females *been* fighting for respect, we've been fighting for equality since back in the Bessie Smith days. Millie Jackson, all that. It's like, why can you get mad at me and say, 'Fuck you,' and I can't say, 'Fuck *you*.' I want to be the type of rapper that stands up for *that*. You have a certain type of rapper that stands up for world peace. You have rappers that stand up more for African-American culture. You have people that are just into party music, you have rappers who are street. I'm just Foxy."

Like she spits on "Niggas Might," a hot track from *Chyna Doll* with Nas all over the hook: "Don't come to me / With no housewife shit / I ain't no spouse-type bitch." Even with that engagement ring on her finger, Foxy's a girl caught in the crosshairs of the new.

"Brown-skinned bitches in a Hummer!" Foxy's talking about her video for the ridiculously catchy single "Hot Spot" from *Chyna Doll*, an album that ended up certified platinum, but because her buzz in New York City was almost nil, tastemakers and hip hop heads acted as if it was wack and still gathering dust on store shelves. By then Lighty and Foxy would have gone their separate ways.

We've limoed over to Bal Harbour Shops, where the people in Gucci know her name, where the people in Prada parade around her with shoes and purses for fall. The old ladies in Chanel act snobby toward her until Lighty pulls out his gold Amex (already smoking hot from all the action). Said ladies—foundation cracking, matte lipstick fading—smile and bring Foxy what Foxy wants, which is mostly shoes, size six and a half for her, seven and a half for Mom back home in Brooklyn.

Judith Marchand divorced early and raised Inga and her brothers Anton and Gavin mostly by herself. "My mother wasn't strict," Foxy says. "She would leave notes for me and my two brothers. One day I'd have the dishes—we'd rotate days. Everything was organized. Wherever we went, we had to call. She'd never sweat us."

"Right now I'm in awe of my daughter," says Mrs. Marchand. "Inga was very bright. She's been in gifted programs since preschool. She kept you on your toes. She was always reading and talking. We had a special relationship. She's my only daughter. When she got to be a teenager, we went through changes. She was getting to know herself. I call it her creative period."

Between Louis Vuitton and Sergio Rossi, I ask what she would tell a girl who said, "Foxy, my man is tripping." First she allows that she's not the one to be talking. "I need all the advice I can get," she says, and pauses. Then she takes a stab at it: "Basically, don't chase. Let it go. It'll come back. I got that from my mother. If that person isn't putting in the time and love and effort he should be, you need to back off for a minute.

"You need to be like, Why is it every time I go off on a business trip, I can think that much of you to go out and pick up something, but you go away for two weeks and you ain't even thinking about me? All your friends are coming home with things for their girls and their wives, and you're just like, Oh, baby, I didn't know what you liked. You know

says Grier, "Foxy Brown represents the women in my family who taught me how to be independent. We fight for ourselves, for our family, and we fight for our man."

The Tides Hotel looks like a Calvin Klein wedding cake: white with squares of mauve and pale blue. Umbrella'd tables. You can forget how hot it is when you're sitting in the hotel sipping lemonade made with sparkling water. Ninety-one degrees at 3:15 P.M. Lighty is on the phone again: "Tell them South Beach is on some *Art Deco* shit. These aren't like the usual hotels we stay at. Everything is small."

At South Beach Studios inside the Marlin Hotel, the blue walls are stenciled with gold stars. Nine Inch Nails and Jimmy Buffett have recorded here. This is where Hanson did "MMMBop." The Violator crew comes down here to get away from New York and L.A. and Atlanta. Not as many distractions. Foxy says in L.A., there's a celebrity on every corner.

It's time to go to the studio. Foxy's hyped about it, but resisting. Besides, we want to talk about guys.

Foxy was seven years old when Janet Jackson hit with "What Have You Done for Me Lately." Five when Madonna broke it down with "Material Girl." No wonder she's so consumed with consuming.

what I mean? You need to be like, Let me step back for a little while. You do *you*. Come back when you're ready to do me."

So until he's ready, you toss them titties around. Shake that ass—but watch yourself. Make that money. Cultivate that brassy soul-sister shit everybody applauds you for. Yes. Foxy Brown is a *star*. Be nasty. Be classy. Be extravagant. Be everybody's fantasy. Be Millie, be Pearl, be Whitney, be Diahann, be Donna, be Janet, be like your girl Kim. Stare down the old rules. Run with the big dogs. Hey, soul sister! Be superstrong, supersexy, supertalented, supersatisfied. Be supergirl.

Be like Pam "Original Foxy" Grier. Foxy handed me, at some point, a video of the 1975 film *Friday Foster*, starring Pam Grier and *Homicide*'s Yaphet Kotto. "Brings Foxy into the focus of danger!" screamed the box copy. Foxy says Pam and her are buddies. That Pam calls and tells her when she's doing well. And tells her when she's fucking up. "For me,"

You didn't quite answer me before. Could you date a guy who's not paid?

I'd *rather* meet someone who's cool and not in the limelight. But when you do it—and I've tried—it doesn't balance itself out. It's always like four o'clock in the morning and I'm getting calls from Russell Simmons and [the guy'll be] waking up like, "Niggas is trying to get some *sleep*"—you know? We can't go to the movies unless it's "Ohmigod, it's Foxy." People want autographs. He'll be feeling, like, left out. And I wouldn't want to feel that way. I totally understand.

My first love, Rayshawn, he's a part of Junior M.A.F.I.A., but he's not in the limelight. And for a while we could keep it together. But then my fame just *went*. And that kinda messed it up. He was reminding me, 24-7, *I was with you when you didn't have shit*. And I was like, I'm trying to be with you and you ain't *got* shit. But I'm trying to *still* get mine. It didn't work out. But I ain't looking for nothing. I'm still young and I got a lot of time. I ain't in no rush.

Lauryn Hill once said that a guy she was going out with felt like he never had to tell her she was special or dope, because the whole world was telling her that every day.

I never had that problem. But I have been in a lot of situations where I felt like I was ridin' for niggas, like no matter what, that's my nigga, I'm riding for them no matter what, and then they're like, "Ahh . . . yeah, she's my [shrugs]"—and that hurts. That shit is so mean. You have no idea.

I've been hearing that you're going out with DMX.

You know what? D is a real special friend. He's been there for me through hard times and I've been there for him through hard times.

Is there any reason for anyone to believe anything could ever happen between you and DMX?

[Grins.] Nah, we're just friends.

year-old to be herself. Foxy Brown's not a bad girl; she really is a good girl. I thought it was fun and games what she does, but she works hard. She's using the talent she's been blessed with. I respect her. I don't always agree with her—what mother agrees with everything her daughter does?"

If Foxy is fast, if she fucks who she wants when she wants, if she rides on niggas as well as for them, I don't wonder what went wrong, I wonder, as I have been wondering forever, why when she does it she's super-wrong, but when the brothers she's boning do it, it's cool as shit?

So is it all good for Foxy Brown? Not if you listen carefully to songs like "The Letter" from Foxy's remarkable 2001 album *Broken Silence*. It's part of a tradition of hip hop suicide songs. Biggie recorded one; so did the Geto Boys. Eminem flirts with the subject all the time. But this is the first such song by a woman, and also somehow the most disturbing. Colored girls don't consider suicide—they cry, they pull it together, they keep moving toward the rainbow. Right? *Broken Silence* is an intensely personal album, the best of Foxy's young career. Many of the lines seem to have been written with her old ex-friend

Is it bad to be what the brothers call a hoochie mama? Or is the hoochie moment an awesome one? An instant of true equality between man and woman. Love, for a brief, glittery moment, supreme.

So you and Andre Rison did a song together on the NFL album?

We did a song called "Burning Down the House."

That's a little controversial by itself, considering his and Left Eye's dramas.

It was his idea. He came to me and asked me to do the record and the song was crazy. But he's got a little bit of rapping skills. He's kinda all right.

I hear he was checking for you.

Yeah. I heard that, too.

I ask Foxy's mom if she'd want a 15-year-old to grow up and become Foxy Brown, and she says: "Foxy is Foxy. I'd prefer someone to wanna be like Inga. I would tell a fifteen-

in mind. And Foxy's much-hyped beef with Kim might help sell a few extra CDs. Unless of course somebody really gets hurt, in which case it'll sell a *lot* of extra CDs.

"I really don't know how it started," Brown told *MTV News* a few days after Kim got caught up in the crossfire. She said that Russell Simmons tried to make peace with Lil' Kim's camp, who "weren't responsive." Still, Foxy persevered. "I want to call a truce. I want to have a sit-down with Kim," she said, reaching out to a long-lost friend through the all-consuming media machine. "I don't care what it is. Let's just end it. We can even do a collaboration. We're bigger than this. If it has to start with me, let it start with me."

There is a sense in which even this heartfelt plea is surreal. Perhaps it would be different if these were men trying to settle their differences. Beef is considered some sort of male right/rite. When women do it, it's somehow less serious, not ladylike. Even Noreaga, who rhymed with Foxy on "Bang Bang," seemed to take the conflict with Kim lightly. "We ain't got no beef, we just representin'," he said, a few months before bullets started flying. "Let the females cat fight, and whatever happens, happens."

On her new album Foxy turns personal drama into art. "Basically," she raps, "I'm the female Pac."

We've seen male bodies drop for good—in hip hop and around the way. We resist imagining what happens—artistically and actually—when female anger, so often reserved for wayward boyfriends and absent parents, is shoved at another "sister." Whatever happens, happens, indeed. Perhaps Nore reduces women to cats because to imagine true human female anger is frightening even to the most cold of cool-ass MCs.

I've mostly seen Foxy rocking purple eyeshadow, skinny super-plucked eyebrows, blue mascara. Flowing black hair down the middle of her back. Fly-ass weave-o-rama. Hazel contact lenses. Deep dark glossy lipstick. Foxy's a big pop superstar baby. Don't sleep. In South Beach, where everybody's at least close to cool and good-looking, brothas stared her down, boys begged for a snapshot. Girls nervously approached. Graying men verged on cardiac arrest. They stumbled, even, trying to get a look at Foxy Brown, hot child in the city. Is it bad to be what the brothers call a hoochie mama? Or is the hoochie moment an awesome one? An instant of true equality between man and woman. Power testing power on a rough but level field. Love, for a brief, glittery moment, supreme.

I've seen Foxy, too, though—right before her VIBE cover shoot—with no makeup, weave in a lopsided ponytail, old jean shorts and a tan tube top washed too many times. In so many ways, she's a total girl. No doubt, even at that moment, the most beautifullest thing in this world.

I am a
diamond-cluster
hustler Queen
Bitch supreme
bitch kill a
nigga for my
nigga by any
means bitch
murder scene
bitch

KIM

what price queen bee?

by Rob Marriott

onsider Kimberly Jones, exalted nasty girl turned glamour baby, sitting quietly in Daddy's House, Sean "Puffy" Combs' midtown Manhattan recording studio, sporting a shoulder-length platinum-blond ponytail with eyebrows dyed to match, sitting cross-legged in her favorite jeans decorated with ostrich feathers. The 4-foot-11 rap star stands up to kiss Puffy's mother, Janice Combs, good-bye. "Thank you, Mama, for coming to see me," she says in her sweetest little-girl voice, blinking her lashes, smiling from ear to ear. She's ready to enter the booth and lay down vocals for a track on what will become her sophomore album, the first one she's recorded since her lover and mèntor, the black genius Notorious B.I.G., was shot to death.

A lurching, uneven beat engulfs the studio. Lil' Kim, now in character, delivers the prototypical raunch that's made her so infamous: "Just lay me on this bed and give me some head / Got the camcorder laying on the drawer where he can't see / Can't wait to show my girls / He sucked the piss out my pussy . . ."

Lil' Kim's mythology is about pussy, really: the power, pleasure, and politics of it, the murky mixture of emotions and commerce that sex has become circa 2000. Like a priestess out of some ancient matriarchy she makes songs that deify it, demanding that her male (and female) public respect, revere, and glorify the sacred punaney.

She is, perhaps, the greatest public purveyor of the female hustle this side of Madonna, successfully parlaying ghetto pain, pomp, and circumstance into mainstream fame and fortune. So much for the myth.

Kim's reality, on the other hand, is about love. It is her true currency. She trades in love the way Mary J. Blige trades in survival, Lauryn Hill in consciousness, and Missy Elliot in invention. The entirety of her appeal has much to do with the fact that love—carnal, familial, self-destructive, or spiritual—is the root of who Kim is. Pussy is just the most marketable aspect of it. Kim gives and craves love equally, her devotees ranging from luxury-tank-pushing street niggas who lust for her to transvestites whose masquerades she inspires, to the silent legions of dispossessed women—stripping, ho'ing, and hustling—to whom she has given an urgent, uncensored voice.

Her capacity to calculate what you want her to be and then become it—a skill she honed in the streets of Brooklyn—makes her damn near interactive. Raunchy, vulnerable, demure. Mae West. Bessie Smith. Lady Godiva. Blue-eyed Barbarella, aqua-haired ghetto mermaid—she's the virtual black girl staring at you from billboards and magazine covers in a dazzling array of guises.

But as her stature as pop and fashion icon grows, as her hair and eyes take on new colors, the raw street survivalist she once signified must now be perceived through shiny layers of artifice. At times it's difficult to determine whether she's the hustler (subversive manipulator) or the hustled (sacrificial black girl, complicit in her own exploitation). It's precisely her ability to thrive within this web of cosmic dilemmas that makes her one of the last truly charismatic figures left in the aging machinery of hip pop.

Kim's unquenchable charisma is the result of her lifelong struggle with and for love.

lash back to the dawning age of hip hop, 1980 or so. Imagine six-year-old Kimberly in her mama's bedroom playing with a black Barbie—one of a large, multicultured collection of dolls and accessories—in her parents' Bed-Stuy, Brooklyn, apartment. You hear loud bickering in the background as cherubic Kim, covered in her mother's makeup, leafs through fashion magazines with a pair of scissors. She cuts out the models' eyes and lips. Standing in front of a mirror she places their eyes against her eyes, their lips against her lips. It begins there: Kimberly Jones discovers Lil' Kim.

"I watched *Mahogany* over and over again," she says. "In fact, my mom kinda looked like Mahogany."

Two years later her cousin Renee watches Kim dancing around the apartment, belting out radio tunes. "Kim is gonna be something," she predicts. Gifted at sports, Kimberly wins medals at the Colgate Women's Games in track and field, while attending the Queen of All Saints Catholic School in Fort Greene, Brooklyn. Her mother, Ruby Jones, then a fashion-conscious department store clerk, remembers Kim running with her cousins and brother, the only girl among all the little boys: "She was always independent.

She was always aggressive. I never worried about leaving her. I knew she could take care of herself."

Her father, Leon Jones, was a dark brown man with a penchant for Member's Only jackets and Marc Buchanans. A bus driver and member of the Air Force Reserve, he was a provider and disciplinarian. "My father was kind of an outcast in his family," Kim recalls. "His sister was light-skinned so she was favored. I think he kinda brought that to his children. He was so sweet when I was a baby. I would jump into his arms when he would come home." Kim rarely speaks to him now. "He's a good person," she says. "But he has a lot of fucked-up ways."

Divorce tears the family apart in 1984. Kim and her older brother must fend for themselves emotionally. Ruby Jones: "I wasn't financially ready, but I had to choose between leaving and my sanity." Heavy legal bills force Ruby into a transient life; living out of her car, from couch to couch, Kim in tow. They stay with a friend in New Rochelle where Kim attends Jefferson Elementary, a lonely black girl in a class full of white kids. Kim: "That's when I realized there was still prejudiced people. I beat up these girls that were coming at me and I got suspended. But even then I didn't hold a grudge. I did well, though, and they wanted me to stay, but I left after a year."

Shortly thereafter Leon wins custody of Kim. Blaming herself and struggling with her self-esteem, Ruby falls in with a bad crowd, losing herself in the smoky music of Marvin Gaye and Gladys Knight. Kim returns to her father's house angry, regularly talking to herself. "I would tell myself stories. It would make me feel better. He thought I was crazy. I knew I wasn't."

There is serious tension at home. During one argument Kim's father calls her a bitch. Hearing the word from his mouth cuts her to the core. He throws away her Barbie pool set cause she is making a mess, prompting Kim to call her mother. "I was like, 'He is such a fucking asshole!'" Kim says. "My mother was like, 'What did you say?'"

Flashing police lights dance across the windows. Leon Jones sits bleeding, looking at the stranger his daughter has become. They had been fighting. ("My father would fight me like a man," Kim remembers.) Amid the tussling, she picked up a pair of scissors and stabbed him in the shoulder. Kim: "The police were there and said, 'Well, what do you want to do with her, Mr. Jones? We can put her in a home.' And honestly, I just wanted to be away from him so I said, 'I wanna go.' He looked really sad, like he wanted to cry. He turned to them and said, 'No, no I'll handle it.'"

Kim's father and his new wife bring her to a therapist. Kim, now 12 years old, reads a racial tinge in the white psychiatrist's questioning. "You know what, lady?" she says. "I

don't like you." When her father chides her, she curses him. "Some people might think that was fucked up of me," Kim reflects, "but I didn't know how else to let my father know that I wasn't a stupid girl."

It's 1988. Some older girls take Kim out. She's thinking it's some kid's birthday party, instead she finds herself at Manhattan's Latin Quarter nightclub in its heyday. Underage but welcomed by the older hustlers, she witnesses the dark extravagances of the drug game. Kim sees cats dressed in thick gold ropes, custom-tailored Louis Vuitton- and Gucci-style leathers made at Dapper Dan's, the infamous clothier of Mike Tyson, L.L., and a generation of young capitalists growing rich from the crack trade. Kim and the older girls roll with big money players, cats pushing Rolls-Royces, heading to the Rooftop, an uptown after-hours spot where the glamorous niggas showed out.

Kim soon runs away from home to live with her Panamanian boyfriend. She still talks to herself sometimes. "I feel that voice inside to this day," Kim says. "I think that was God speaking to me, but I wasn't listening. I was wild, doing what I felt I had to do."

Kim's lessons in hustling begin. "At that time I always had a man to take care of me," she remembers. "Sometimes if I thought I could get some more out of a guy, I'd sleep with him. And I got kinda caught in that mentality." She starts transporting drugs. Lives from boyfriend to boyfriend, learning hard lessons, getting betrayed. "I would be doing it out of love," says Kim about muling for her men. "I mean, sometimes there would be some other guy that could give me more money, but I would stay with the guy I was with. And they would say, if I ever got locked up I'ma do this and that for you, but when I almost got caught the nigga seemed like he didn't really give a fuck."

Imagine Kim, black-haired, brown eyed, flat-chested, chocolate, walking down Brooklyn's Fulton Street on her way home from her job as a clerk at Bloomingdale's in Manhattan. On this day she meets the man who would change not just her hustle, but her entire life. Sitting on a garbage can in front of a liquor store on St. James Place, a young Christopher Wallace strikes up a conversation with her. Kim: "We were just there talking. He was not the kinda guy I was used to talking to. I would deal with niggas with money. But he had this confidence about him. This was around the time he did that Mary J. remix. He was the biggest manipulator in the world. Later he got me to rhyme for him. After I rhymed he said, 'I'm fucking with you, Ma. We gonna make some money.'"

Kim finds a father figure in the Notorious B.I.G. "It was everything I wanted in a relationship," she says. "Biggie gave me his keys and I remember thinking, he wasn't doing this for other broads." She sleeps with him on his single twin bed in a tiny corner room in his mother's apartment. "We would lie together talking about what we was gonna do the next day," Kim recalls. "He was always romantic. When you don't have money, you can think of more romantic things to do. One Valentine's Day I went over to his house and he said he was gonna buy a bunch of roses and put them on the bed, but he didn't have enough money. So he wanted to put a bunch of pennies on the bed instead, in the shape of a heart, but he thought I'd be mad."

By '95, Biggie's plans for her become clear. He and Lance "Understanding" Rivera, a former drug dealer turned music executive, form Kim's first group, Junior M.A.F.I.A. and release their gold-selling *Conspiracy* album on the Undeas Recordings label in association with Atlantic Records (the musical home of Aretha Franklin and Led Zeppelin). Her performances on the hit "Player's Anthem" and the million-selling smash "Get Money" create enough buzz to make Un and Big start working on her solo album.

They begin recording her seminal debut, *Hard Core*. Around that time, Biggie describes Kim as "the dopest female MC that's coming out ever. She gets busy like a nigga, that's why I like her style. Hard shit! She speaks on suckin' niggas, shooting niggas, real shit that real bitches do that they are just scared to talk about—just how I came out, on some real shit."

"Kim grew up in the studio," says Un. "It's like she took all the bricks, all the heartache, all the pain, and used them as stepping-stones. We started getting real good records."

They shoot a promotional poster of Lil' Kim with her legs akimbo, displaying the outlines of her punaney through leopard-skin panties. Her primordial matriarchal pose provides the first glimpse of Kim's specific brand of alchemy. Prey playing predator, doe-eyed lamb dressed in a lacy wolf getup. She is an empowered sexual vixen, wielding the mysterious power of pussy like a weapon. She becomes the self-described "Queen Bitch," claiming the word she once hated hearing from her father. "You wanna be this Queen Bee," she rhymes on one song, "But you can't be / That's why you're mad at me."

And her struggles with love continue. Kim busts in on Biggie in bed with other women. Then Kim watches Big marry Faith Evans nine days after meeting her. "I was so hurt," says Kim. Un says he used to take care of her when her relationship with Biggie turned abusive. "I used to even want to beat Big up when he beat her," says the entertainment entrepreneur. "I used to always tell Kim, 'Yo, whatever you do, don't give Big no pussy.' She never understood why. Because Big had a mentality, in terms of control, that was powerful over women. I used to tell her, 'Mentally he will destroy you.' And he did. Once upon a time, she was on the edge. If niggas wasn't there to pull her back. . . ."

"I never brought another man around Biggie," says Kim. "I never felt the need to fuck with another man. Even though Biggie may have been doing things on his own, I felt like if I showed real love, one day I'd win my prize.

"When you're in love with someone," Kim continues, her voice dropping to a whisper, "you find yourself going back to them. You find yourself still doing stuff for them. You find yourself having sex with them even though you told yourself you wasn't going to."

In March 1997, Biggie is shot to death in Los Angeles. Kim is tormented by his memory every day. "When he died, it was like the record skipped," says Kim. "God shook me to let me know what he gave me." The title of her second album, *The Notorious K.I.M.*, is a further attempt by Kim to create a symbiosis with her mentor, like a moon to his sun. She plays Isis to his Osiris, the queen rising from his ashes. "I just want to stay with him," she says. "I just want him to know that I loved him."

While Faith, his mother, and his children inherit Big's estate, Kim shoulders the burdens of his musical legacy. "It's been on me for the last three years," she says of her obligations to the Junior M.A.F.I.A. family. Kim shares her Englewood, New Jersey, home with extended crew: L'il Cease, Damion "D-Roc" Butler, C-Gutta, and Larce Banger.

Kim and Un Rivera no longer speak, although she remains contractually obligated to Undeas for another four albums. "The split with Un was a little bit of everything," explains her manager, Hillary Weston. "After Big died, he didn't stay true. Un had his priorities and he gave the M.A.F.I.A. a shitty deal. It was not just the business thing. Un really hurt her."

Pushing the release date of her album back was the result of the contractual chaos left in the wake of Biggie's death (both Biggie's widow and Un own a piece of Kim's music). There was also a boycott against Atlantic Records because of the label's perceived lack of marketing support for Lil' Cease's 1999 album, *The Wonderful World of Cease A Leo*, and a series of mishaps that culminated in bootleggers getting hold of seven songs. "It was an inside job, but I won't mention no names," Kim says. "But that is why they are suffering now. It don't matter 'cause I got all new songs."

Back at Daddy's House, Kim's newly completed "Suck My Dick!," a transgressive response to male cat-calling, bangs up the studio. Cease and C-Gutta are on a roll, cracking jokes about the size of a Bad Boy employee's head. Kim laughs, released for the moment from the intense pressure she feels. "We're like a family now," she says. "I'm like the mother. D-Roc is like the father, Hillary is the aunt, C-Gutta is like the uncle, the M.A.F.I.A. are like the children, and Puffy's like that uncle who ain't shit, but we love his stank ass." With Big gone and Un out of the picture, Puffy is the project's surrogate executive. Mostly, he's trying to push Kim to finish.

"What are we going to do about getting a singer for the 'Fuck You Better' song?" Puff asks. "Something will come to me by tomorrow," Kim says, shaking her head to a number of suggestions.

"Kim is a true artist," says Puffy. "The reason why the album's so late is because sometimes she'll go on a dry spell for three months. She's a perfectionist. Sometimes she's lazy and I have to crack that whip." Kim smiles. "I do be lazy," she says. "I can't front. But you know what it is? I'm a dreamer." Plus she was going through problems: "personal and business."

It's decided that "Suck My Dick!" is too raw to include on the album. Instead it will be a white label 12-inch released to DJs. The X-rated blast plays like a sequel to her cameo on Mobb Deep's epic "Quiet Storm" remix. After hearing the track Prodigy of Mobb Deep confides: "You keeping my girl in the streets, where she belongs."

Lil' Kim with Big Poppa and Puff.

But Kim is no longer just in the streets. She is fabulous now, darling of the fashion elite, a card-carrying member of the glittering ghettorati. Her hairpieces are custom cut. Her blue eyes are hand-painted laminated contacts costing $1,250 a pair. "You could buy a car with the pieces Kim buys," says her rock dealer, Jacob the Jeweler. She counts Donatella Versace, Giorgio Armani, and *Vogue*'s Andre Léon Talley among her friends and associates. Prodigy's concern—that hip hop's raw bitch will be lost to that illusory world of glitz—is one Kim weighs carefully these days. "All I can do is remain myself," she reasons. "There's two sides to me and I can get ghetto red and let a nigga have it or let a girl have it. But I can also be civilized enough to deal with the Caucasians that are fabulous."

Kim knows what works and for whom. Inside the ritzy midtown Manhattan eatery Mr. Chow, it's one of *those* events: the steaming plates of lobster, the clinking glasses, the murmur of aimless banter. The heavy-lidded beautiful people throwing their heads back in forced laughter. Missy, Maxwell, Puffy, and MTV's Ananda Lewis await the guests of honor: M.A.C. spokeswomen Mary J. Blige and L'il Kim. Above the crowd hangs an oversized, heavily airbrushed photograph from the ad campaign for M.A.C.'s new lipstick, Viva Glam III (the proceeds of whose sale would raise some $4 million for AIDS charities in a single year).

The ad shows Mary and Kim as twin divas draped in gold, surrounded by several near-naked models painted with kisses. Similar models are hired to stand outside Mr. Chow and their bare flesh shivers in the February air as they wait to escort that platinum bitch into a dark fluttering mob of international paparazzi.

Kim enters wearing a Misa Hylton-Brim custom-made leopard-print minidress, her blond flip falling just past her shoulders, and steps with a dramatic pause onto the red carpet. Lil' Kim is on her game and the flashes eat her alive. Surrounded by bodyguards and onlookers and photographers and handlers, she is ushered into the restaurant and presented to the president of M.A.C. cosmetics, John Demsey, a distinguished-looking white-haired man. She offers her hand. He grips her fist, soul brother–like. They exchange wide smiles in the flashes of light, dollar signs glistening in their eyes.

In the treacherous world of glamour where the rules are always changing and the racism is in the details, Kim's blond wigs and subtle nose contouring gives the army of stylists, photographers, and editors permission to erase race from her equation. It is the unspoken price of entry. "I'm so obsessed with her hardcore sexuality," says David LaChapelle, who shot Kim for her August 2000 VIBE cover story. "Kim is like Betty Boop meets Marilyn Monroe, hanging out on 125th Street in Harlem, about to go downtown to Fifth Avenue to shop."

Then comes the disturbing moment when Kim's image is unrecognizable as a young black woman. *Vanity Fair* photographer Annie Leibovitz says of the portrait of Kim that she included in her and Susan Sontag's collection *Women,* "Sociologically, [this picture of Lil' Kim] is really fascinating because she is not only dressing up to be a woman, but she's dressing up to be a white woman, with that blond wig."

Kim dismisses any suggestion that she wants to be white. "I'm a black girl," she says firmly. "All we try to do is give people something to hold on to and then move on." But if there's a tendency to lean in a light-skinned direction, Kim is complicit. "I think I'm beautiful because of my heart," she says, but her choices speak of a longing for mainstream appeal. "Halle Berry, Sally Richardson, Stacy Dash, Jada Pinkett? I used to wish I look like them motherfuckers!"

Smoothing down the serrated edges of her race and class is not the only adjustment made for fashion, and Kim is not immune to the less-than-subtle suggestions. In a vanity industry, her breasts, or lack thereof, quickly became an issue. "It started out as a joke," explains Kim. Hector Extravaganza, the furrier, would size her up. "Girl, you be rocking them pictures," Hector would say. "But how the hell you gonna be modeling with no fucking titties! You are so fucking flat-chested! You better get yourself some titties!" Kim reflects, "I laughed at first. But then I went home and really thought about it. I went to the best, most expensive doctor available, but that was the most pain I ever felt in my life."

It's nighttime in the heart of Bed-Stuy, March 9, 2000. Three years to the moment Big was gunned down in Los Angeles, there's a raucous murmur on St. James between Gates Avenue and Fulton Street, his old stomping grounds. Junior M.A.F.I.A. is shooting the video for "Biggie," their tribute song on his multiplatinum-selling posthumous record, *Born Again.* The block is lit up in a surreal mix of orange and blue. Expeditions and Navigators and Black 500

Benzes crowd the block. A sizable gathering of Brooklynites materializes: Cripped-out, Blooded-up, plaited, dyed, fried, and dreaded. Inside a trailer Kim and crew sit in the dark, hugging up Biggie's six-year-old daughter, T'yanna, quietly reeling from a recent betrayal by someone Kim considered a close friend. Betrayal, the counterpoint to love, has also been a theme in her life. She smiles through her pain and anger. "I hurt real hard, you know. When I was young, I'd take it there. You get stabbed. You get shot. I didn't give a fuck," she says, the frustration rising in her voice. "But I got to think about my actions now. I got everybody depending on me now. I got kids who depend on me. I got my family depending on me. I got God depending on me."

Outside, children and acquaintances crowd around the darkened trailer hoping for a glimpse of the starlet. Wearing a tight white T-shirt with tiny rips at the chest, aquamarine Versace boots to go with her wig of the same color, and skintight shorts with dangling straps, Kim descends into the anxious crowd—a tumult of neighbors and fans of every age. Klieg lights swing wildly. Little girls squeal her name and beg for a hug. Kim is lifted to her pedestal atop a gleaming white Cadillac Escalade. Biggie's voice rises up from powerful stereo speakers, booming and echoing down the block. Kim gyrates, twists, and pops, opening her legs and bouncing in an intricate pantomime. Tonight, she is the queen of all lost girls, looking ghetto angelic, resurrecting her king. Once the shot is done, the lights go down and security engulfs her, whisking her into a white Navigator.

From the moment she entered the stage, Lil' Kim was a heavy dose of estrogen injected into a particularly male space. Surrounded by the rest of the Junior M.A.F.I.A., a set of true BK hardrocks, Kim armed herself with the female hustler's womanness. Her fluid teasing and cajoling on sexified tracks like the classic "Get Money" were entirely feminine but, as she reminded us on Bad Boy's 1997 mega-hit "It's All About the Benjamins," she could still "kick shit like a nigga do." Kim rapped with force and verve without resorting to the butch gesturing of lesser MCs. She'd been blessed with tremendous gifts: ghetto-honed candor, an authentic personal history of struggle, and a way with cuss words. While true microphone womanhood had been achieved before (Kim followed squarely in the tradition of Salt-N-Pepa), never had such a load of rhyme skills, femininity, and sex come together in one dynamic package.

Like Nina Simone or Millie Jackson, Kim's appeal was in her rawness. She could be a willing participant in male fantasizing, could even get a little too crass. She played to a gangsta's narcissism, spoke to his masked vulnerabilities. In lieu of old-timey courtship and love, she offered the prostitute's alternative: mutual exploitation.

For women living on the fringes of society—victims of sexual abuse, misbegotten daddy's girls, and others who survived with limited options—Kim articulated specific feelings of betrayal, contempt, and hope that had not been voiced in quite that way before. She spoke about and embodied the ambition and desperation of women who aren't above using their body as a weapon. Even women who rejected the recklessness of Kim's attitudes toward sex and violence could be inspired by her bold confrontations with male power: "Now you wanna pistol whip me / Pull out your nine, while I cock on mine / Yeah what nigga? I ain't got time for this." Hers was a new womanhood, rife with contradictions, but dynamic nonetheless.

In contrast, Kim's ongoing conflict with her former schoolyard friend Foxy Brown seems sadly predictable. It started as an aesthetic battle between two women occupying a very similar space. (According to the laws of physics, as Lauryn Hill once pointed out, "Two MCs can't occupy the same place at the same time.") It turned into a war of insults over who has true claim to the gangstress throne. "They get into character," Chuck D observed, "and they get caught up in the paradigm." The rivalry blossomed into the Sunday afternoon gunfight between entourages that left one man wounded in February 2001.

Some trace the static back to a certain sheer designer pantsuit that both women wore in the photo shoots for their debut CDs. Then on the song "Paper Chase" from Jay-Z's 1998 album *Vol. 2: Hard Knock Life*, Foxy delivered her rhyme with a timbre and cadence that was eerily similar to Kim's. On Lil' Cease's "Play Around" (the first single on Kim's Queen Bee imprint), Kim said her verse, then Puffy added a subliminal response: ". . . and stop trying to sound like her too."

And there were other barbs, both real and imagined. So much of the MC's art consists of putting rivals in their place that hard feelings have a way of escalating. But the whole melodramatic episode has only succeeded in diminishing the shine of both women. Most of us are weary of the violence. Kim and Foxy's conflict seems like a tragic mirroring of the fatal Biggie/Tupac confrontation, regressing from friendship to rivalry to mortal combat.

Where is the love?

Imagine Kimberly Jones, survivalist turned surrogate mother, baby-sitting D-Roc's son, little Damion. She's happy to be home, not working for once. "In this world, money is power, but if I was in the land of paradise, love would be power to me," she says. "You know what I mean? But in this world you can't get nothing off of love. People don't show you love back. But if I can get a Queen Bee island one day, love would be power."

Little Damion starts to cry. "Come 'ere pookie pumpkin," Kim says, soothing his tears and promising him they'll go roller-skating later. "I think God has a plan for me," she says. "It's revealing itself slowly. There are some people who don't understand, but I know by the end of my fulfillment they will."

To those of us who've made it their business to examine the ritual terrain of African America, hip hop has proven to be a kind of trickster god. A come-again-go-again deity committed solely to the perpetual transformation of self. As with all matters of magic, it's impossible to know the deity in full or to accurately predict when and where it will manifest. The deity chooses when, how, and through whom it speaks.

Put it this way: we know hip hop when we feel it. But who could have predicted Grandmaster Flash or Rakim or Eazy-E or Tupac Shakur? We recognize the chosen because the deity demands so much from them, great sacrifices of mind and body, courage and audacity, and full-out submission to the hurricane winds of change. Hip hop can be unmerciful. Trespass against it, betray it to commercial forces and the holy funk will leave your ass, exhausted, uninspired, incapable of articulating the rhythmic truth that once came so naturally.

> For I am the first and the last,
> I am the honored one and the scorned one,
> I am the whore and the holy one,
> I am shame and boldness,
> I am shameless; I am ashamed.
> I am the judgment and the acquittal.
> —"Ancient Whore Wisdom from the Whore-Mother Goddess" excerpted from the Gnostic text *The Thunder: Perfect Mind*, circa A.D. 1

Through Lil' Kim, hip hop came in the guise of Ishtar-Asherah-Mari-Anath, carnal deity of antiquity; dimly perceptible through the veil of Brooklyn street-girl fantasies. We hear the goddess voice rising from the din surrounding her; the click and whirr of cameras and the *kah-kah-kah* of automatics, the moans and groans of alleyway sex and stairwell trysts. On *Hard Core*, Lil' Kim is a nasty girl with a dirty mouth, but more important, she is the catalyst for a new chapter in hip hop's ongoing transubstantiation.

It's a wonder to behold when the deity possesses a body, especially when it takes feminine form. Considering how male-dominated the ritual terrain has become over the years, an explosion of true female energy was necessary and overdue. Since hip hop's earliest gestation period—when groups like the Mercedes Ladies, Sequence, and other overlooked founding mothers did their thing—women in the culture have struggled to define themselves outside of male constrictions. Some may recall the audacious energy of Salt-N-Pepa's "I'll Take Your Man," the bold simplicity of Roxanne Shanté's "Have a Nice Day," or even "Stop, Look, Listen," MC Lyte's elegant exegesis of the Brooklyn b-girl cosmology in three easy steps. But despite these breakthroughs, for the first fifteen years of hip hop, pimps and players ruled while the goddess remained in hiding.

The '90s were a revelation. Spurred by the efforts of Mary J. Blige, Yo Yo, Latifah, and others, a new generation of women began to reveal the deity's feminine side. These developments—coming just as male MCs were beginning to exhaust their narrative possibilities—led inevitably to the deity's possession of a teenage girl named Kimberly Denise Jones, and ushered in the phenomenon of the Queen Bitch.

> Never before have you seen such magnificence
> In the black princess, yesss
> Flow's phenom, I'm the bomb-diggy
> Ask Biggie . . .
> —"Drugs," 1996

Kim's relationship to her mentor and greatest love was complex. The tiny woman was at once a reflection and perfect counterbalance to Biggie's enormous Bed-Stuy genius and the ego that came with it.

BIGGIE: "I used to get feels on a bitch / Now I throw shields on the dick / To stop me from that HIV shit."

KIM: "I used to be scared of the dick / Now I throw lips to the shit / Handle it like a real bitch."

Biggie played pimp to Kim's whore and shared a number of charged exchanges with her on record. That was Kim in the sex skit with Biggie on *Ready to Die*—her recording debut—crying out, "Oh fuck me you chicken-gristle-eating Slim-Fast-drinking motherfucker." That was Kim on "I Can Love You," declaring her devotion: "Ruger by the thigh for ya, right hand high for ya."

But the violent exchanges detailed on tracks like "Get Money" laid bare not just the dark realities of love gone awry, but also what was special about Kim. She was perfectly suited to grapple with wounded, exaggerated manhood, Venus rising from a crack and Kevlar wasteland. Her and Biggie's lyrical conversation made for some of the most challenging music ever recorded—they put it all out there. It was a barbed interaction that was nevertheless full of love. Traumatized love, angry and misdirected at times, but love all the same. That love defined her. "I loved him with all my heart," she said after he was killed. "Like I've never loved anyone in my life. I still feel his spirit with me, like right now he's sittin' right here. I could be on the toilet and I feel his spirit. I talk to him every night and I feel like he's telling me a lot more of the truth. I just feel blessed because Biggie has been with me every step of the way."

Without Biggie, Kim seems rudderless, floating through a purgatory of cameos, photo shoots, and red carpets. *Notorious K.I.M.* has none of the freshness of her debut, which Biggie executive produced along with Un. Rehashed and unsure of who she is without him, she is more dependent than ever on sampling from his body of work as if still seeking his guidance.

Biggie understood that Kim's wanton displays of pussy power would strike an ancient chord. *Hard Core* offered a fully integrated, unpoliced sexuality, rare in this nation's public spaces. As America continues to struggle with its tortured sexual history, from the Puritan witch trails to the sordid legacy of slavery, perhaps figures like Kim will one day be seen as forerunners of a time when women would harness the full potential of their sexuality—harbingers of harlot possibilities.

Even so, we sense that Kim has not yet grasped the fullness herself. Kim revels in her ability to turn men to swine. "Got buffoons eatin' my pussy while I watch cartoons," she boasts, but at what cost? Her Queen Bitch role begs the question: What is the true nature of pussy power? And who will claim it? Both Lauryn Hill and Mary J. Blige dabble in aspects of it. (Remember when Mary sang "Come into my bedroom honey / What I've got will make you spend money"?) But it is through Kim that we confront all the contradictions of using sex as a means to power—or the trappings of power. Isn't "That Thing" worth more than access to money and car keys? What about love and procreation and the capacity for healing?

But I digress.

Lil' Kim, manifestation of the female aspect of hip hop, is not the Lil' Kim who sacrificed herself to the blue-eyed idol of fashion. Her attempts to move beyond hip hop, musically and aesthetically, have lent a tragic dimension to her story. In the strange netherworld of commercial sex, white women are an easier sell, black girls a niche commodity. In the media flesh market Kim became an anomaly, a mildly interesting sideshow act rather than the crescendo of rhyme, rhythm, and sexuality she had been within the ritualized terrain of hip hop. In the blander context of pop machinery, the deity, it seems, let her go it alone.

Kim is such the little black girl, the media and fashion world instinctively forced her into aesthetic subservience. She would answer Regis Philbin's most inane interview question with sweet sincerity. The challenge she once posed to fashion's assumptions of beauty was made moot by her plastic surgery. And Kim, unaware of her own power, was seduced by the con of "ghetto fabulousness."

Where once she set trends, she's become a follower, or worse, a parody. Victim to the fashion world's fickleness, Kim has also become a stranger to her more charismatic former self. In the hands of the "fabulous," Kim turned into a dumping ground for misplaced concepts of what a black girl could and should be. Despite isolated moments of beautiful imagery, her styling became excessive, gaudy, and tragically overwrought.

But Kim's role in the ever-churning world of ghetto pop is more complicated than it seems at first glance. She did more than give us music to fuck and fantasize to. Her ultimate importance is less as fashion icon, more as a representative of revolutionary change happening in the sexual politics of not just hip hop but the world.

Kim outlined the woman's dilemma in modern America. In these middle years after feminism and before the onslaught of a second woman's revolution, young women are addressing issues of love, money, power, and sex in radically different ways than their grandmothers. Kim is a transitional figure to what comes next. At her best, she implies a new woman, one more in touch with the power of her sexuality, more able to integrate her capacity to love with her desire to be strong and independent. But even in her failures, her lapses of self-esteem, Kim succeeds in revealing painful truths concerning modern womanhood, changing society, and the eternities of love. And really that's all the Goddess ever required of her.

Miss Trina Z3 Beamer open up my legs stick your head in between them till I bust like lead from a heater make sure you got bread for the diva

TRINA

miami
vice *by Erica Kennedy*

It's been 16 years since Roxanne Shanté vied for the coveted title Queen of the Dis, and as Biggie Smalls once said, things done changed. Today's raptresses seem more concerned with looks than lyrics. No hooded sweatshirts for the 21st-century rap diva. Promoted by mostly male record execs peddling CDs in an overcrowded market to a mostly male audience, female artists must come equipped with a glamour-girl image burnished to an MTV-ready high shine.

Not that lyrical content has totally gone by the wayside, but the rules have been redefined. When Latifah posed the question, "Who you calling a bitch?" on her 1993 Grammy-winner "U.N.I.T.Y.," she was calling out the misogyny of her male peers. The new breed of female MCs embrace the B-word as a symbol of post-feminist empowerment. In fact, adopting the freaky bitch persona helped the debut albums of Foxy Brown and Lil' Kim hit platinum in a matter of weeks. Their success defined a clear formula for new female rappers—one adopted from the world's oldest profession—just sound fuckable and dress accordingly.

Might the sluggish sales of Kim's sophomore disc suggest that the once-potent challenge to hip hop patriarchy posed by these sexually liberated self-described bitches is losing its edge? Their explicit wordplay and never-ending theatrics do seem more gimmicky than outrageous the second time 'round. It's a scary prospect for those following in their well-worn path.

Enter Trina, whose salacious verse on fellow Miamian Trick Daddy's 1998 club-rocker "Nann Nigga" proved her to be a worthy rival for the crown of Raunchiest Bitch, if not the one she claims—Baddest. It's no surprise that a sista hailing from Miami, home of Luke and 2 Live Crew, would be the one who upped the panty ante.

Luke and his nasty-as-they-wanna-be brethren caught national flak for objectifying women—proving that if sex sells, then pimping controversy sells even more. It was only a matter of time before ladies like Kim, Foxy, and Trina pilfered the "me so horny" business plan to pay for their own Gucci pocketbooks.

Trina grew up listening to Luke, knew Miami's resident baller personally, and before launching her rap career even recorded a spoken interlude on one of his records, "It's Your Birthday." With the photogenic look and sexual bravado necessary for a female to compete in the booty-rap game, Trina hit the scene proudly carrying on the tradition of freaky Florida bass music pioneers with two big differences: Nobody bothers to make the old pornography versus free speech argument anymore. And now, sisters are doing it for themselves.

Heads turn as Trina saunters into Tony Roma's in the Palmetto section of Miami. She's got a red belly-baring halter, tight-ass jeans, zebra print mules going click-clack, and Versace shades perched atop perfectly coifed hair. Before her bountiful booty even slides into a booth, two middle-aged black men approach. "So when you coming out with something," one asks, damn near panting. It's been this way since Katrina Taylor, 24, blipped onto the rap radar with lyrics that made Lil' Kim seem tame—"Now you don't know nann ho / That'll ride the dick on the dime / Who love to fuck all the time / One who's pussy fatter than mine."

Thoroughly unfazed—after all, attracting men is part of what she does—Trina makes polite chitchat before sending the admirer on his way. Then suddenly he's back, having noticed this reporter's tape recorder. "Just so you know," he declares, pointing at the object of his lust, "she's the baddest bitch."

How serendipitous! Trina thinks so, too. She even used the phrase for the title of her first solo joint and first single, "Da Baddest Bitch," to be exact. It's a moniker she wears like a badge. "When you hear males rap about it they're not talking about a diva bitch, they're talking about a bitch in another sense," she says, digging into a slab of baby back ribs. "But when a woman uses that word, it's like empowerment. A bitch is a strong woman who's not going to take no shit. Like a diva. It means control."

Maybe so, but in hip hop, as in the Book of Genesis (where God made Eve from Adam's rib), man begets woman. With few exceptions, an established male star ushers a female protégé into the boy's club by introducing her on a guest spot on their album. It happened with Ice Cube and Yo Yo, Jermaine Dupri and Da Brat, Biggie and Kim, Jay-Z and Foxy Brown, Master P and Mia X. And so it was with Trina, whose name will be forever be linked with Trick Daddy.

Funny thing is, even though Trina has the look and demeanor of a woman born for stardom, her involvement with the whole rap thing was something of a fluke. She knew Trick from the gritty Liberty City neighborhood where they both grew up, he in the projects and she in a more stable home nearby. She did write rhymes, but only as a hobby. Even though her spoken interludes (especially the dialogue on "Talk Some Shit" from JT Money's first album) seemed like a prelude of things to come, rapping wasn't the vocation she had in mind when she dreamed of living in the spotlight. When Trick approached her to record an answer verse on his record, she says, "I just did the song for him as a favor because he needed a girl."

"She always had a smart little mouth," says Ted Lucas, the 29-year-old CEO of Miami's Slip-n-Slide Records, who's known Trina and Trick since childhood. "She was always able to cuss your ass out."

As fate would have it, "Nann Nigga" blew up—due in large part to the scandalous lines that Trina had written in one day. Before long, the young woman who had been studying for her real estate license was doing concert dates with Miami's freakiest thug. "The first show, it had to be at least two thousand people there," she recalls. "I was so scared, *shaking*. But I just did it. And that was when the song had just come out and people were going crazy, so we had to back it up and do it again. I was like, 'Oh my God.'"

After that it was on. "At the shows," she says, "I was getting so much support from the audience I was like, 'This is nothing. I could tear this shit up.'" But when Slip-n-Slide came calling with a solo offer, she had a hard time deciding. "I was hiding from them, not answering the phone," Trina recalls. "It was so crazy. I had a real estate job lined up! I put them off for at least two months. Then I said, 'Okay fuck it,' and I signed. That's when I really took it serious."

With all the wannabe rappers willing to sacrifice their firstborn for a deal, it's hard to imagine someone saying, "I'll get back to you." But Trina's always been something of a ghetto superstar. She was the popular girl in high school, always wearing an off-the-chain outfit, the one

Trick Daddy and Trina.

who had all the niggas open. "I grew up feeling like I was the shit," she says in a tone so casual it doesn't even sound like bragging, just statement of fact.

"You could call her Miss Miami," Lucas says with admiration. "There ain't a person in Miami that don't know Trina and this was before the music. She was the most beautiful girl in the 'hood."

The enormous chunk of ice on her ring finger is a testament to her popularity with the boys. "It was a gift," she says coyly. "I'm not married. I'm not engaged. I'm just happy. I get all kinds of gifts—lots of diamonds." It turns out that she is indeed engaged, but prefers to keep her private life separate from her public persona.

Though her lyrics will undoubtedly lead most to believe Trina is a stone-cold freak, most of the stories told on *Da Baddest Bitch* are borrowed from her wild child youth—things she experienced and tales she heard when she and her girls used to run the streets all night, sneaking into clubs and shaking her designer-clad ass when Mama wanted her home.

There was even a brief period, back in '97, when honey tricked bank as a dancer at Miami's World Famous Rolexxx Exotic Night Club. The designer fanatic's dance name was Versace, naturally. "I didn't really do it for money," she says cautiously. "I did it because I was so fascinated with myself. I knew I could intimidate men with my body. I was fascinated by the costumes; I was making $1,000 a week but I said, 'This is not a life for me. I'm better than this.'" Trina says she has no regrets today. As she looks back on her stripper days, saying that she "got caught up in the hype," it's not hard to imagine 40-year-old Trina looking back on her music career. "My New Year's resolution was that I wasn't gonna be caught in the strip club when 1998 gets here," she says proudly. "And I wasn't."

Trina's current incarnation as a rapper allows her to keep the best parts of her old gig—the outrageous wardrobe and the attention—and jettison the feeling of powerlessness that ultimately overcame her as a nude dancer. Unlike Foxy Brown, who once complained to *Essence* that even when she wanted to tone it down, her hypersexual image was mandated by men at her record label, Trina revels in her flamboyant attire. "I love the glitter and glitz, it's so Hollywood," she says, citing her favorite movie, *Showgirls,* as sartorial inspiration.

"The one thing about me is that Trina speaks for Trina," she says. "Ain't nobody gonna make up my mind for me. With my record company, management, and everyone around me, I basically control everything. I tell *them* I'm not gonna wear this, I'm not doing this, I'm not doing that." Considering the things she *does* wear and do, the rejects must be something else. "I don't even ask their opinion 'cause I don't need it," she insists. "I feel like if I buy something and I'm comfortable with it, that's what I'm gonna put on, straight up."

While Foxy publicly lamented the crotch-grabbing shot that made the cover of VIBE in 1998 and brought her schoolteacher mom plenty of grief, Trina bragged about the photos that would appear on the pages of *Blaze*'s May 2000 issue. "They got a shot of me and Trick in a bathtub. It looks like he's going down on me. You're gonna love it," she says, barely able to contain her glee.

Even though he assures me it was merely a simulation, there's no doubt that Trick, a professed lover of cunnilingus, adored that shot as well. His fascination with freak-chasing and Henny-swilling make it almost impossible for Trick to talk coherently about his music. He and Trina kept in touch while he was in jail, and they spent many months on the road together, but she doesn't really roll in the same circles he does when they're home. It soon becomes clear why.

On Ali Baba Avenue in Miami's Opalaka section, small rooms sitting next to a commuter railroad track rent for $300 a month. This dead-end fortress looks like a run-down army barracks; they call it the Tank. It's the kind of locale you see every night on *Cops*. It's also where 25-year-old Maurice Young, a.k.a. Trick Daddy, feels most comfortable.

Trick is on his way with a truckload of treats to barbecue with his soldiers, who reside at the Tank. That's the plan, anyway, but when he pulls up in a black Ford Excursion, no one looks festive. Tony, Trick's soft-spoken manager, scopes out the scene and returns with a grim look on his face. "Oh this ain't good," he says. "Somebody got shot."

Across the street a young man lies in a pool of his own blood, grasping the leg that's been hit. Soon there are police on the scene, two fire rescue trucks, and a helicopter overhead. Dressed in red and black track pants, a matching jersey, and Nikes, Trick flashes a mouthful of gold slugs. It seems as if Trick Daddy is always in the wrong place at the wrong time.

Twenty minutes after making a getaway from the crime scene, Trick is safely ensconced in his new home inside a gated community called Miami Lakes. The house is a pagan shrine to the thug life. Visitors are greeted by an enormous poster of Trick's hero, Tony Montana, the fictional blow-merchant in *Scarface,* and framed memorabilia from the movie hangs everywhere. The coffee table is piled high with rap and porno mags.

Despite the gangsta decor, the comfortable home with a pool out back is a long way from Liberty City's "Pork-n-Beans" projects where Trick was raised with 11 brothers and sisters. Beginning at age 14, he spent most of his adolescence in the penal system. It took a tragic event, the murder of his brother Hollywood, a street hustler whom Trick idolized, to turn Trick's life around. "He was a ghetto millionaire," Trick says reverently. "He made it to a certain level, was able to support his mama, me, and the kids—all without a college education." Once Trick made parole and got his legitimate hustle together, he would do the same. By his second album, *www.thug.com,* he was able to bring Hollywood's former flame, Trina, along for the ride. Hollywood's death had an equally dramatic effect on her.

Trina was only 16 when they began dating. He was two years older, kept her freshly dipped in designer clothes, picked her up at school in his Benz (or let her tool around town in it), and made sure she had everything she wanted. She knew he was a hustler but even now protects his memory by not explaining the exact nature of the hustle. "He did whatever he had to do to survive," she demurs.

But she knew enough about his dangerous life to worry

one night when he didn't show up to collect her from her mother's house. After Hollywood's sister heard that the friend he had been with that night was killed in a drive-by, Trina, then 19, went into a complete panic. It wasn't until she went over to his mother's house that her fears were confirmed. "When my eyes met hers, I just fell out," Trina recounts. "They didn't even say nothing. By the time they woke me up they told me, 'Trina, he was in the car.' That's all I could remember."

It was a defining moment—"The worst thing that ever happened to me," she says. Even though she had always been confident and brash, the sudden death of the man she thought she'd marry toughened her into the no-nonsense woman she is today. "I was miserable and distraught, lost and lonely. But he always told me, 'No matter what I do for you, I want you to be able to do for yourself. Don't ever depend on a man to do 100 percent for you.'" After Hollywood's death, his advice came back to her: "The first thing I thought afterward was, What am I going to do with myself?"

When Trick coaxed her to provide the female verse on

"No, I'm not bisexual," Trina says dismissively the next day after an afternoon of shopping at the ritzy Bal Harbour Shops, where she drops $400 in cash—pulled from a bank envelope inside her Gucci purse—on a pair of Chanel slides. She seems to regard her labelmate with a weary "he so crazy" attitude. "Trick loves a lot of women and everywhere he goes, they flock," she says. "We went to New York, we didn't even check in, two girls meeting him at the hotel. I was like, 'Damn, how you know them?' And he said, 'I met them one time on the plane.' He never comes back after a show without a girl." But she steers clear of the freakfest when she's offstage. "I'm in the room watching TV. He's in his room too . . . watching pornos." Or, it would seem, making his own.

And why would he think she was bisexual? "Trick knows that I have a lot of friends that are bisexual and he likes that freaky shit," she says, showing an open mind. "If I chose to be bisexual then, oh well, but it doesn't really attract me like that. But you never know what you gonna do in life. Never say never."

"Who cares if I'm half-naked onstage?" Trina asks. "If you're a model you're half-naked onstage. Nobody's talking about Naomi Campbell and she's in a bikini on-stage. What's the difference if it's a rapper?"

"Nann," that question was answered. It was Trina's natural quick wit that earned his respect, but it's what he imagines she does behind closed doors that keeps him intrigued. "She's an animal like the rest of us," he says by way of a compliment. "Naughty thoughts, freaky friends. And I love bisexual women!"

Many a female rapper gets dogged by rumors of lesbianism—MC Lyte, Latifah, Da Brat. Back in the day, that was a straight dis. It was as if a woman who's aggressive, opinionated, and didn't dress to impress the fellas had to be unwomanly. But in today's anything-goes climate, Trina raps that she's "Quick to deep-throat the dick / And let another bitch straight lick the clit." The tease of bisexuality is just another way to make a fella's ears (if not other body parts) perk up.

"Oh, she didn't tell you?" Trick says about Trina's alleged bisexuality, a sudden twinkle illuminating his normally dead eyes. "Ask her."

It's this kind of self-assurance that allows Trina to spit hardcore lyrics, don flamboyant stage outfits, and live up to her bitch status. "Guys can say bitch or ho, but if a woman says *she's* a bitch then it's a problem," she complains. "It's annoying because who's to say that men should have so much to say and women shouldn't? I feel like women have just as much power as men. Who cares if I'm half-naked onstage? If you're a model you're half-naked onstage. Nobody's talking about Naomi Campbell and she's in a bikini onstage. So what's the difference if it's a rapper?"

Tiffany, Trina's 18-year-old assistant and diva-in-training, chimes in: "Trick can say, 'You like the dick to be locked, cocked, and shot all over yo' forehead.' Don't nobody ask him nothing about that!"

"Yeah, like I heard DMX say he fucked a corpse," Trina agrees. "Then you hear a female rapper talk about fucking or oral sex and it becomes such a big deal. Everybody fucks. Yo' mama fucked! That's how you got here. So I feel like it's nothing to be ashamed of. Like people say you sinning if you having sex when you're not married? That means there's a lot of sinners." As for Trina, she has an active sex life to be sure, but she insists it's more tame than most would believe. "I may choose to be a freak with my partner but I'm a one-on-one girl," she says.

Men have been quick to respond to Trina's sex on wax for obvious reasons, but it's hard to imagine that she would find an audience among female hip hop heads, who are plenty tired of being objectified as sperm receptacles in rap songs and shimmying body parts in the accompanying videos. But Trina claims that ladies do show love when she hits the road. It seems freaks need a role model, too.

"Every single show that I've done, every girl in the audience is singing the verse on "Nann Nigga," she says. "That's life. That's not something to take home to Mama. This is not something you walk to the altar saying. But obviously there are many people who live this type of life and they know exactly what I'm talking about. They get so deep with it. One girl ran up on me like, 'You don't know no ho that can deep-throat the dick like me.' And I was like, 'Okay, Ma. It's cool. Don't beat me up.'"

Trina maintains that she's giving a voice to other women's tales, not her own. At times she admits to being confounded by the debauchery she's witnessed—or at least heard about—while on the road with Trick. "What can you gain from chasing an artist?" she asks when the subject of groupies comes up. "What's your purpose? Sex is something everybody does, but it should be with someone you feel comfortable with, someone you know. That's like personal, private shit. I've talked to a couple of girls and their answers are that they are fascinated by the stars, Trick or whatever. I mean to each her own but that's something I would never do even if I wasn't in this business."

Still, Trina gave her fans—male and female—exactly what they lusted for on *Da Baddest Bitch*. There was more pussy-popping and dick-sucking on this album than in any porn flick, but Trina's rhymes were pretty tight for a debut effort: On "69 Ways": "Ghetto Superstar niggas eat the pussy like a sushi bar / Never let a nigga hit the coochie raw / Might bust a nut on my Gucci bra."

It's certainly not a song you'll hear on the radio, because even if there was a clean version, it would be mostly bleeps. But Florida's audience, weaned on Luke records, has grown immune to shocking lyrics and happily embrace Trina as their own. "She ain't run from the 'hood," says B.B. Lewis of Miami's Circle House Studio, the black-owned state-of-the-art sound lab where Trick and Trina recorded many of their hits. "She didn't get rich and switch." She has, however, sold

more than 500,000 copies of *Da Baddest Bitch* on the strength of mostly regional airplay down south.

"We definitely love her," says Khaled the Arab Attack, a Miami club and radio DJ. "She's explicit but it's more of a fun-type thing. She's got an ego. She let niggas know that if they ain't gonna treat her top dollar then she ain't fuckin' with them. She's representing the women and I ain't mad at her. Her songs are dance or party records and the club is all about that sexy vibe."

Trina has also recorded less lascivious tracks, including "Dear Mama," her personal favorite, which is dedicated to the woman who was always there for her. "When I was wrong, I was wrong," Trina says in the song, "but she made it right." Mrs. Taylor was understandably touched by "Dear Mama," and she says the other raunchy lyrics her daughter spews don't bother her. "There's a lot that people experience but they keep it behind closed doors," she says diplomatically.

The nymphet image has brought Mrs. Taylor's daughter the attention she craves, earned her a certified-gold LP, and paid for a new four-bedroom home in the Plantation section of Miami. It houses a walk-in closet filled with a designer shoe collection worthy of Imelda Marcos. Now that there's some dough to be made, playing the ghetto superstar is all right, but Trina admits that it was once a burden. "When I was growing up, being so popular, I always had to live up to this image," she says. "I wished I could just go somewhere, go to the mall and be another fucking person. It was so bad that I wouldn't go nowhere if I didn't buy something new to wear. I wouldn't go to the club if I didn't have on something bangin'" Now, she says, "My image is everything. But the funny thing is that now I really don't give a fuck."

But look closer and you'll see that there are chinks in Trina's bitch armor that suggest she might grow weary of maintaining an image that's at odds with her true self. In today's music marketplace, an artist can't be blamed for trying to maximize sales, but a quick listen to "Take Me," her collaboration with Pam from the girl group Total, makes you wonder whether Trina has made peace with the alter ego she has adopted. The chorus (sung by Pam) goes: "Baby I wanna go to a world where I ain't gotta be a freaky ho / Just so I can be noticed by people / Please tell me if you know / Because I wanna go."

Whereas Trick is exactly the same person on record as he is off, there is a distinct inconsistency between the reality of Katrina Taylor, the young woman who prays daily and spends her nights watching reruns of *Martin, Sanford and Son,* and *Good Times,* and the sex-bomb fantasy Trina peddles to her audience.

"Sometimes it is a real big conflict because there was a

time when I was surrounded by all that—the clubs, the guys," she says. "I have seen it all." But that was the past. As she prepares to record a follow-up album, Miami's hot girl is wisely branching out to different subjects. "With my second album, I still have the sexuality but it's a whole different era of *me*. Anything that I said that was really raw, I said it already. And I don't intend on saying it over and over again."

Nevertheless, the Lil' Kim and Foxy comparisons will likely persist. "Coming up I listened to Foxy all the time. Kim, I love her music, her style. I don't care about the competition because it doesn't matter to me who's on top, who's outshining who. There's enough space for everybody. I'm just making sure I do my thing." On that note, Trina says her greatest role model is a more mainstream pop diva. Madonna's blatant materialism and carefully crafted sexual persona—outrageous in her heyday—was a far cry from her own middle-class, Catholic-girl roots. She courted controversy, played it to the hilt, and even during her artistically lean years, staged public stunts that kept her afloat. Trina seems to be following a hip hop version of this game plan.

She has a third album in mind but would like to move on to television and film and plans to take acting lessons so she can do so. In the world of hip hop, three well-received albums is considered a successful career, and Trina definitely has the fire and energy to reach that benchmark. If she can keep the tease going and sustain the interest of listeners half as long as the original material girl, this rap thing may turn out to be a stepping-stone to another entertainment medium. One that will keep her exactly where she wants to be—front and center with the spotlight shining brightly on her, the baddest bitch.

MISSY

Oh what a night

you should be like Missy

'stead of bein' like Mike

I like to ride ponies

instead of riding bikes

Photograph by Lyle Ashton Harris

feeling bitchy

by Karen Renee Good

The New Negro is an inventive amalgamation of past and future trends that are indigenous to black American style. Generally, the New Negro—who is "new" every decade or so—is female, a woman who considers her marginal status a form of freedom and a challenge: she takes the little she has been given and transforms it into something complex, outrageous, and, ultimately, fashionable. She is outrageous because no one cares what she does—until, that is, she begins to make money. Missy (Misdemeanor) Elliott, the 25-year-old hip-hop performer who is energetically redefining the boundaries of rap music, is a singer, a songwriter, an arranger, a producer, and a talent scout. Six months ago, few people outside the music industry had heard of her: six months from now it will be necessary to pretend that you've known about Missy Elliott for years. She is the biggest and blackest female rap star that Middle America has ever seen. She is the latest incarnation of the New Negro.

—former VIBE editor Hilton Als, *The New Yorker,* 1997

Missy believes she can fly. And when given the chance, she does. These flights are not restricted to the magical space of the video screen—a space she has conquered like nobody since Michael Jackson—instead they go on inside the rich, fanciful world of her imagination. She's weightless and transcendent here, time-warping past physicality, gender, race, and all their attendant ruts. Behold the innervision whereby Missy, master of illusion, becomes a celebration of herself.

The Missy story is all about Possibility with a capital *P* and the heartfelt conviction that you are whoever you think you are. Octavia Butler, the science-fiction scribe who writes about black people in the future, might call her Shapeshifter—a powerful woman who quietly morphs from one persona to another right before your eyes. *She* something else, ain't she?

Not quite 30, Missy Elliott runs her own record label, The Gold Mind, Inc., a freaky subdivision of the Elektra Entertainment Group. Elektra CEO Sylvia Rhone pronounced her a "genius" and gave her the label deal before Missy had even released her first album. Since 1997, Missy has delivered two multiplatinum discs (her breakthrough *Supa Dupa Fly* and 1999's darker *Da Real World*). Of the hotly anticipated third installment, 2001's *Miss E . . . So Addic-* *tive,* she says this: "If ecstasy is the hottest drug, then consider me your pusher."

Just what makes Elliott so hot may not be entirely obvious. She isn't an exceptional rapper like Lauryn or a particularly gifted singer, like Erykah Badu. "My lines aren't all that fly," she admitted in a moment of self-critique. "But as far as flows, I can give you flows all day." Her entire body of recorded work sounds like one long freestyle. Her lyrics sometimes appear nonsensical. She specializes in onomatopoetics, sounds that communicate more directly than words. She's been known to write a tune in 20 minutes. It's the voices in her head that make her Supa Dupa, the way she surrenders herself totally to do their bidding. Plus her marketing savvy, which is no small part of her genius.

Missy's as pure an artist as there ever was, but she's all about that paper. "I am so much more than a rapper or a singer," she wrote in the liner notes for *Supa Dupa Fly.* "I am a songwriter, a producer, and an entertainer." But the real bottom line is simply this: "I am a businesswoman *first.* "

Missy's control over her art and her destiny is a kind of suffrage, what Destiny's Child was really talking about in their anthem "Independent Women Part I." After 25 years of hip hop heroines getting used up, ripped off, beat down, and pimped in every sense of the word, the tide is turning. In Missy we see this flagrant disregard for glass ceilings and patriarchy—and it's thrilling. Missy was once courted by Puff Daddy but turned him down. "As much as I love Puffy and I know he makes stars, I didn't want to be under him," she explained later. "I wanted to be at the same table as him drinking the same champagne. I wanted to buy *him* drinks."

Fearless as she may appear, Missy Elliott is painfully shy. She hates to stand onstage. She hardly ever does concerts, and when she does appear on TV awards shows—only under duress—she says, "And the winner is . . ." and jets.

She kinda snuck up on us, though we might have seen her coming, maybe in some *X-Men* comic book, light years away. Her music is a lot like her distinctive way of movement: stop and start, losing, then catching the beat and her balance, moving in bullet-time like something out of *The Matrix.* And always, there's that undeniable bounce. Hers is a twist on the Bankhead Bounce, which really ain't nothing but an '80s dance called the Prep, which really ain't nothing Patti LaBelle hasn't been doing with her shoulders for years, which really ain't nothin' but what happens every Sunday high noon in the black Baptist church when someone catches the Holy Ghost.

Still, in hip hop circa 2001, capturing the churchical spirit is no small feat. "Today's hip hop concert is like twenty people onstage with you," Elliott laments. "And everybody screaming." The problem Missy confronts is this: Being a woman who loves and performs hip hop has mostly meant one of two things: either stomping back and forth across stages grabbing virtual dicks or acting like you want to get fucked. It has meant turning a deaf ear and a blind eye to the most ridiculous double standards, historical, sociological, mind-boggling, bamboozling disrespect of and by your own all for the sake of the bass. (Ladies, hear this: if the music doesn't entertain or empower you, if it makes you feel bad or disrespected, skip to the next track, turn the shit off, or leave.)

Selling out and dumbing down has gotten the culture of hip hop nowhere but, as Missy often says, shaking her head, "stuck." The situation calls for fresh beats and rhymes, and for nothing less than the rediscovery of feminine leadership, to save the men from themselves. On the backs of ladies like Sha Rock, Salt-N-Pepa, and MC Lyte come warrior women who are not born from Adam's rib or content with sidekick status. From Latifah (Who you callin' a bitch?) to Left Eye (Burn baby, burn!) to Missy ("Don't Be Commin' [In My Face]"), the battle cry has been sounded: We will retaliate. So you must understand if Missy's feeling bitchy these days. (Is this substantiated?)

In one of the opening shots for her classic dark video "She's a Bitch," all you see of Missy are her hands. Loosely clasped, they are bound in shiny leather gauntlets, fingertips jutting out into sharp, fierce tips. She slowly rubs her hands together as if she has a plan; at first, it seems a masculine gesture, what with the rawhide, covertness and implied villainy. Then you remember that this pressing of hands, whether in preparation or as salve, implies witchery, as in the ill-reputed "practice" of timeless women who would be magic, be they the Yoruba goddess Ochun or—another Missy muse—*titans*. And sure enough, that's what she is, in the very next scene: a mythological giant rises out of a murky silver sea, dancing on a giant *M*. The supernatural powers—the sheer largeness—of these women were considered dangerous by patriarchal law. Punishable by death. And as we all know, Missy is a large bitch.

Accordingly, she plays subversive games with androgyny, hence her proclivity for long pants, the latest Nikes, and colorful suits festooned with glittering Tweety birds or

rolling dice. Her heresy renders gender barriers (hip hop and worldwide) moot. She has as much money, power, and respect as any man. In only four years, Missy's ability to morph between businesswoman and artist has resulted in a multiplatinum franchise. She is producer and writer, lyricist and bankroller. Hear her roar.

Missy's ways are tomboyish, freaky, country, and a little butch. But even with her freakiness, she clearly has drawn a line of demarcation between herself and the exploited women disrespecting themselves and their sexuality in hip hop because of desperation. "Is that *your* chick?" she asked in Memphis Bleek's song of the same name. In other words, don't play yourself.

Wildly feminine and damn cocky, Missy's a woman who fearlessly explores her creativity and sensuality, who thinks body-as-bribe is lazy, and whose business is and ever will be her own. To reign supreme, or at least effectively, a woman must know subtlety, grace, posture, and her power. If this movement must have a label, call it *Eat Me Feminism*—and mean that shit! The offended, the scared, and the 'bout it 'bout it call her *bitch*.

Even with the name's multiple meanings—loosely: female, coward, difficult adversary, best friend—Missy has embraced *bitch* in all its delicious, prohibited vulgarity. Not merely for purposes of reverse psychology, which has always been a means of survival in the black community, but because she knows what the offended *really* mean.

"I became a bitch in power because when I walked in, I asked for what I wanted. And at the end of the day, if this is the way I want it, this is the way I'm going to have it," she says. There it is, who Missy truly is. "I wanna be like a female Quincy Jones!" she's said more than once. Don't be lulled by the shy demeanor, she's just private. And don't get lost in her beautiful, almond, geisha eyes; she knows they enchant. Missy is a woman unquestionably, enviably in charge. She knows her business and she knows her numbers and that excites her.

Missy rhymes about sex, money, and power like most men in hip hop (hip pop) do—prowling tales peppered with glittering toys. Her music is highly sexually charged (less come-hither than come-do-me). She has been known to enter a song fucking, moaning, like getting hit from the back. (Listen to the beginning of "Hot Boyz.")

Her ridiculously hot single "Get Ur Freak On" is hip hop for the club that bounces with a little bit of rockers and a little bit of rock and roll. Just goes to prove what I've been saying for years. Missy's a freak, y'all. Like, give her 20 more years to get her raunch up and she could be Millie Jackson. Listen to songs like "Don't Be Commin' (In My Face)" or her lyrics on SWV's "Can We" off the, ahem, *Booty Call* soundtrack. "Don't ask me if I'm nasty / Freaky deaky / See, y'all cain't see me." Flirt. All Missy wants is for you to use your imagination. Let her talk about it, and she gets shy. "Um, I mean, it's undercover. Everybody got a lil' nastiness in 'em. But I don't want people to look at how I'm dressed. I want them to see there's a talent. Although you might think I'm in a G-string with what I'm talkin' about."

You know Missy goes to the strip club. The dancers (so bored with niggas) are her girls. Da Brat and her hot ass is probably there. Herewith, Bad Bitches who fuck men when and if they please. And they are having a good time. Take note, this is the new generation: sexy, brilliant women making power moves, getting free. The sexuality you *feel* first. Women who *loooooooove* to make money and have a good time doing it. Women who have their wits about them. Missy is one such woman. The reason she can be so cocky and not have a dick is because those cars in the videos are hers. What did dead prez say? "Po' folks got the millions and my woman's disrespected." Not this woman. Missy makes millions, her way. Say what you want about her writing, her artistic depth, whatever. Missy cannot be denied.

Missy was really born in a galaxy far, far away. In her Cancerian imagination—a tad outrageous no matter how conservative—she is a superhero.

She was one of those dreamy, creative girls, sensitive as they come, a little crazy. You must be all those things to dress like Michael Jackson. (Remember the yellow poster? Yellow vest, bowtie, fresh Jheri curl? Hands in pockets, the picture of peace? You'd remember if you were a real fan.) And you know she had an asymmetric like Salt-N-Pepa. You know she could not decide whether she was Chaka or Boogaloo Shrimp in the "I Feel For You" video.

Even with a population of 100,565, Portsmouth, Virginia—really just citified country—could not contain Missy Arnette Elliott. Like all the greats from small towns, like Oprah and Janis Joplin, she sensed this early on. Her father was a former marine; her mother, Patrica, was a dispatcher for the utility company. Missy came up in the '70s, when some folks could still leave their doors unlocked and the summer breeze felt good floating through the tore-up screen. Her parents' marriage was violent, abusive, and deteriorating; Missy says her home environment was the kind where "you need to run to the shelter." Baptist church on Sunday, hell on Monday. Lost her virginity at eight to a teenage cousin.

So Missy, who just knew something better was coming, dreamt dreams bigger than her reality and made up songs to sing. She sang for her mother and cousins, sang for and with her dolls—Baby Alive, GI Joe, various stuffed animals.

She sang songs by the Jacksons on top of upside-down trash cans in front of her house as cars drove by. In junior high, Missy dressed like Michael Jackson, seeing as he was her best friend and would be here any minute now, his glittering glove beckoning, to take her away from all this.

When Missy turned 13, her momma left her daddy, which, despite lean days of pork and beans and buttered bread, taught her self-sufficiency, strength, and possibility. Missy also became aware of her black-girl body and her black-girl self and did not find herself wanting. So in an effort to take the attention off herself and make the others comfortable, she became class clown. But inside there were urges, blood, growth, and private inclinations. Like all the girls, she wanted a boyfriend, nice clothes, and to be taken seriously. Finally, reluctantly, Missy admitted to herself that her beloved Michael wasn't ever going to pick her up. Not in Portsmouth. She would at least have to meet him halfway.

First thing she did was go to three of her best girls—Radiah, Chonita, LaShawn—and they formed a group called Fay Z, which would later change to Sista. It was also around that time Missy's friend Magoo also introduced her to one of his boys, Tim Mosely, who was the DJ in Magoo's group, Surrounded By Idiots. "He happened to play some stuff. He was just playing songs and it was still rap tracks, but I could sing over them and I started writing songs," she recalls of the fateful meeting with Timbaland. "From that point on, we just kept working together." Still do.

Sista did talent shows and, in 1991, after a Jodeci concert, Missy persuaded DeVante to let Sista audition for him. Girlfriends had "long ass weaves" and matching short sets and canes lookin' like Kappas or Boyz II Men or, yes, Jodeci. DeVante liked to be called DeVante Swing; he was the "de" of Jodeci, an R&B quartet composed of brothers who love hip hop and thrived on new jack swing. Sista had talent and he liked their style; a few days later he flew them to New York and they soon signed with Elektra.

She introduced Timbaland to DeVante as "this new cat who got a sound I never heard before, and I want him to do the Sista album." Tim built the beats, and the album was executive-produced by DeVante, who also directed their cheesy rooftop video. Missy was so self-conscious when Sista was filming their video that when the cameraman pulled in for a close-up, she freaked out because she thought DeVante would be mad. All these emotions swirled inside her, agonies and ecstasies expressed and repressed, her most lurid fantasies, dramas, and passions. Missy wrote them down. Sista was eventually dropped from Elektra for unspecified reasons, their album described by one critic as "one of the greatest hip hop records never released." But she continued to make music with Tim, back in Portsmouth, light-years away and moving even faster.

Missy was still working with DeVante as a songwriter too, having penned a few sweaty tracks for Jodeci's *Diary of a Mad Band* and other artists on his roster. He eventually moved Missy and Timbaland to New Jersey to join his songwriting team. One night in a Manhattan studio, she bumped into Faith Evans, R&B chanteuse and fellow writer. Faith explained their relationship via cell phone from her new Atlanta home, all three of her children in tow. "I had already heard about her from Misa [Lil' Kim's stylist and mother of Puffy's son Justin] and different people that were working with DeVante, and they would all talk about how talented Missy was. And then I heard some of the stuff she was writing and was just floored, like, 'Oh my God. You are ridiculous!' I guess she knew it, but didn't know what she could do with all that at the time. 'Cause she was definitely not thinking about being an artist."

The two women became friends, talking on the phone, hanging out, and when Missy started coming back and forth to New York, writing more frequently—bunking on the couches of studios and some producers—Faith invited her to stay with her. "It was just me and my little girl, and I probably just moved from Brooklyn, I had got separated from my first husband, so it wasn't like I didn't want the company. Missy was funny as hell, so she was like my homegirl. We were really, really cool."

"I think Faith Evans broke me out of my shyness," Missy told VIBE. "I used to live with her and I used to play her songs before I had become 'Missy Elliott' to the world. I used to be embarrassed and I used to always hold my head down when I played them because I didn't think they were hot. And she used to be like, 'Why you always hang your head down? Your shit is hot!'"

So Missy haunted studio halls with her notebook and, flowing like a deep river, wrote down whatever came to her. She wrote until she was writing songs for Aaliyah and 702. Missy did Puffy a solid by guesting on Gina Thompson's single, "The Things You Do (Remix)." The song was sexy and Missy blessed it with a rhyme. In this and nearly every song she was writing Missy scattered excerpts from one long, well-crafted freestyle. She was always creating these silly sounds, like cartoons, one such sound, a giggle—"hee-hee-hee-hee-*haoow*" would prove to be a kind of sonic logo, a

Missy Elliot in the studio with R&B singer Tamia.

glimpse of a new marketing strategy bordering on genius. Call her Goldfinger because baby girl's got the touch, perhaps only rivaled by King Midas himself, Puff Daddy.

I remember wondering to myself, Who is that *hee hee haoow* girl? I was assistant music editor at VIBE, where I put together the Next section, little 300-word pieces on new artists, people on the verge. We decided to cover the *hee hee haoow* girl who had no management, no record label, no album. We had to find her through Gina Thompson's label, Mercury Records. The publicist had to track Missy down and, eventually, Missy called me on a cell phone, from Virginia, crackling with a quiet buzz. She was warm, sweet, businesslike, and busy. She apologized for not having a manager or publicist. "It's just me right now. My lawyer [at the time, Louise West] is going to help me out with that." She said that although she was perfectly content being a writer and doing the occasional guest spot, there was an overwhelming demand for her to record her own album. "People think I did this for the money, but I was comfortable just writing for people," she says. "And I mean *really* comfortable."

A major bidding war between several labels ensued when Missy, at the behest of critics, fans, and colleagues decided to make her own record—a move for which she never thought she would have the bravery or inclination. "I'd rather give another artist one of my songs," she says. "At the end of the day, it still represents me." Elektra Entertainment Group CEO Sylvia Rhone, who became Missy's mentor, won by offering Missy a recording contract *and* her own label—an unprecedented deal for a new artist (who was, incidentally, managing herself). The venture would be called The Gold Mind, Inc., giving Missy an opportunity to develop her songwriting and producing abilities. Missy would oversee. She signed herself on as her first artist.

"Missy continues to amaze me," says Rhone. "She demonstrates a great sense of adventure, a willingness to take risks. In that regard she's peerless. She continues to give hip hop a change of face and in doing so she keeps altering the landscape of popular music."

Listening to *Supa Dupa Fly* was a little like going off to see the Wizard. Executive producer Elliott (who says there are no female producers?) and beat visionary Timbaland crafted a hip hop "sheets of sound" to crib a Coltrane reference: sleek R&B tracks blended with jungle, drum 'n' bass, and percussion a la Howard Grimes/Al Jackson on Al Green's 1972 "I'm Glad You're Mine." They plucked a few strings off Jamiroquai's gorgeous harp from "Morning Glory" then mixed in some cartoons, busted beat boxes, and onomatopoetics galore. A whirr out of nowhere; goblins 'n' shit. The record debuted at No. 3 on the pop charts and went on to sell over a million copies, which doesn't even begin to describe its transformative influence on the possibilities for hip hop in the next millennium. They recorded it in the spring of 1997 in a week or so. "What people doin' now with samples, we was doin' five years ago," Elliott said then. "On *Supa*, there's none of those *tik-kat-tik-kat-tik* beats like on Aaliyah's *One in a Million* because Tim noticed that people were starting to copy that. It's all good, though," she continued. "People know where it came from." There must be something in the air below the Mason-Dixon—something to do with country living and hearing crickets at night.

As a production team, Missy and Timbaland are comparable to some of the best duos: Jimmy Jam and Terry Lewis (for their crossover sensibility), Dr. Dre and Snoop Doggy Dogg (because they are a great team); and Ashford and Simpson (although Missy and Tim aren't married, they might as well be). They have a respect for each other's process and tell each other the truth. They love each other. "We so tight that you get our styles tangled," Missy once rhymed about her friend.

"I think we bring a fresh new sound. We're leaders," Missy says. "And we've always tried to do the opposite of what we hear on the radio. I think we're risky and edgy and never scared to do whatever we feel. The people are either gonna love it or hate it. And we don't wanna be the ones to wait. Because you'll always be mad at yourself if someone else end up doin' it. So we always gotta take that chance."

She says her influences are Japanese animé and sci-fi. What's inspiring her these days? "Orbit," she said in *Seventeen*. "I'm trying to create orbit sounds in the studio. Like what a Martian would sound like if it landed in the studio."

Missy and her crew represent the collective, entrepreneurial spirit of hip hop, the cipher and the economics. And of course she sits at the head of the table. "They can't make one move without confirming it with me," she says of her label. "I have creative control over my stuff no matter what. So if they want to put out a single for 'Rain' I can say, 'No, they got to buy the whole album.' Everything, I have creative control over everything." Bitch.

I had a moment the other night. It was a full moon and I was feeling irie, watching the video for "Hit 'Em Wit Da Hee," directed by Hype Williams. Set in medieval days, it begins with a steel Trojan horse trying to shake itself alive and Missy rhyming, walking through an enchanted forest alternately as warrior princess and spirit in white. Cut to a sequence where Missy and dancers tap and fly up off the ground in three-piece striped suits with matching hats. The choreography and mood reflect a place where Gene Kelly's *Singin' in the Rain* and Michael Jackson's "Smooth Criminal" meet. Dramatic close-ups of the Virginia family—Nicole Wray, Mocha, Ginuwine—with the wind in their face and amulets levitating around their heads.

On the break, a small chorus of pale ladies stand in a circle playing violins over the quiet boom of an 808, creating a beat that has me just yielding. Timbaland walks through this dominion in a wizard's cloak, repeating an old candy bar jingle like a mystical spell: *Sometimes I feel like doing a beat, sometimes I don't. Sometimes I feel like moving your feet, sometimes I won't.* Cut to Missy again, dancing her ass off, tapping her Nikes in the rain, everyone really *in* the moment. This is their offering. Proper, southern presentation of something utterly their own. They came together and made a sound and this is how it made them feel, this is where the music took them, to an enchanted forest, and they *went there*. Worked hard. Believed every minute of it. So I cried.

Thriller in all its momentous, innovative glory, was never, ever wasted on Missy. The video for her debut single "The Rain (Supa Dupa Fly)" would challenge notions of race, beauty, sociology, and psychology. There's Missy in an inflatable black vinyl jumpsuit with dark red sunglasses attached to a rhinestone headpiece sporting finger waves. In another scene, she sits high atop a grassy, trippy knoll, saying the simple nonsensical: "I feel the wind / Five six seven eight nine ten / Begin / I sit on hills like Lauryn / Until the rain starts comin' down pourin'." Her eyes and lips morph with choice words. She has on a long blond wig, and flips her head and rolls her eyes like a white girl.

"I want my videos to be different and cutting edge," Missy says. "I just got tired of seeing all these rappers in videos driving around in Mercedes and drinking champagne. Artists are usually more concerned about looking nice than making a video that's fun and interesting. I want people to look at my videos and say, 'What's she gonna do next?'"

Well how about 1999's "Hot Boyz"? It was an all-star posse cut, with braveheart Nas in the area, Eve before she went red and blew up, and pretty, lively Lil' Mo—who's blowing up now with her own album, *Based on a True Story.* The song was exciting (like an oncoming hurricane) and sexy, with Missy front and center rocking like Elvis, suit glittering red, her usual asymmetric longer and more dramatic, the better to toss off her face. The song became the highest charting rap single in the history of *Billboard,* holding the No. 1 spot for 18 weeks, breaking the 11-week record shared by Puffy, Coolio, and Da Brat.

Missy flows on whatever she's feeling at the moment, rhymes so subtle and tight you wouldn't suspect that they require close attention. It almost seems like she's toying with you. She's invented her own patois, a kind of southern dozens, like when she says:

Izzzy izzzy izzzy ahhh zzziiizzzaaah zizzaaa zzaaah
Bitches be talking like they all rah rah

Simple rhymes, yet highly effective at making an ass out of the competition. Because Missy will take it there. What are you going to do, whirr and beep back at her? There is also Missy's very soulful voice, a beautiful alto that knows yearning, from a girl who went to church a lot, listened to Prince and Teena Marie and *feeeels* things. Her movement is a lot like her music: stop and start; losing, then catching the beat and her balance. This movement creates that undeniable bounce. For Missy, this bounce represents freedom, the body's natural fall, that feeling of being at home, a place where you can raise your hands, close your eyes. The rhythm will do the rest.

A moan here, giggle there, a warm tongue lick behind your ear. Uhh. Uhh. Uhh. Missy comes from a long line of

nasty—in mind and expertise. Missy is a woman who grew up around guys, not quite a tomboy but she could get down, and was privy to certain information, which can make you a mack. She understands real sexiness is never tasteless or overt or desperate. It is in the mind, what you're saying, how you move your body, what you're doing with your life.

Missy understands that crossover does not necessarily mean compromise. She was the first hip hop artist to perform at Lilith Fair; she has been featured in Sprite and Gap commercials; she has her own shade of lipstick with Iman Cosmetics called Misdemeanor and part of the profits go to battered teens. She is a spokeswoman for Break the Cycle, an organization for victims of domestic violence. Because she is a young, eager businesswoman, she sometimes contradicts (like having all-round hater Eminem rhyme on *Da Real World*'s "Busa Rhyme": "Three things I hate: girls, women and bitches," and also: "Punch a bitch in the nose till the whole face explodes," like that didn't happen to her mama). Or, flying in the face of self-sufficiency on "All in My Grill," she sings, "If you want me, where's my dough? Give me money, buy me clothes!" Then on "Hot Boyz" she rhymes: "I'ma dig in your pockets, dig in your wallet, is that money I'm foundin'? Yeah you got my heart poundin' . . ."

Even as artists like Keith Richards sweat her for beats, Missy keeps her music as raw as ever. "This album is 3000," she says, skipping ahead. "And it's real street. The beats are crazy." She wants to talk about "where black folks are from, and where we're going." She knows about lack firsthand and satisfies the need for luxury in her life. Missy is dark and sexy, glamorous, international, and elemental. She likes leather, diamonds, and fast cars that move like lightning. And she has earned every bauble.

Missy Elliott embodies a charm that breaks down barriers. She's a dancer who taught television another way to move and see. She is always the subject, never an object. She has challenged America's notions of what is sexy (she rubs herself at whim and still makes people notice her eyes). She is a creator, not just an interpreter of other people's words. She is a dark-skinned, big-body girl who manages not only to challenge historical stereotypes but mocks, exaggerates, and celebrates herself in the process. The result is something soulful, yet industrial, correct and exact. It's the stuff of which Shapeshifters, superheroes, titans, and bitches are made. As she said at the end of "The Rain": *To have me, yes you lucky.*

She was in
love and I'd
ask her how?
I mean why?
What kind of
love from a
nigga would
black your eye?

Photograph by Marc Joseph

all
about
eve *by Greg Tate*

"**S**trictly dickly" is what an off-the-air Eve has to tell a deflated and disappointed caller to Funkmaster Flex's radio show who can't believe she's not a lesbian. "How can you not be a lesbian when you have so many lesbian fans?" the heartbroken voice on the other end of the line wants to know.

Inside the downtown Manhattan studios of Hot 97 FM, Eve struggles to explain why she loves men, who are so, so, so . . . *something* to her that she's at a loss for words to explain at the moment. Whereupon the caller takes the opportunity to pounce on all the Y-chromosome carriers in the house, admonishing the dog in them. "Yes, men are dogs," says Eve, nodding in agreement with homegirl's wise observation. "But I can train a dog."

As the First Lady of the Ruff Ryders (per the title of her 1999 platinum debut), and a veteran of tours with Juvenile (of "Back That Azz Up" fame) and the Cash Money crew, Eve has had ample opportunity to hone her canine-taming skills. Earl "DMX" Simmons calls her "the meanest female pit bull in a skirt." But a big part of Eve Jihan Jeffers's charm is that like most of what you'd call Real Black Women, gay and straight alike, she seems quite unfazed by the company of such certified roughnecks as DMX, Ja Rule, the Lox, and their assorted entourages. She even seems to thrive on the challenge, gracefully negotiating monstrous mounds of Nubian testosterone with her femininity and Scorpio wiles intact.

Like her song says, Eve's "Gotta Man." Producer Stevie J, who built many a blazing hot beat as one of Puffy's Hit Men, looks like the kind of cat you don't want to hear found out you were bothering his woman. It also can't hurt that unlike a lot of folk in the game, Eve's also got a life. Meaning close family ties, good friends, and deep roots in Philadelphia's projects and its black middle-class 'hoods, too.

Those who've listened closely to the *First Lady* album have realized Eve's not just rhyming for the sake of riddlin'. Coded in her lyrics are hardcore messages of homegirl empowerment. "I don't even know you and I'd kill you myself," Eve spits in "Love Is Blind," a damn-near operatic showdown between a wicked baby-father and a homegirl vigilante. "Played with her like a doll and put her back on the shelf / Wouldn't let her go to school and better herself / She had a baby by your ass and you ain't giving no help.")

Though she wouldn't call herself a "womanist" a la Alice Walker, I will, extracting from her lines a vision of inner-city sisterhood that may be understandably lost on folk all caught up in her platinum blond (or, more recently, hot-pink) butch haircut, pouty lips, and breast-stalking paw-print tattoos.

On the brief boulevard of superstar women MCs, 22-year-old Eve has rapidly established a place for herself somewhere between Lauryn Hill's House of Afrocentric Spirits and Lil' Kim's Rough Sex and Magick Shoppe. Being neither a roots goddess nor an urban bush nymph, Eve had to present another recipe for becoming a household name: Mix three parts keep-it-raw with five parts skillz, pour on seven parts ghetto-glamorous-and-gangsta-friendly, sprinkle liberally with megadoses of down-for-all-my-girls-holding-it-down-in-the-'hood, then stir and strut.

Up close and personal Eve is all that and a bag of sweet potato chips. She's got the kind of star charisma that arrives in the room before she does. And when she does arrive—in her glitter-mesh silver hoody, booty-hugging fashion jeans, seriously stylish silver stiletto-heeled black suede boots with pockmarked metal toe braces, metallic gold nails, her head and carriage more erect than a racing stallion—it's obvious why she's hip hop's No. 1 It Girl.

Eve has just got that thang which separates the true diva from those desperately seeking the title. She's more petite than the camera would have us believe (the lens likes its Eve about 10 pounds thicker). And as my wife and co-interviewer Tamar-Kali noted, she's more cherubic about the face than the rice-burner-riding mama in the video snarling, "What y'all niggas want / Can't touch / All y'all niggas need . . ." like her love was about to mow down your battlefield.

She's also become the darling of fashionistas like the

head designer for Chanel. "Karl Lagerfeld just loves her," Eve's stylist Brewster told VIBE. "He's the one who invited her to pick clothes to wear to the Chanel party." Did she just borrow $20,000 worth of gear? "Oh, no," Brewster said, beaming. "She gets to keep them. Ghetto fabulous is over. Now we're just fabulous."

The place Eve has carved out for herself at the intersection of counterculture and couture-culture that is hip hop lies in that place between bona fide supermodel and roughneck female MC. In many ways Eve is what we've all been waiting for in a female lyricist: someone with the stage presence and rhyme prowess to go toe to toe with the guys plus the kundalini charisma of a DMX, a Method Man, or a Jay-Z.

After the initial furor around her debut died down, Eve wisely stayed out of the public eye so the release of her sophomore joint *Scorpion* would not suffer from being overhyped. What was available for hearing at this writing displayed a sure stepping up of her game not only in terms of lyrics and production but unexpected guest appearances. Yes, her man Stevie J provided her with a couple of hot joints. Dr. Dre contributed two tracks as well, one of which ("Let Me Blow Ya Mind") features Eve singing with No Doubt's Gwen Stefani. She actually does a considerable bit of crooning on the album, laying down a sweet lead on a remake of Jamaican Dawn Penn's "No, No, No" (produced by Damian and Stephen Marley). Her chat-style rhymes on this track are quite credible, too. All in all it's precisely the kind of quality second album Eve's die-hard fans are expecting, a sure solidifier of her position as the undisputed queen of hip hop MCs.

Given the way Lil' Kim overexposed herself, not just flesh-wise but media-wise, long before her second joint came out, and the near retirement of Salt-N-Pepa and Latifah from the game, and Lauryn Hill's seeming withdrawal from public life after her multiplatinum multi-Grammy conquests of 1999—not to mention the failure of contenders like Amil and Rah Digga to catch fire . . . well, given all that, it's clear Eve pretty much has the field to herself, with the possible exception of Missy and Foxy. Besides, who else is there that can give you bad girl, beauty queen, and high school sweetheart all in the same breath?

Perhaps the most intriguing thing about Eve is her refusal to let the hoopla demolish her human touch. Down at Flex's show she's hanging with her best friend and fellow Illadelphian Diona. Though Dee's an 18-year-old Saggitarius, they appear to have been separated at birth. They've developed a unique way of communicating that has its own sign and body language, is likely to break into two-part harmony at will, and drops crazy inside jokes you'd need a cryptographer to crack. One such exchange seems to recall a night spent making crank calls with Dee adopting names that sounded like condiments and foodstuffs. You had to be there, and even if you were it would be their world and you'd be the Squirrel, so don't trip. The point is they'z girlz.

The radio station was also where I first noticed Eve's effect on your average brother (be he young, not-so-old, Geritolic, or bound for Jurassic Park). The general tendency among the young'uns is to just not look at her—they stare at the floor when she's around and don't even dare sneak a peek. Middle-aged cats, like the guards in the lobby, will shout her out, but only when she's walking away from them. Call it respectfully awestruck.

The same male behavior recurs in Philly, where I've been sent to scope sis on her old stomping grounds. As she's leaving a luxury hotel after Sunday brunch with her six-year-old baby brother Farrod, a whole bunch of blue-collar O.G. gather behind the entrance's double doors to watch her limo pull off. It would seem that Eve really has got this dog-training thing down to a science.

Set down in Philly at Eve's family's crib and you really get to see normalcy in action. The star's equally fly mom invites this writer and his traveling wife to partake of some home cookin' like we're regulars: a tangy spiced whiting, house salad, and lemonade, all spread out for the gang of friends and family who will roll through on this particular evening.

Mom, stepdad, and baby brother live in Philly's Germantown, an immaculate district where they own a two-floor house on a hilly street whose pavement and lawns are blanketed by torrents of autumn leaves. Their home is warm, attractive, and tastefully decorated. Mom coordinates fashion shows in the area and he's a designer who was once Minister Louis Farrakhan's tailor. A portrait of Dad and the Minister beams brotherhood over the family dining room.

Eve hasn't stepped out of the limo for two seconds before a group of barely adolescent little brothers across the street begins arguing among themselves whether or not it's really her. The debate rages on even after they've inched their caravan a bit more up the block and Eve jumps the gun on their asses, offering up autographs if they've got a pen. Once the question of her true identity gets settled, they decide to wait outside her door for hours. They're just young enough to not be intimidated by her sheer presence.

Eve (who bought herself a three-bedroom house in an exclusive community in northern New Jersey) did not grow up in Germantown but in West Philly, a much rougher side of town. As we drive into her and her mom's original base, the Mill Creek projects, Eve recalls her childhood here as a "pretty normal one of playing baseball, running around, and basically acting like a boy." Her mother and father separated when Eve was twelve, and Eve spent a few years as a self-described "goddamn delinquent." She even did a month-long bid as a stripper (stage name: "Mystique") before turning to a life of rhyme. Eve credits former Bad Boy all-star Mase with straightening her out. "He talked to me for like two hours," she explains. "He said, 'You are too smart to be doing this. You wanna rap, you want a career. You need to get away from this.'"

'Tis the season when Philly gets chilly and choppy so Eve is wearing a Muppet-furry orange mink hoody that she says makes her feel like "a monster." She makes a mental note to acquire a goose down and a few sweaters before winter rolls in for real. The landscape around Mill Creek is bleak, desolate, and foreboding in that peculiar way of project environments. You're not sure people live there until you're right up in their faces. The side of one tower has so many broken windows scarring its facade you just know the place is vacant—except that the scarification pattern isn't repeated on the next one.

actions with Farrod, who goes into tantrum mode whenever his big sister has to leave him behind). This little acre of Mill Creek being full of "de youths," Eve is enveloped by "Jah pickney" as her entourage is trying to break out.

Asked about the burden of being a role model, she replies calmly: "It comes along with the job. You don't ask for it. People don't want to admit it, but you can't deny it, it's there. Every entertainer knows little kids look up to them. I think we just have to be more careful. That's how I feel about the situation. There are artists I like who are pretty out there but I got a little brother, I got little cousins and I love kids a lot."

While the women and children of Mill Creek smother Eve in affection, the neighborhood hardrocks stay behind an invisible perimeter line, cautiously gawking without having to be so uncool as to toss a hearty "Wassup" her way. Observing Eve at this stage of her career ride is like watching a devious science experiment on the effects of instant fame and celebrity on a single human life. What happens when pop stardom happens to sensible people? Repeat the

"A little ten-year-old girl was telling me how she told her dad she was going to dress just like me when she grew up," says Eve. "That's dope. I like that parents feel good about their kids liking me."

As our white stretch Lincoln glides past the somber monoliths, Eve points out a smaller building as her former address. We pull into the narrow alleyway behind a complex of duplexes, and a denim-clad young blood starts motioning at the vehicle like he's guiding in a 747. This would-be clown turns out to be J'vonne Pierson, professional comedian and one of Eve's best friends since childhood. His tapes of *Showtime* and *Def Comedy Jam* appearances have us rolling when we stop by his mom's house. J'vonne remembers Eve as a blur of motion, and her mom being even more in the wind. The less-traveled road from Mill Creek to Germantown is a race for the swift, no doubt. In J'vonne's mother's house, surrounded by siblings and adoring elders, Eve's remembered as "a good girl."

Children start spilling out of the woodwork soon as Eve appears—one little mama jetting out her back door with no shoes on, paper in hand, dead-set on getting an autograph. Eve is majorly kid-friendly (as we've already seen in her inter-

old saying about how "You don't change so much as the people around you do," and Eve will concur. She detests it when people she's known for years roll up in her face screaming and cheesing. "They'll go, 'It's Eve!' like they think I must want that," she says. "But I don't."

Success has also found her compiling a file of knuckleheaded remarks from brothers who just don't know no better, the poor dears. "One guy told me, 'I've always thought you were fine but now that you're a star you're the sexiest motherfucker in the world to me.' Another one said, 'Before you got famous I always wanted to talk to you.'" Somebody tell them to give it a rest. The irony is that Eve's truly down to earth enough to roll up in the PJs in a mink and a stretch and still make everybody feel as if there's nothing abnormal going on. By the same token she and her management team, Philly-based Black Friday, also recognize that her status demands a Fruit of Islam security team with Secret Service–level skills. Not to mention a home with enough back entrances that "no one will ever know I'm there."

You want Eve in a nutshell? Try chill, calm, confident, and uncontrivedly style-conscious. She's been rocking her short 'do for six years because she just got tired of going to the hairdresser every week: "It just took too much time in the morning, so I said let me just cut it and slap some gel on it." These days Eve's got a hair specialist named Treasure whom she flies everywhere to hook up the mini-braids and spikes. "Now people bug out if they even think I'm about to change my hair."

Inquiries from Tamar-Kali about the cornrows in the "What Y'all Want" video elicit a response that's pure comedy. "I was like, man, I'm doing this Spanish song with all these Spanish *mamís* with all this hair so I need some hair, too. I said let me get some braids, girl. After that people were like, 'Girl you need to get those braids back because I went and got braids because of you.'"

Eve became an urban fashion trendsetter without really trying. "My image is Eve as I really am," she says. "The things I wear now are things I would've worn before I got signed if I had the money. I always saw myself as sexy but not vulgar. To make people say, like, 'I don't know what it is about Shorty, but *damn.'* That's how I always wanted to be. Because sexy is not the little teeny shirt I got on, it's the attitude. The ugliest person in the world can be sexy. One thing that worried me when I came out was whether or not the world was going to like me because I'm not naked. But people always tell me I represent for real females. Like, 'Girl, you got your clothes on, and that's great because we wear clothes, too.'"

Without losing her hardcore fans, Eve was quickly embraced by the mainstream showbiz machine, appearing on the cover of mags like *Teen People*. "A little ten-year-old girl was telling me how she told her dad she was going to dress just like me when she grew up," she says. "That's dope. I like that parents feel good about their kids liking me. I feel like I'm doing something right if parents listen to my CD with their kids. I apologize to parents for the cursing but I'm not extra out there. I talk like regular people and regular people curse during the day. You got to talk like your people to get through to your people."

That Eve is fanatically focused on handling her business

Eve with Chivon and Wah Dean of Ruff Ryders and producer Swizz Beats.

is the quality that keeps her appealing to the Black Friday management team of Mark and Sherman Byers, Siddiq Knox, and Troy Carter, who also handle Jay-Z protégé Beanie Siegal. Experience taught them to appreciate an artist who "comes ready to do work and still makes every sound check on time." Black Friday was responsible for Eve's first deal, an ill-fated stint with Dr. Dre's Aftermath label. After six months, and the release of "Eve of Destruction" on the *Bulworth* soundtrack, the Aftermath deal seemed to be going nowhere fast, as Dre was preoccupied with producing Eminem and his own comeback album. So Black Friday brought her to Ruff Ryders, where her audition entailed an on-the-spot freestyle battle with Drag-On and Infa-Red. Eve showed and proved her readiness for battle, "Rhyme for rhyme, skill for skill," as she relates it. Fellow Ruff Ryder Drag On acknowledged that "she had the ill potential."

This proved, however, to be only the first rung of winning over the company's nonbelievers. "When I first got with Ruff Ryders, Chivon [the co-CEO] was like, 'Whatever, so we signed a girl.' Now she loves me to death. They'd had other girls there before who turned out to be groupies, but they saw that I worked like this was my life *and* my business. There were people there who believed I was going to be the next one and they helped me believe in myself. But there were bets on me. People around the company were betting on whether or not I could do the album. It's all good because I proved myself and those who bet against me lost their money."

Addressing the difference between an MC and a rapper, Eve hits the nail squarely on the head. "An MC's thing comes from within them—MCs are artists, they're deeper, they're about always mentally expanding. A rapper is someone who gets their stuff written for them. Someone who's just . . . rappin'." Though Eve has always written her own material she hadn't really defined herself as an artist until she tried recording a whole album.

"I discovered my flow and voice and character when I got signed to Ruff Ryders. I dropped the Eve of Destruction name that I'd used on the *Bulworth* track and became Eve. Just being around DMX and the Lox, the type of people they are, when they build with you as an artist they want

One reason success hasn't gone straight to Eve's head is because she hardly sees platinum as the be-all and end-all of her vision quest. Blinded by the fast-fading glare of this hip hop game, Eve is not. Eyes wide shut? Honey, she ain't even. And to cap it all off she has already made her peace with the short shelf life of an MC and is already plotting her exit far in advance.

"Some of the guys who are rapping now, all they can see is right now," she says as a Philadelphia nightscape flies past her tinted windows. "It's about their music and that's it. They don't have a vision. I know because I ask questions like, 'What are your plans?' and there is no plan." But like a certain New Orleans rap mogul, Eve sees a future with no limit. "I feel that this is just a stepping-stone. But they don't see it like that. They think they're going to be around forever. I'm not going to be spitting bars for the rest of my life. I don't see me with a record deal at thirty-five. I see a lot of properties, a lot of investments. I see me as a businesswoman, maybe in music, but maybe not."

Somewhere down the line, she wants to take the whole

"Women in hip hop need more unity," says Eve. "When I met Pepa I wouldn't let her go I hugged her so hard. I was like, I love you, man. Roxanne Shanté, Queen Latifah—you must respect them. You just must."

to know who you are. They say, 'Write about what you know, write about what you're feeling.' When I started keepin' it real is when I realized, 'All right, I don't have to try and be nobody else.' The world can accept it or not accept it, but it feels good just being me. That *Bulworth* track was me trying anything to get signed, shouting out Dre and Aftermath, whatever. I was younger, and hungrier in a different kind of way then. I'm hungry now because I have a purpose. Before I was just . . . rappin'."

Pursuit of a greater purpose is also moving Eve toward a full embrace of the Sunni Muslim faith. "Islam is peace," she says. "I've been through Jehovah's Witnesses, the Baptist church thing, Catholicism . . . couldn't do it. I went to Catholic school for two years wondering, 'What is this Trinity thing?' They were like 'Shut up already.' I got into Islam because of a friend of mine across the street. I liked praying and learning. I don't know hardly enough about the Koran, but when I say the prayers, I feel peace."

wife and motherhood trip. "To me, it's a blessing, but it's really not in my plans now," Eve says. "Maybe in two years, when I'm twenty-four." Married or not, she says she'll continue being her own woman: "On the new album I say, 'Got my own money now / Ain't got to be nobody's wife. / Only if I want to, not 'cause I need you.'"

The film *The Terminator* describes a creature known as the Infiltrator model, a humanoid assassin capable of blending in with the underground rebel population before blowtorching their asses and blowing up the whole spot. Eve's near-perfect combination of brains, beauty, and spit lends her an Infiltrator-like profile in the dick-dominated world of hip hop. It's as if she was on a mission to stand the game on its little head by going where no other female MC has gone, rolling raw-dogg with the hardest of the hard, stacking her papes and breaking the hell out of Bucktown long before she reaches that age when most MCs are plotting their third and most pathetic comeback attempt.

This may make her seem like a mercenary to some, but hip hop, quiet as its kept, has always been a three-headed beast—art form, culture, and business enterprise. The fact that Eve is keeping a tight rein on all these areas is a sign of how much her hip hop generation has in common with the billion-dollar babies of the Internet. Eve's arrived in an era where realness is measured in Benjamins, and representin' for hip hop means you're getting love from the fickle-ass streets and fickle-ass MTV and taking it to the bank pronto. Having ascended the biz's slippery slopes, Eve would be a fool not to have a plan worked out for the downside. Judging from the evidence we've seen, mama didn't raise no fool.

She's signed a modeling contract with the Ford agency though Eve generally hates looking at herself in photos ("I see every detail that's wrong"), and she agrees with me that the public would probably like to see the "Seven Deadly Venoms" Sprite commercial (featuring her, Roxanne Shanté, Mia X, and Angie Martinez) made into a feature film. When we talk she's all about her hit CD *Scorpio*, but for future recordings, her wish list includes Premier ("gotta get a joint from him because I just gotta") as well as duets with Jay-Z, Lil' Kim, and a new acquaintance, Lauryn Hill.

"Talking with Lauryn was like a motivational speech," says Eve with a warm glow. "She told me to be strong, and that I was gifted and I need to do things wisely. It was dope to be talking to her that day because I was having issues with myself about the game. I'd love to do a big sister–little sister thing with her where she's teaching something. Women in hip hop need more unity. I love the women in hip hop. When I met Pepa I wouldn't let her go I hugged her so hard. I was like, I love you, man. Roxanne Shanté, Queen Latifah—you must respect them, you just must."

HIP
HER
74757677787980818283848586 8

HOP
STORY

VIBE TIMELINE: 28 YEARS OF WOMEN IN HIP HOP

8899009192939495969798990001

Sequence

By Sun Singleton

I f ever there was a woman who personified the resiliency and all-around fierceness that have come to define a hip hop legend, it has to be Ms. Angie Stone. The only child of protective, working-class parents in Columbia, South Carolina, Angie's performing life began as a cheerleading captain in high school. Along with fellow pom-pom girls Cheryl "The Pearl" Cook and Gwendolyn "MC Blondie" Chisolm, Stone was able to flip rah-rah cheers into funky-fresh raps that nabbed them a deal with Sugar Hill Records and a new life as the rap trio Sequence.

Breaking ground for future sassy-mouthed chicks like Salt-N-Pepa and the velvet-voiced renaissance woman Lauryn Hill, Sequence was among the first to lay the black-girl pizzazz on hip hop vinyl. Their song "Funk You Up" was the second record released on the Sugar Hill label in 1980. A tough-talking honeydip with much attitude to spare, Angie B. was the vicious to Cheryl's hot and Blondie's cool, and their high-octane mix of rapping and singing scorched a path of womanfire right through the manicured lawns of early '80s black radio.

"We're definitely the first females to integrate rap and singing together," says Stone. "You hear that in every hip hop song on the radio, from Jay-Z and Dr. Dre to Lauryn Hill and Queen Latifah—everything is a signature of what Sequence started." The fact that most of today's hip hop fans have never even heard of Sequence is something Angie, in her own words, "takes personal." Especially after the Fugees blew up and people began telling Stone that she sounded like Lauryn. "Don't get it twisted," she told them. "I know it's been a long time but, obviously Lauryn Hill reminds you of Angie Stone."

Stone has gone on to become an R&B diva in her own right, and the trio still keeps in touch, but don't look for any comeback attempts from Sequence. "After you've done it for five or ten years, consider yourself a pioneer," says Stone. "You're not fresh. You're not hot. You're just keepin' it goin'."

1974
Georgia-born and Brooklyn-based R&B singer Millie Jackson delivers salty spoken-word monologues on her R&B album *Caught Up*, which receives a Grammy nomination. She says she wasn't trying to be a rapper, but began talking on records because she didn't think she could sing well.

1976
A Bronx high school student named Sharon Jackson changes her name to Sha Rock and becomes the sole female member of a new rap group called the Funky Four.

1977
The Mercedes Ladies, the first all-girl hip hop crew—featuring as many as four MCs and two DJs—premier in the South Bronx.

1978
Harlem-based doo-wop producer Paul Winley records his school-age daughters—Paulette Tee and Sweet Tee (not to be confused with the Sweet Tee who would later rap with DJ Jazzy Joyce)—performing "Vicious Rap," one of the first rap records ever, and the first to feature female talent.

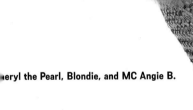

...eryl the Pearl, Blondie, and MC Angie B.

1979
Former R&B singer
Sylvia Robinson founds
the seminal rap label,
Sugar Hill Records.
Their first release is
"Rapper's Delight" by
the Sugarhill Gang,
which enters the *Bill-board* pop charts,
becoming hip hop's
first hit record.

1979
Sequence, a glamorous
rap trio featuring future
R&B star Angie Stone,
releases "Funk You
Up," the first of 10
singles for Sugar Hill,
and becomes the label's
first all-girl group.

1979
Lady B, a Philadelphia
rapper and radio per-
sonality, releases "To
the Beat, Y'All," making
her the first woman
outside of New York to
make a record.

1980
Queen Lisa Lee, a
member of Afrika
Bambaataa's Cosmic
Force, shines on the
first recorded tribute to
Bam's Zulu Nation,
"Zulu Nation Throw-
down."

Jazzy Joyce
By Cristina Verán

This Bronx-born turntable veteran wins the prize for staying power in the hip hop game. She began DJing in 1981, learning the ropes from her cousin Chovie-Chove and DJ Whiz Kid at the tender age of 11. From her earliest appearances at 'round-the-way jams, she defied all doubters who had low expectations for a female on the wheels of steel. Joyce cherishes her memories of those early days. "Hip hop was the bomb back then," says Joyce. "The breakers were in the house and I'd mix records like Apache with some Talking Heads and Billy Squier rock cuts for them."

Hooking up with a group called The Sweet Trio, she recorded "Non Stop" for Tommy Boy Records in 1986, and soon thereafter got together with an MC counterpart named Sweet Tee. Their hit "It's My Beat," released on the same label, became a classic selection that solidified Joyce's reputation for good. "You don't wanna miss / Jazzy Joyce on the mix," Sweet Tee rapped, and she wasn't lying.

When the record blew up, it also opened up other avenues for Joyce, including live shows, mix tapes, and radio work that led to her current gig, "Ladies' Night" on N.Y.C.'s HOT 97 FM. Every Friday night finds Joyce holding court with Nuyorican rap *mamí* Angie Martinez and DJ Cocoa Chanel in one of the few all-female rap shows on the radio.

"What was your struggle?" Monie Love once asked Joyce during a recent TV interview. "Just being considered wack before you start," she replied with an note of exasperation in her voice. "But I guess I got thick skin now." Joyce has learned to move carefully through the male-dominated rap arena. "There's always this element of I wanna fuck you," she has lamented. But she has no regrets about the path she's chosen: "Without this I do not know how I would have expressed myself artistically, I would have been living or dying in the 'hood." Joyce is currently making forays into the area of production, a natural next step for the woman to whom "music is life."

168 HIP HOP HERSTORY

1980
Soulful funkstress Teena Marie, Rick James's Caucasian protégée, busts a few rhymes as alter-ego "Lady Tee" on her hit single "Square Biz."

1981
Funky 4 + 1 More, featuring Sha Rock, becomes the first rap group on national television when guest host Debbie Harry invites them to perform on *Saturday Night Live*.

1981
British promoter (and later Rock Steady Crew manager) Ruza "Cool Lady" Blue begins hip hop's first cross-cultural exchange program at downtown Manhattan's Club Negril, where open-minded new wavers blend with b-boys and Bambaataa's breakbeats.

1982
A white, French-speaking woman who calls herself Bee Side records "Change the Beat," the first non-English rap record.

1982
Sugar Hill exec Sylvia Robinson turns rapper for "It's Good to Be Queen," her response to a Mel Brooks's comedy rap "It's Good to Be King."

1982
Lisa Lee busts a rhyme in the classic underground hip hop movie *Wild Style.*

1983
Baby Love from New York's Rock Steady Crew rhymes on the single "Hey You, the Rocksteady Crew," becoming the first b-girl dancer to rap on wax.

1984
Sha Rock, Lisa Lee, and Debbie Dee—together known as Us Girls—perform in the movie *Beat Street,* making them the first female rappers to appear in a major motion picture. DJ Wanda Dee has a cameo in the movie, too, repping for female turntablists.

Debbie Harry *By Cristina Verán*

There's no denying that Debbie Harry has deep roots—not just in her trademark platinum-bleached coif, but in New York's musical underground. Her band Blondie embodied the open-minded punk-meets-pop attitude of the late '70s and early '80s. This was a time when discotheques and Top 40 radio stations were still willing to mix and blend different genres of music on the regular.

In the days when hip hop stars first headed downtown from the Bronx and upper Manhattan, Harry encountered this inner-city youthquake at spots like The Roxy and the Mudd Club, where DJs like Afrika Bambaataa rocked roomfuls of spiky-haired, safety-pin-pierced punk types along with the customary assortment of MCs, DJs, graffiti artists, and breakers. The disparate tribes were united by a love of cool sounds, and a common search for an alternative to the stifling monotony of disco.

Blondie became the first nonrap group to pay tribute to hip hop culture—years before most black R&B stars would even consider such a thing. On her 1980 hit "Rapture" she rhymed in her own unique fashion, dropping references that proved she was not just biting a style but paying homage to a culture: "Fab Five Freddy told me everybody's fly / DJ spinning I said 'My My' / Flash is fast, Flash is cool . . ."

In subsequent years, Harry's bandmate and life-partner, Chris Stein, went on to coproduce the music for the seminal hip hop film *Wildstyle*. Harry herself did a brief cameo in the film *Krush Groove* and contributed "Feel the Spin" to its soundtrack. She was even invited to appear at Sugar Hill Records' First Anniversary Rap Convention alongside the likes of Sha Rock and Sequence. Any lingering doubts about Harry's contributions to hip hop culture were blown away when KRS-One adapted the melody of "Rapture" for his 1997 hit, "Step Into a World (Rapture's Delight)."

In the final analysis, Debbie Harry matters because she did more than just dabble in hip hop; she helped spread it far and wide, opening up whole new audiences for rap music decades before the invasion of the Limp Bizkits.

1984
Salsa songstress Brenda K. Starr—born as the Puerto Rican–Jewish Brenda Kaplan—sings and raps her song "Vicious Beat" in the movie *Beat Street*. Starr would later give Mariah Carey her start in the music biz as a backup singer.

1984
Inspired by UTFO's 1984 hit "Roxanne, Roxanne," a Roxanne craze sweeps the hip hop nation, introducing the likes of Roxanne Shanté, *two* "Real" Roxannes, Sparky D, and a host of forgettables who couldn't resist jumping into the dis-fest.

1984
Puerto Rican MC Joanne Martinez, better known as the (second) Real Roxanne, becomes the first Latina MC on wax with the release of "The Real Roxanne."

1985
Sparky D snags the first commercial endorsement for a rapper, appearing in a Mountain Dew radio ad 16 years before Busta Rhymes does the Dew.

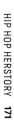

1985
The girl group Supernature is born, dropping "The Show Stoppa (Is Stupid Fresh)," their answer to Doug E. Fresh and Slick Rick's smash hit "The Show." Supernature would eventually morph into the platinum rap crew Salt-N-Pepa.

1985
Queens-bred K-Love rocks the first female human beat box on wax in the song "Bad Boys" (a.k.a. "Inspector Gadget").

1985
Shaunie Dee, the white girl who danced in Malcolm McLaren's classic 1981 "Buffalo Gals" video along with the Rock Steady Crew, becomes the first female rapper to throw down in the New Music Seminar's MC Battle for World Supremacy—against future Ultramagnetics star Kool Keith, no less.

1986
Ann Carli signs DJ Jazzy Jeff and the Fresh Prince to Jive Records, launching the career of megastar Will Smith. She goes on to work with A Tribe Called Quest and, later, Britney Spears.

J.J. Fad *By Cristina Verán*

Rocking fresh Nike volleyball jerseys and big dark sunglasses, MCJ.B., Baby-D, and Sassy C—three 'round-the-way girls from Compton, CA—became J.J. Fad, the first female rap ensemble to sell a million records. Their 1988 platinum album *Supersonic* on Ruthless Records was also a milestone for a young producer known as Dr. Dre, who went on to define the sound of hip hop through his work with N.W.A, Snoop Dogg, and Eminem. This girl group may not have been Dre's greatest artistic achievement, but there's no denying that J.J. Fad helped prove that rap music had a rightful place on the pop charts. Their music was totally nonthreatening—unlike their gangstafied label mates.

Originally an acronym of each member's first name, J.J. Fad was eventually flipped to spell out the casually boastful motto, "Just Jammin' Fresh and Def." Their new moniker also hinted at the fad-like frenzy their single "Supersonic" would inspire. The tune boasted a dance-able bass-heavy beat and spirited, rapid-fire rhymes like: "Supersonic motivating rhymes are creating / And everybody knows that J.J. Fad is devastating."

Drawn like moths to a flame, J.J. Fad jumped into the already heated battles of their East Coast counterparts, releasing the track "Anotha Ho" to dis Sparky D, Roxanne Shanté, The Real Roxanne, and Salt-N-Pepa. This may have been a mistake, since few listeners ever considered them serious competition. But J.J. Fad maintained loyal ties to their South Central roots throughout, featuring a cameo rap from Ice Cube on their song "Ya Goin' Down"—a brutal dis aimed at Shanté—while also getting down on the banger-truce anthem "We're All in the Same Gang."

For a minute, they promised to be more than just a fad, but the group disbanded once and for all in 1992. But their influence lived on—for better or worse—when Ruthless Records founder Eazy E unveiled another female trio, Hoez With Attitude.

87

1987
On the strength of spicy songs like "Shake Your Thang," Salt-N-Pepa sells half a million copies of their album *A Salt with a Deadly Pepa.*

1987
California's J.J. Fad becomes the first female rap group to sell a million records—for N.W.A founder Eazy E's Ruthless label—with their single "Supersonic."

1987
B-Boy Records (the same label that launched Boogie Down Productions) releases the first all-female rap compilation, *B-Girls Live & Kickin',* featuring L.A. Star and Sparky D.

1987
Anquette becomes the first female MC to represent for Miami with "Do the 61st," "Throw the P," and "Ghetto Style" on porn-rap mogul Luther Campbell's Luke Skyywalker label. She would later immortalize Janet Reno in song for her work to enforce child support payments.

J.J. Fad with
Whodini (left) and
Big Daddy Kane
(right).

1987
Antoinette lashes out at
an unsuspecting MC
Lyte with her hit single,
"I Got an Attitude,"
sparking an epic battle
between the two
women.

1988
Lyte gets the better of
Antoinette with "10%
Dis"—just one of the
outstanding tracks
from her take-no-
prisoners debut album,
Lyte as a Rock.

1988
The U.K.'s Wee Papa
Girl Rappers become
the first overseas rap
group to score a hit
record in the U.S. with
the reggae dancehall–
inflected "Wee Rule."

1988
South Florida rap cuties
L'Trimm—Bunny D. and
Lady Tigra—drop their
silly, unforgettable hit
"Cars with the Boom."

Antoinette *By Michael A. Gonzales*

First introduced on producer Hurby "Luv Bug" Azor's funky 1988 compilation, *Hurby's Machine,* the b-girl wild child who went by the name Antoinette was definitely no joke. With a voice as cool as an iceberg, she repped the tougher side of Girls Town on "I Got an Attitude." Riding a raw, hardcore beat as though it were a bucking bronco, Antoinette boasted that she was "the mike smoker of chicks." Forget about sisterhood, this bad mama from Queens—who later adopted the title "the gangstress of rap"—was ready to attack all rivals at the drop of a hat.

Obsessed with the skills of Brooklyn bomber MC Lyte, Antoinette spent much of her 1989 debut, *Who's the Boss* (Next Plateau), trying to drag her competitor's name through the mud. Dressed in 'round-the-way-girl chic on the album cover, Antoinette's denims and fat gold chain were reminiscent of Big Daddy Kane with lipstick. Produced by I.G. Off, Jay Ellis, and Cedric Miller from Ultramagnetics, *Who's the Boss* was a rather lackluster affair in comparison to her blazing leadoff single.

But her sophomore disc, *Burnin' at 20 Below,* proved that not only could Antoinette snap, she could shine, too. Pulling no punches, she kept throwing fits at Lyte on "The Fox That Rox the Box." But at least she tried to expand her horizons beyond the land of cat fights. On the leadoff track, "I Wanna Be Me," she dropped some truly independent funk amidst tumbling drums, syrupy bass, and slippery synth notes. "Has anybody ever tried to change ya / Shape ya, mix and twist—rearrange ya?" asked Antoinette. These lyrics could have been the mantra for a generation of women rappers who felt like puppets on the strings of male producers. Antoinette also teamed with Spinderella and Pepa on the splashy asphalt-shaker "Never Get Enough," later hooking up with machine-dreamer Curtis Mantronik on the smooth pre-techno electro jam "From the Top."

Although many years have passed since hip hop America has heard a peep from Antoinette—according to an old associate, she's now an officer of the NYPD—wherever she might be, it's safe to say she still has an attitude.

1988
Finnese and Synquis become the first women to put fashion at the forefront of their game by rocking Dapper Dan's faux MCM and Gucci suits. Unfortunately, their style was the most appealing thing about them.

1988
On his album *Lovesexy,* Prince enlists the services of a female rapper identified only as Cat, who urges listeners to "jerk your body like a horny pony would."

1988
Yo! MTV Raps host Fab 5 Freddy passes a tape of Latifah's "Princess of the Posse" demo to Tommy Boy's Monica Lynch. Swayed by the sounds, and the support of A&R Dante Ross and DJ Mark the 45 King, she offers the New Jersey teenager a deal.

1989
Most Americans have no idea what she's talking about, but that doesn't stop them from embracing the fly British import Neneh Cherry and her quasi-rap hit "Buffalo Stance."

1989
Tairrie B, another Eazy-E protégée, releases *Power of a Woman,* perfecting the whole white-trash image years before Kid Rock strikes platinum with it.

1989
With her majestic debut album, *All Hail the Queen*, Queen Latifah feeds a hip hop nation hungry for a dose of righteous sister power. The single "Ladies First" announces a new era for women in rap.

1989
Nichelle Strong, a.k.a. Nikki D, becomes the first rapper to record a song about abortion from a woman's point of view with her Def Jam release "Daddy's Little Girl."

1989
MC Hammer turns two of his dancers into the rapping duo Oaktown 3-5-7. On their debut album, *Wild and Loose,* Sweet L.D. and Terrible T drop bombs like "Juicy Gotcha Krazy" and "We Like It" before disappearing—along with spandex—some-where around '91.

Ms. Melodie *By Omoronke Idowu*

Long before the brief and troubled marriage of Notorious B.I.G. and Faith Evans, there was only one first couple of hip hop: KRS-One and Ms. Melodie. He was Kris Parker, the righteous Blastmaster of the Bronx's legendary Boogie Down Productions. She was Ramona Parker, born in Flatbush, Brooklyn, and brought to worldwide attention as an affiliate of the BDP family (which also included Harmonie, D-Nice, and Heather B). In the late 1980s, as BDP's righteous brand of all-killer-no-filler hip hop served as a soundtrack for an angst-filled generation trying to survive New York's crack wars, Ms. Melodie emerged as the proverbial strong woman behind the man.

She released just one solo work, 1989's *Diva* (which contained the semi-hit "Live On Stage"), but was omnipresent in BDP's recordings as both rapper and writer. Images of Ms. Melodie during this period were always towering, strong, and proud. Her round, impeccably made-up face batted long eyelashes while she gave verbal lashings in various BDP videos, holding court in the Stop the Violence All-Stars East Coast peace anthem, "Self Destruction," and the 1987 comedy movie *I'm Gonna Git You Sucka*.

Before Queen Latifah, Monie Love, or Lauryn Hill, Ms. Melodie was blending rap and raggamuffin reggae styles. More important, she was down for the womanist movement in hip hop, and vocal about sisters' place in rap history. "It wasn't that the male started rap, the male was just the first to be put on wax," she says with her usual gusto. "Females were always into rap, and always had their little crews. We were always known for rocking house parties, streets, schoolyards, the corner park, or whatever it was." Her song "Remember When" put the growth of hip hop into proper perspective: "The street is the root of the tree," she asserted, "that branches out to R&B."

By 1993, KRS-One had whittled down BDP and parted ways with his Mrs., which had the unfortunate effect of thrusting her out of the spotlight. But Melodie will always occupy a special place in hearts of the hip hop faithful.

1989
Born This Way, the first album from South London's Cookie Crew, brings fast-paced electro-funk samples and silly rap hooks for the teenybopper nation. After one more album, the cookies crumbled.

1990
As chief executive of EastWest Records, Sylvia Rhone sells millions of records with such artists as En Vogue, Yo Yo, MC Lyte, and Das EFX. Later, she is promoted to CEO of Elektra Entertainment, becoming the first African-American woman to hold such a position at a major label.

1990
Choreographed by future movie star (and VIBE cover girl) Rosie Perez, the Fly Girls bring hip hop dance moves to national television on the Fox TV series *In Living Color*. A year later, Jennifer Lopez joins the crew.

1990
Luther Campbell and 2 Live Crew's successful merger of rap and porn helps *Video Music Box* hit its stride. The sight of gyrating black women with big butts and little bikinis becomes commonplace on television, paving the way for Sir Mix-a-Lot's "Put 'Em on the Glass" and taking the "art" of the booty video to a new level.

1990
Carmelita Sanchez
becomes VP of Inter-
scope's Poetic Groove
imprint, which features
lady rapper the Poet-
ess, and Nueva York's
pan-Latino crew
Powerule. Sanchez
goes on to produce and
cohost the most lis-
tened to hip hop radio
program in the world,
"The WakeUp Show"
on L.A.'s KKBT FM.

1990
Shazzy rocks a high-
top fade on the cover of
her album *Attitude: A
Hip Hop Rapsody,*
featuring the single
"Giggahoe." Her 1993
follow-up, *Ghettosburg
Address,* is not as
warmly received.

1990
Borrowing a beat from
Public Enemy, Madon-
na makes MTV blush
with her steamy rap
hybrid "Justify My
Love."

1991
MC Lyte undergoes
a more feminine
makeover before
the release of her
third album, *Act
Like You Know.*

Monica Lynch *By Cristina Verán*

Monica Lynch arrived in New York City as a Chicago native with bigger-city dreams, never suspecting that hip hop was going to shape her destiny, and vice versa. Stints as a topless dancer and downtown club diva gave her an ear for the underground music vibe that would serve her well in years to come. But she found her true calling after answering a Village Voice ad for the fledgling label Tommy Boy Records. Working with founder Tom Silverman as the label's first and only employee, she arrived in time to witness the start of Afrika Bambaataa's T-Boy recording career.

Doing every job there was to be done, Lynch repped at industry conventions, took telephone orders from distributors, and dropped off the latest test pressings at Mr. Magic's original WHBI radio show. And she did it all for love. At the end of most 16-hour workdays, she'd head out to live the hip hop experience. The statuesque redhead was a regular at all the hot spots, from Negril to The Roxy to the T Connection, where director Martin Scorsese once accompanied her to check out the scene.

While Lynch and a handful of other white hipsters eagerly embraced hip hop for its multicultural vibe, many of rap's harshest critics came from the prevailing bourgeois black media. Her marketing wizardry flew in the face of those who viewed hip hop as a ghettofied "disgrace to the race," rather than the most innovative sound to come out of America since rock 'n' roll. In 17 years at Tommy Boy (where she eventually rose to the level of president), Lynch would help boost the careers of artists like De La Soul, Naughty By Nature, Digital Underground, House of Pain, and of course the great Queen Latifah.

While she still works on select projects for the label, Lynch went on a lengthy sabbatical from the daily grind of music-as-business in 1998. She now hosts her own radio show on New York's WFMU, playing an eclectic melange of diverse records as if to recall hip hop's early experimental years. Whatever else happens, Monica Lynch promises to be very much in the mix.

91

1991
Mary J. Blige sings a karaoke demo of Anita Baker's "Rapture" in a White Plains, New York, mall. Her dad passes the tape to a friend of a friend at MCA Records, and a year later "Real Love" is released.

1991
Yo Yo's hit single "You Can't Play with My Yo Yo" (featuring Ice Cube) gains respect for West Coast female MCs with a winning mix of sex appeal and hardcore rhymes.

1991
After the pioneering rap TV show *Pump It Up* aired a not-so-flattering segment about his group N.W.A, Dr. Dre assaults the show's host, Dee Barnes, during a Los Angeles record release party. Barnes files a $22 million lawsuit, which is settled out of court.

1991
Barnes hosts *Sisters in the Name of Rap*, the first nationally televised hip hop concert featuring 13 strictly female MCs, including Queen Latifah, Salt-N-Pepa, MC Lyte, Silk Tymes Leather, Nefertiti, Yo Yo, Shanté, and dancehall diva Shelly Thunder.

1991

"Two Minute Brother" by the rap duo Bytches With Problems hits number 6 on the *Billboard* rap chart. Their name, they explain, is a plural acronym for "Beautiful Young Talented College Honey."

1991

Just a year after she releases the singles "Get a Grip" and "I Wanna Make You Mine" on Motown Records, LaTasha Sheron Rogers, a.k.a. MC Trouble, dies in Los Angeles of heart failure after an epileptic seizure, at the age of 21.

1991

"Let's Talk About AIDS," Salt-N-Pepa's remix of their biggest hit to date ("Let's Talk About Sex"), breaks a deafening silence in the black community about the coming plague.

1992

TLC makes it okay for girls to carry condoms when they sport rubbers as fashion accessories in their breakout video "Ain't 2 Proud 2 Beg."

Heather B. *By Ayana D. Byrd*

Back in 1992, during that historic first season of MTV's *The Real World*, millions of viewers learned that housemate Heather B. was secure enough in her "blackness" to 1) befriend the crazy white girl from Alabama who wondered if this black girl was a drug dealer because she had a beeper, and 2) not care if anybody else thought that wasn't cool. Although she hinted at being a rapper during the show, most people didn't learn that she really had skills until the 1996 release of the grimy, hardcore "All Glocks Down," from her banging debut album, *Takin' Mine*.

In fact, Heather had already launched herself as an associate of Boogie Down Productions, rocking live shows throughout the late '80s with her booming voice box. She says she was inspired to try rapping after a chance meeting with Fab 5 Freddy at a bagel shop in Bed-Stuy, Brooklyn. Before long she had abandoned her bass clarinet lessons and taken up the mike in earnest.

But 1996, the year of hardcore Ill Na Nas, was not an easy time for fully clothed female MCs, and after one hit single, Heather's album grew dusty on store shelves. Instead of trading the mike in for a string of post-MTV appearances (although there have been plenty of those, too) the Jersey City native has stayed committed to music. Since closing the full-service Newark beauty salon she opened in 1994, B. has appeared on countless mix tapes, collaborated with Brownsville hypemasters MOP, and released the 1998 single "Do You" (MCA). In 1998 Heather B., Lady of Rage, and Nikki D formed the Underdogs, an all-female collective and support group for female MCs. Her next album, forthcoming on Sai Records, is the aptly titled *Eternal Affairs*.

A product of a hip hop generation that was forever screaming about the importance of "keepin' it real," Heather B. was that rare woman who could truly, uncompromisingly hold her own with the men—yet always seemed genuinely concerned with holding it down for the ladies.

1992
Bilingual *boricua* MC Hurricane G—best known for her opening lines on Redman's "Tonight's the Night"—has a baby with EPMD's Erick Sermon, and keeps right on rhyming.

1992
Lyte's thug-love shout-out "Ruffneck" becomes the first song by a solo female rapper to sell half a million copies.

1992
After President Clinton criticized her at a Rainbow Coalition event, Sister Souljah tells NBC's Bryant Gumbel that "Clinton is like a lot of white politicians. They eat soul food, party with black women, and play the saxophone, but when it comes to policy, they make the same decisions that are destructive to African people in this country."

1992
Yo Yo and MC Lyte confront Roxanne Shanté on the *Jane* show after she dissed them on her record "Big Mama."

1993
Despite controversy
over the fact that Dr.
Dre's *The Chronic* got
robbed, many fans
quietly cheer as Mecca
becomes the first
woman to win a rap
Grammy as part of the
jazzy trio Digable
Planets.

1993
Years after appearing in
the video for "Rox-
anne's Revenge," X-
Clan's Princess Isis
splits from the Afrocen-
tric group and gets
down with MC Lyte and
her short-lived Duke Da
Moon label, dropping
the underground hit
"Let It Fall."

1993
De La Soul releases the
complex *Buhloone
Mindstate,* and this
much is clear—spunky
MC Shorty No Mas is
one to watch. Inexplica-
bly, Shorty's solo
career stalls, but
Buhloone stands as a
testament to her tall
appeal.

1993
Queen Latifah exits
Tommy Boy and bolts to
Motown. She soon
drops her introspective
album *Black Reign* with
its Grammy-winning
single "U.N.I.T.Y.," in
which La punches a
disrespectful man in
the eye as she asks,
"Who you callin' a
bitch?"

Monie Love *By Omoronke Idowu*

In a single breath, Monie Love could spew complicated, witty, and conscious rhymes with a blazing-fast delivery that forced any MC, male or female, to rewind her tape for a second or third listen. The British rapper (born Simone Johnson) earned a spot in the U.K. underground as a teenager, but found her creative home on U.S. shores after linking up with the Native Tongues, a movement pioneered by her musical brethren De La Soul and The Jungle Brothers. Her classic duet with Queen Latifah, the sister anthem "Ladies First," along with her sassy solo hit "Monie in the Middle," propelled her to stardom and raised issues that still resonate for women in hip hop today. "So few of us are taken seriously," she says. "So few of us are paid any attention to outside of the way we look."

Love was always one of those rappers who took the time to weave social issues like AIDS, teen suicide, and violence into her lyrical repetoire. She also added layers of complexity to her work and image by becoming the poster girl for motherhood and family values at age 22. But family commitments did not cool her passion for all forms of music. Love has the unique distinction of having been produced by both hip hop mastermind Marley Marl and pop wunderkind Prince. She's collaborated with funk forefather Bootsy Collins and saxophonist Maceo Parker, as well as contributing vocals to Common's 2000 album *Like Water for Chocolate.* She's also tried her hand as a radio DJ and a host on the New York cable variety show *Studio Y,* all while working on a new album.

Nowadays, when so many popular female rappers bling-bling without rhyme or reason, the name Monie Love evokes a style, time, and space in hip hop that is precious, essential, and thought-provoking. But Love's not trying to disrespect any of her rap sistren. "I love the bigness of hip hop," she says. "I feel like that's the result of what my genre did, and we got what we had from the blood, sweat, and tears of those before us. Others have taken it in a million directions, whether it's 'I'm gonna be naked,' or whether it's 'I'm gonna concentrate on flow, style and attitude.' And the next woman after all these chicks will take it and run with it." After all these years, it's still all Love.

93

1993
East Oakland's the Coup, featuring the turntable skills of DJ Pam the Funkstress, bring straight-up revolutionary messages on their debut album *Kill My Landlord.*

1993
Conscious Daughters release *Ear to the Street,* the biggest-selling record on Paris's Scarface Records imprint. CMG and Special One are two funked-up girls from Oakland who rap about cars, gats, and ganja. Three years later, their follow-up fizzles.

1994
With *Keep It on the Real,* Champ MC brings straight-out-the-projects flavor to EastWest Records. Some time after her single "Sisters Better Recognize" goes mostly unrecognized, she teams up with the Wu Tang–affiliated girl group the Deadly Venoms.

1994
After warming up crowds for Louis Farrakhan and Public Enemy, Nefertiti releases her debut album *L.I.F.E. (Living In Fear of Extinction).* Always an intelligent rapper, her contract stipulated that Mercury Records pay her way through college.

1994

The Lady of Rage shines on Death Row's *Above the Rim* soundtrack with her Dr. Dre–produced banger "Afro Puffs." The song also makes her the first woman to rhyme about her period on wax: "I flow like the monthly, you can't cramp my style."

1994

TLC's Lisa "Left Eye" Lopes torches the $2 million mansion of her boyfriend Andre Rison during a drunken argument. Months later the group appears on the cover of VIBE in fireman's outfits.

1994

Chicana MC JV represents for Aztlán and every *ése* therein with her Thump Records debut *Nayba 'Hood Queen*, featuring true-life tracks like "Stompin' on the Concrete (Like I Own the Street)."

1994

Bahamadia, a staple of Philadelphia's underground scene, releases her long-awaited debute *Kollage*, featuring the buttery single "Total Wreck." Her precise lyrics and distinctive vocal tone distinguish Bahamadia as a dope MC regardless of gender.

Rage *By Ayana D. Byrd*

Whether weaved, braided or bald-headed, in the summer of 1994 the entire hip hop nation was rocking rough and tough with "Afro Puffs," a blistering hit by the Lady of Rage. She emerged as the first lady of Death Row Records at a time when the label was just hinting at the ironclad grasp that it would soon have on rap culture.

But Rage always had big things in mind. She owes at least some of her success to the unlikeliest of role models—Madonna Ciccone. Born in the cow town of Farmsville, Virginia, young Robin Allen read a magazine article about the pop superstar's Blond Ambition. She remembers telling herself, "If this bitch could move to New York, broke as hell and starving for what she wanted, I could do the same." So she set her sights on the epicenter of hip hop, getting a job at the legendary Chung King studio, where she used to sleep on the couch. But in 1992 it was off to Cali after her verse on an L.A. Posse album caught the attention of Dr. Dre, cofounder of Death Row. With a style that defied anything feminine or sweet, Rage's ferocity was heard on such clas-

sics as Dre's *The Chronic,* Snoop's *Tha Doggfather,* and the sound track to *Above the Rim.*

Despite the mounting hype around the label's sole female, Rage's project was continually pushed back, and her album, *Necessary Roughness,* was not released until 1997. By that time Death Row was a mere shadow of its former self, and *Necessary* suffered, selling less than 200,000 copies. "It left a bad taste in my mouth, the things that I went through with Death Row—Tupac dying, Dre leaving, [label chief] Suge [Knight] getting locked up, you know, it was like, 'Man, just at the time my album was comin' out!' Since then, Rage had branched out, appearing in a recurring role as a school bully on UPN's *Steve Harvey Show.* Although she enjoys acting, she can't get the boom-bap out of her head. "For a while I was like, forget this!" she confesses. "But now, it's calling me, so I'm going to go ahead and do it." Her recent appearance on "Set it Off" alongside MC Ren, Ice Cube and Nate Dogg on Snoop Dogg's *The Last Meal* served as a reminder of just how effective a little well-directed Rage can be.

1994
Talking smack, puffing chronic, and coming off as a cute girl who could beat anyone's ass, Da Brat fuses her Chi-town roots and Jermaine Dupri's bouncy Atlanta sound to create the first million-selling record by a solo female rapper, *Funkdafied.*

1994
"The Boom poetic" Sha Key releases the slept-on masterpiece, *A Head Nodda's Journey to Adidi Skizm.* After her album tanks, she goes on to publish a sharp-edged hip hop website called The Guillotine.

1995
Lisa Cortes, the A&R exec who signed Black Sheep and Buju Banton among other notable artists, forms her own Loose Cannon imprint within PolyGram Records.

1995
Leshaun does it well on L.L. Cool J's "Doin' It" (a remake of a song she originally recorded in 1988 as Almond Joy), but gets dissed when L.L. refuses to feature her in the video, allegedly because of her maternal figure.

1995
Brooklyn teenager Lil' Kim outshines the rest of her Junior M.A.F.I.A. brethren with her outrageous duet with the Notorious B.I.G. on "Get Money."

1995
Foxy Brown, another young Brooklynite, drops her first recorded rhyme on L.L.'s "I Shot Ya (remix)" and instantly becomes a wild child to watch.

1995
VIBE's "20 Questions" column asks of the Fugees: "When is Lauryn gonna go solo and leave those two non-rhyming cats alone?"

1995
The various artists album *Project Blowed: Sector 21310* captures the energy of the L.A. freestyle scene, with blazing performances by underground empresses like Ganja K, Medusa, and Nefertiti, among others.

Boss *By Omoronke Idowu*

Was she a response to the whorish images of women depicted in rap music videos—or perhaps a female answer to the male studio gangsta MCs who gained popularity in the early '90s? Regardless of what motivated Michelle Laws to fabricate the thuggish persona that made her momentarily famous and ultimately laughable, there is no doubt that some folks were eating her style up—at least in the beginning.

Shortly after Apache began searching for a "Gangsta Bitch," Michelle created her own with Boss, whose debut album, *Born Gangstaz*, featured hooks like "I don't give a fuck, not a single fuck, not a single solitary fuck . . ." Whatever she lacked in complexity, Boss compensated for with a major dose of shamelessness.

Spitting a barrage of lyrical odes to Glocks, Uzis, and cheeba smoke on songs like "Run, Catch, and Kill," Boss matched her male counterparts lick for lick, right down to her androgynous attire. She wore her pants and tops so baggy that the slightest curve was undetectable, her dark wraparound shades obscured much of her face as well as the windows to her soul, and of course the costume would not have been complete without the mandatory bandanna on her head. Boss creeped and prowled her way through videos with a carefully honed menace that alternately awed and alarmed viewers.

And just like a real G, Boss's glory days ended rather abruptly. One day her career simply disappeared, egged on by the embarrassing disclosure of her middle-class roots. She had studied ballet and modern dance. She had gone to college to study business. Then she decided she was going to become an MC. "I tried the straight-up nice girl approach," she said, after her secret was revealed. "It didn't work."

She turned up again, briefly, as an on-air personality at a Texas radio station. By being a rebel, a moral contradiction, and a choking breath of fresh air, Boss put yet another face of black womanhood into the colorful mosaic that is rap culture.

96

1996
R&B diva Mariah Carey enters the rap arena by collaborating with Wu Tang Clan's Ol' Dirty Bastard on the remix version of "Fantasy." The success of this appearance spawns future teamings with Puff Daddy, Mase, Mobb Deep, M.O.P., and Bone Thugs-N-Harmony.

1996
The Fugees dis VIBE on their 17-million-selling *The Score:* "These cats can't rap, Mr. Author I feel no vibe / The magazine said the girl should go solo."

1996
Suga T (sister of rap mogul E-40) starts an Oakland, California, telephone service line 900-28-SUGAT offering kids' entertainment, spiritual advice, and gossip. She says she started it as a backup in case her album *Paper Chasin'* didn't take off. (It didn't.)

1996
Nonchalant keeps the positive themes flowing, and becomes one of the first MCs to blow up out of Washington, D.C., with her hit "5 O'Clock."

1996
Dr. Dre tells *Newsweek,* "Black women are the strongest, most hard-working people on earth. The shit I talk on records about women is just that: shit."

1997
Toi Jackson, formerly Sweet Tee, who record-ed the hit "It's My Beat" back in 1986, featuring DJ Jazzy Joyce—changes her name to Suga, and has the biggest hit of her career with "What's Up Star?"

1997
NYC's Hot 97 FM radio personality Angie Martinez makes her rapping debut on KRS-One's album, *I Got Next* with "Heartbeat" featuring her and Redman. This leads to an appearance on Lil' Kim's 1998 single "Ladies Night," also featuring Missy Elliott, Da Brat, and Left Eye.

1997
Lisa Cortes, former president of Loose Cannon Records, files suit against PolyGram Records charging racial and sexual discrimina-tion. Cortes contends she lacked access to information her white male colleagues were given. The suit is set-tled out of court.

Rah Digga *By Ayana D. Byrd*

Rah Digga is blessed with the MC's rarest gift: a distinctive voice. Hers is so deep that it might be mistaken for a man's, except that it also displays a feminine sensuality. Her lyrical skills—she's a wicked freestyler who also writes her own powerful rhymes—earned her street credibility, while her stylish appearance made her attractive to magazines and television. It's this ability to combine sexiness with edgy, hardcore flavor that distinguishes her from other rapstresses.

Rashia Fisher, the single mother who sprouted from the fertile rap soil of New Jeru (a.k.a. New Jersey, which also reared stars like Latifah and Lauryn), is painfully aware of the precarious fence she straddles in today's musical landscape of booty-jiggling female rappers. "I don't have a problem exploiting my youth and my looks to sell my rhymes," she said shortly before the release of her 2000 debut album, *Dirty Harriet*, "but I'd rather push my MC skills. If you do happen to notice that I look good or that I got bodacious ta-tas, that's all good too."

What Q-Tip noticed one night in 1997 was that she could rhyme her ass off. Digga was shining that night at N.Y.C.'s famous Lyricist Lounge, and she was also eight months pregnant. Tip introduced Digga to Busta Rhymes, and she soon became a part of his Flipmode Squad. She was already the only female member of the esteemed Jersey crew Da Outsidaz (her daughter's father, Young Zee, is also a member, as is Eminem). In the years it took for her to get her own major-label solo deal, Rah collaborated with the Fugees on "Cowboys" from their breakout album *The Score*.

While Bahamadia and Heather B. have opted to take the independent label route, Rah is one of the few women who's been able to transform subterranean dues-paying into real commercial appeal. She's managed to keep from being dwarfed by mentor Busta Rhymes—who oversaw her debut, *Dirty Harriet*—and has gained respect from an industry that isn't always quick to recognize diverse forms of female talent. Her album's title was not only a reference to Clint Eastwood's gun-toting vigilante cop but also, she points out, a homage to Underground Railroad heroine Harriet Tubman. Digga may not be leading any slaves to freedom, but by her very presence she's helped unshackle the stereotypes that keep too many female MCs underground.

'97

1997
Lauryn Hill travels to Kenya, Uganda, and Tanzania to show support for refugees from the war in Zaire.

1997
After being snubbed in the local press and criticized by Jamaican politicians for her X-rated performances, dancehall donnette Lady Saw blasts back with "What Is Slackness?" a sophisticated musical argument that details her critics' hypocrisy.

1997
N.Y.C.'s Hot 97 FM shock jock Wendy Williams is pulled from the air, but not released from her contract, after questioning the sexuality of Sean "Puffy" Combs on her midday gossip show.

1997
Hype Williams's video for Missy Elliott's "The Rain (Supa Dupa Fly)" blows everybody's mind, and Missy's career blows up bigger than that patent-leather balloon suit.

1998
Queen Pen sparks controversy with "Girlfriend," the first rap song to adopt an openly lesbian persona. Soon after the release of her album *My Melody,* the mother of two becomes evasive about her own sexuality.

1998
Hip hop's first couple, Pepa and Treach, celebrate the birth of their daughter, Egypt, and tie the knot.

1998
Rhino Records releases *Fat Beats and Bra Straps,* an exhaustive 3-CD "salute to women in hip hop" that begins a long overdue reassessment of sisterly contributions to the culture.

1998
"In the twenty-plus-year history of hip hop on record," writes Nelson George in his book *Hip Hop America,* "there are no women who have contributed profoundly to rap's artistic growth. I would argue that if none of these female rap artists had ever made a record, hip hop's development would have been no different."

Mia X *By Ayana D. Byrd*

For a few memorable moments during the last years of the twentieth century, hip hop was in the grips of a love affair with Master P's Louisiana-based No Limit Records. And the matriarch of No Limit clan, Mia X, blazed a trail for female Southern rappers. From her 1995 debut, *Good Girl Gone Bad*, through 1998's *Mama Drama*, the self-proclaimed Mouth of the South came with her own spicy recipe for hip hop gumbo.

Mia Young hails from New Orleans's Seventh Ward, the only child of parents who instilled her with black pride and the teachings of Marcus Garvey. After a few years as part of Queens' New York Incorporated rap group, she returned to Louisiana and made a couple of bounce songs that afforded her a degree of local celebrity.

The story goes that when Percy "Master P" Miller came knocking to sign her to his fledgling No Limit label she was at home under the hair dryer. Because she liked something about the rising entrepreneur and sensed that he could really follow through on his dreams, Mia joined the No Limit family, provided it could be on her terms. That meant writing her own lyrics and projecting an image that was not going to be tinkered with by the men around her. (And please don't make the mistake of telling her she sounds good for a girl.) It was a stance not often taken at that time by female rappers, but it worked.

Mia now has one platinum album under her belt and a place in the hearts of thugged-out rap fans around the world. "'Bout It, 'Bout It" and "Make 'em Say Ughhh" may be catchphrases that some folks are now embarrassed to admit they once uttered, but with Mia X No Limit gave hip hop its most endearing down home rapper.

When she got signed to the upstart label, the former welfare mom framed her last government check for $155 alongside a copy of her first No Limit advance for a quarter million dollars. The documents serve as a vivid reminder of the power of hip hop, and as proof that wherever you may be coming from, there's nowhere you cannot go.

1998
Lauryn Hill eventually does go solo. Her album, *The Miseducation of Lauryn Hill*, sells over six million copies in the U.S. alone and wins five Grammys, including Album of the Year and Best New Artist.

1998
Haida becomes the first Native American female to release an album, *The Haida Way* (Red Vinyl Records), featuring collaborations with Cherokee rapper Litefoot, Chicano veteran A.L.T., and "Promiseland," which features the voice of imprisoned activist Leonard Peltier.

1998
New-Ark Productions (Vadia Nobles, Rasheem Pugh, Tejumold and Jahari Newton) file suit against Lauryn Hill claiming they did not receive proper credit for arranging, producing, and writing songs on *Miseducation*.

1998
Charli Baltimore, another of Notorious B.I.G.'s former consorts, comes out with a single, "For the Love of Money." Her plans to release an album never materialize.

1998

Wendy Day, founder of the Rap Coalition, helps negotiate a multi-million-dollar deal with Universal Records that lets Juvenile and the Cash Money crew keep more of their cash money.

1998

Apani B-Fly MC, Helixx C. Armageddon, Ayana Soyini, What? What?, Pri the Honey Dark, Yejide the Night Queen, Heroine, and Lyric "flex their double-X chromosomes" and rock the New York underground with the first rap song named after a hormone, "Estragen."

1999

After winning a phone-in MC battle on Hot 97 FM for five days in a row, 18-year-old Lady Luck is signed to Def Jam with a little help from fellow New Jersey native Redman.

1999

Despite one of the most degrading CD covers in recent memory—did they really have to put the center hole right *there*?—*Rear End*, the debut disc from No Limit hottie Mercedes, is actually pretty dope, especially the song "I Can Tell."

Gangsta Boo *By Hyun Kim*

As the only female member of the testosterone-fueled Three Six Mafia camp, Gangsta Boo has it hard. On top of that, she's from Memphis, a city known more for Elvis than cutting-edge hip hop. Still, Lola "Gangsta Boo" Mitchell, a surprisingly soft-spoken Southern belle, has managed to create a special niche for herself. More around-the-way girl than dolled-up rap vixen, Boo's understated sex appeal and confidence are attractive to both men's lustful desires and women's self-esteem. And her distinct rhyme style, first displayed on the 1998 album *Enquiring Minds*, has solidified her place among hip hop's most promising new talents.

"I think I'm blessed," she says. "Some females either have the look and can't rap that good or they got skills and don't look that good. I think that I'm lyrically blessed and blessed with my looks." Boo rhymes for the 'hood, never dropping the names of fancy Italian fashion designers. She prefers to speak about the thugs, strippers, and hustlers who shaped her life growing up in the Black Haven area of North Memphis. She's a pro at giving off both raw sexual and hardcore musical energy. One minute she shocks you, going line for line with her grisly tale-spitting Mafia men. The next she's teasing you, weaving scenarios of the possibility of joining her man in a threesome. "You know how it is on the road. After a show, anything goes," she says. "But I don't ever invite no nigga up to my room."

It's this duality that has led to her cameos with high profile acts like Outkast and Foxy Brown. However, for a variety of reasons, Boo has often gone underappreciated. The fact that Hypnotized Minds' in-house production has its own bass-heavy creepy "Memphis sound" sometimes drowns out Boo's choppy drawling flow doesn't help matters. But it has also kept her preserved, like an undetected time bomb, ticking away before the big bang. Never changing her style to fit with the current trends, Gangsta Boo keeps persevering to try and change them.

1999
Poet/actress/playwright Sarah Jones debuts her one-woman show *Surface Transit* at the American Place Theatre. Its critique of hip hop's rampant sexism turns out everybody from Jay-Z to Gloria Steinem. Lauryn Hill even requests a private performance.

1999
After sparkling on J.T. Money's ghetto anthem "Who Dat," Kansas-born mother of two Solé drops her debut album *Skin Deep*.

1999
Sprite unveils their outlandish Deadly Venoms ad campaign featuring Angie Martinez, Roxanne Shanté, Amil, Eve, and Rah Digga. The Wu Tang Clan–affiliated female rap group Deadly Venoms charge that the soft-drink giant stole their name. The dispute is settled out of court.

1999
Jazzyfatnastees, along with female affiliates of the Roots Crew—namely Nou-Ra, Jaguar, and Leslie Pena—launch the first Black Lily open mike jam session at the club Wetlands in New York City, creating a space for rising female talents like Macy Gray, Erykah Badu, Jill Scott, India Arie, Flo Brown, Floetry, and Kindred.

1999
Bronx Bomber Remy Martin is expelled from high school for spending so much time in the studio with Terror Squad crusher Big Pun. After Pun's untimely death, she goes on to rock the hip hop universe with her skillful flow on M.O.P.'s remix of "Ante Up."

2000
Doggy's Angels, a three-girl crew of Cali rappers hand-picked by Snoop Dogg, drop their debut album, *Pleezebaleevit* (TVT). Producers of the film *Charlie's Angels* file suit for trademark infringement.

2000
Indie director Rachel Raimist premieres her documentary *Nobody Knows My Name*, giving voice to women of hip hop today who are more concerned with keeping it real than getting rich. The film is a showcase for powerful real-life MCs like Medusa, T-Love, and Leschea, as well as DJ Symphony of the Beat Junkies, and b-girl dancer Asia One.

2000
Amil, whose cartoonish voice helped spark Jay-Z's 1998 mega-hit, "Can I Get A . . . ," releases her solo debut, *All Money Is Legal.* The rapper tells VIBE that her newfound religious beliefs make her fundamentally opposed to the materialistic lyrics featured on the record.

Anomolies *By Cristina Verán*

Twenty years after the Mercedes Ladies emerged as the first all-woman MC and DJ crew, the girl-power griots of Anomolies have built upon this still underdeveloped concept, encompassing all four elements of hip hop—not just rapping but turntablism, B-girl dance moves, and the aerosol arts.

Founded in 1997 as a support group for female artists by DJ battle queen (and 5th Platoon member) Kuttin Kandi and MC Helixx C. Armageddon, who knew each other from the New York scene, Anomolies was first featured on "Blacklisted" (Sub Records), a collaboration with The Arsonists in '99. Anomolies members like Pri The Honey Dark (winner of the 1999 *Blaze* MC Battle), Invincible, and Big Tara can be found on numerous mix tapes and compilation albums, including: *No More Prisons, Hip Hop for Respect,* and *Elephant Tracks,* with solo projects for various crew members set to drop in early '02.

True to the dictionary definition of their name, "departure from the common order," Anomolies bypasses gangsta-materialism and hoochie-mama drama to represent hip hop as an all-encompassing, female-empowering art form. "We were all so tired of the negative women who were coming out in the hip hop industry," Kandy explains. "We wanted to show that there are women out there with skills who aren't all about sex, greed, and violence."

The unorthodox spelling of their name is no accident. "There is a message within the word," Kandy explains. "If you look very closely you will see 'No Mo Lies.' That's the message we want to get across to everyone—we're tired of the lies, we're tired of the untold truth, and we're tired of the dishonesty. We Anomolies want to stop the lies in hip-hop and to bring the truth to the masses." Go on girls!

2000
Foxy Brown records "Bang Bang" with Capone-N-Noreaga, a song that appears to dis Lil' Kim. A few months later, the entourages of Capone and Kim get into a gunfight outside the studios of Hot 97 FM in N.Y.C.

2000
A federal judge rules that Brooklyn-bred wordsmith Blade cannot legally call herself "Sonja Blade" because of the *Mortal Kombat* video game character. She changes her named to Blade, and her album is hot regardless.

2000
Tiye Phoenix becomes the first woman signed to indie powerhouse Rawkus Records.

2001
India Arie puts a positive spin on the beat from Akinyele's "Put It in Your Mouth" for her sister-girl anthem "Video."

Invincible, PR,
the Honey Dark,
Kuttin Kandy,
and Big Tara.

2001
As the celebrity
spokeswomen for
M.A.C. cosmetics'
Viva Glam lipstick, Lil'
Kim and Mary J. Blige
help raise $4 million for
AIDS research in
one year.

2001
Singing and rapping
with equal skill, Bay
Area MC and former
Digital Underground
Mystic releases a
remarkable debut
album, *Cuts for Luck
and Scars for Freedom*.

2001
The Real Roxanne
reunites with Lisa Lisa
and Full Force to record
a new version of "Float
On," to be featured on
Full Force's new solo
album.

2001
Lauryn Hill settles out
of court with New-Ark
Productions for an
undisclosed sum, cuts
her dreadlocks, and
camps out at home in
New Jerusalem writing
redemption songs.

Aaliyah  *By Rob Kenner*

January 16, 1979 – August 25, 2001

This is what I always wanted," Aaliyah Dana Haughton told VIBE in May 2001, only three months before being killed in a tragic plane crash. The 22-year-old supernova had just released her third album and wrapped initial shooting on the sequel to *The Matrix,* her third starring film role. "I breathe to perform, to entertain," she said in her first cover story for the magazine. "I can't imagine myself doing anything else. I'm just a really happy girl right now."

Whenever a young person's life is cut short, loved ones are left to cope with painful questions of what might have been. In the case of Aaliyah, who spent half her brief, incandescent life in the spotlight, the only comfort is how much she did accomplish. She made her *Star Search* debut and sang with Gladys Knight in Vegas by age 11. Modeling, movies, and multiplatinum record sales seemed to be preordained.

Her first album, 1994's *Age Ain't Nothing but a Number,* was marked by controversy when the 15-year old singer got married to the record's 25-year-old producer and writer, R&B lothario R. Kelly; their union was soon annulled. Two years later, she joined forces with production wiz Timbaland and songwriting prodigy Missy Elliott to create *One in a Million,* which fused futuristic beats with Aaliyah's alluring voice. That record established the teenager as a bona fide R&B star, and subsequent cutting-edge soundtrack gems like "Are You That Somebody?" and the Grammy-nominated "Try Again" further solidified her reputation as a risk-taker who was equally comfortable with hip hop and jungle beats as she was singing traditional soul.

As her album title suggested, Aaliyah truly was one in a million. And although she is gone, her music—like the love of her family and fans—goes on and on and on.

acknowledgments

From the moment of this book's conception in late 1999, most every person who heard about it considered *Hip Hop Divas* more than just an interesting or worthwhile undertaking. The original impulse has remained constant even as the thing itself evolved: You hold in your hands a heartfelt and long-overdue gesture of thanksgiving to all the women whose names are recorded in these pages. Maximum respect to each and every one of you—daughters, sisters, and mothers. Your words, sounds, and power have kept the spark of inspiration alive through many long dark nights. Rock on. And to the writers who told these women's stories so fearlessly: Write on.

There were, of course, many other crucial contributions, starting with the dynamic duo of contributing editors Mimi Valdés and Shani Saxon, who (with the sage guidance of Emil Wilbekin) charted the course that led this book where it needed to go, even through stormy seas.

The graphic expertise of art director Brandon Kavulla and designer Sue Yoder made every page pop. Picture editor Rayne Roberts (a worthy protégé of Mr. George Pitts) distilled the energy of the book's subjects into provocative and tasteful images that speak almost as eloquently as the MCs themselves.

Researchers Sun Singleton, Gregory "El Juba" Johnson, Abby Addis, and Richard Louissaint went to extraordinary lengths on a daily basis to ensure that every detail contained herein would remain actual and factual. Those efforts were aided and abetted by the tireless reportage and writing of Ayana D. Byrd, Omoronke Idowu, Serena King, Sheena Lester, Amy Linden, Kate Schwartz, and Cristina Verán, not to mention Andrew Gillings, Hyun Kim, O.J. Lima, and Jeff Mao. Editorial intern Xelena González provided the X-factor when it was most necessary.

Kenard Gibbs and Dana Sacher took care of business when it needed taking. Halina Feldsott and Dawn Labriola kept food on folks' tables. Jeff Miller and David Korzenik kept the wolves at bay. (And let us not forget Alan Light, whose lightbulb moment got this whole VIBE Books thing started in the first place.)

Even the best-laid plans of mice and (wo)men would get nowhere without the wise counsel of literary agent Sarah Lazin, who helped guide this idea from the first rough draft of a proposal through the final revision. Also ensuring we got our words' worth was Paula Balzer, who kept an indefatigable eye on the fine print.

Blessings upon the house of Crown, from Steve Ross on down, because they understood the need for this book almost immediately. One could scarcely hope for a better editor than Kristin Kiser, ably assisted by Claudia Gabel. The steadfast production team of Lauren Dong, Jim Walsh, and Jane Searle brought it all home with grace under pressure.

Countless others offered insights, critiques, and encouragement (directly and otherwise) at make-or-break moments. To big up just a few of you: Karla Radford, Joan Morgan, Carol Cooper, Sophia Chang, Jeannine Amber, Kenya Byrd, Raqiyah Mays, Serena Kim, Kim Ford, Teresa Sanders, Anne Kristoff, Michelle Roy, Sharon Gordon, Sarah Weinstein, Jacquie Juceam, Nadine Sutherland, Stephanie Black, Lisa Jones, Lisa Cortes, Lisa West, Lisa Kenner, and Lisa Lisa (courtesy of Bowlegged Lou).

Can't leave out Bob Morales, who cast a colder eye on everyone and everything. Or Cheo Hodari Coker, who kept the BIG picture in focus. Or Kris Ex, whose 24-hour IMs kept respiration going even as inspiration failed. Or Bönz Malone, who reminds us why we still love this game. Or Quincy Jones, who advised us to keep the door open just wide enough for God to walk in.

And the last shall be first: Pele Lanier. Leslie Pitts. Jeffrey Schaire. Anna Bittner. Requiem in pace. See you when we get there.

—Rob Kenner, Editorial Director, VIBE Books

contributors

Harry Allen, hip hop activist and media assassin, is the first member of the hip hop generation to write about hip hop culture as a professional journalist, having done so in a wide range of publications since 1987. Founder of the Hip Hop Hall of Fame & Rhythm Cultural Center, Inc., the world's first 501(c)(3) organization for hip hop culture, he is also well known for his association with the legendary hip hop band Public Enemy. Allen serves on the advisory board of the Archives of African-American Music & Culture at Indiana University, in Bloomington, Indiana. He is currently doing research on a book and film about hip hop.

Andréa Duncan, a West Coast native and UC Berkeley grad, got her start interning at local Bay Area magazines before landing an editorial assistant gig at VIBE in 1995. In 1997, she joined the MTV News team as a reporter/producer. She has profiled some of hip hop's biggest figures, including Jay-Z, Lil' Kim, Eminem, Snoop Dogg, and DMX, with whom she produced a documentary DVD titled *One More Road.* She has written for VIBE, *The Source, XXL, ego trip, Detour,* and *Time Out New York.* She recently produced a special for MTV's 20th anniversary called *Grab the Mic: A Hip Hop History* and has recently taken on the challenge of renovating a brownstone in Harlem.

Urban style warrior **Michael A. Gonzales** is the coauthor of *Bring the Noise,* the pioneering 1991 study of hip hop culture. Former writer-at-large for VIBE magazine, he's also a frequent contributor to *The Source, Mode, XXL,* and *Essence;* in addition, his short fiction has appeared in *ego trip, Untold, Trace,* and *Brown Sugar,* a collection of black erotica. Currently working on two books of urban pulp fiction, *Babies & Fools* and *Platinum,* he resides in Brooklyn.

Karen Renee Good grew up in Prairie View, Texas, and now lives in Bed-Stuy, Brooklyn. She has written for VIBE, *New York, Honey* (the original), and *The Village Voice.* A true visionary, Good is working on a project that unifies all that she loves—music, film, dance, and the written word. "This realization feels right," she says. "My future, in Morrison's words, is shivery and momentous. So keep your hearts open. I'll be by . . ."

dream hampton grew up in Detroit, on the east side, surrounded by vacant lots. She is a writer and a filmmaker, but first a mother and activist. She feels about hip hop the way she feels about this one cat. These feelings fluctuate wildly, but always there is love.

Selwyn Seyfu Hinds is a longstanding editor and writer in the arena of urban media. Most recently he was chief creative officer, executive vice president, and editorial director of 360hiphop.com, the Internet company founded by music magnate Russell Simmons. Prior to joining 360hiphop.com in December 1999, Hinds was the editor-in-chief of *The Source.* An internationally recognized expert on hip hop music and culture whose commentary has been featured in print, television, and radio. Hinds is working on his first book, *Gunshots in My Cookup: Bits and Bites of a Hip-Hop Caribbean Life,* to be published by Pocket Books in 2002. His work has also been featured in several anthologies, including *Best Music Writings 2000,* edited by Peter Guralnick, and *Day of Absence: A Commemorative Anthology of the Million Man March,* edited by Haki Madhubuti and Maulana Karenga. Hinds's articles and criticism have appeared in *Vanity Fair, Spin,* and VIBE, among other periodicals. Hinds also wrote extensively for *The Village Voice,* where he received a 1994 writing fellowship. He is a graduate of Princeton University with degrees in English and African-American studies. He lives in Brooklyn.

Sacha Jenkins is the cofounder of *ego trip* and a former music editor at VIBE, and is currently senior contributing writer for *Spin.* An Astoria, Queens, native who only recently overcame his addiction to graffiti, Jenkins grew up about a mile away from the infamous Queensbridge housing projects. This year, he was awarded a fellowship by the National Arts Journalism Program at Columbia University. He loves you to death.

Erica Kennedy started out writing for the newspapers but *Blaze* was the first mag to give her a shot as a feature writer. Before that she was in the corporate world doing fashion PR. "Let me tell you," she says, "chasing down Trick Daddy in Miami or following Funkmaster Flex on a Sunday night at the Tunnel will shock you out of that corporate mentality in a hurry."

Rob Marriott started writing for *The Village Voice* in high school. He became an editor at *The Source* magazine and was a founding editor at *XXL*. He has been a regular contributor to VIBE magazine and covered the death of Tupac Shakur, for which he won a 1997 ASCAP Award for excellence in music journalism. His work has been included in *Tupac Shakur* and *The VIBE History of Hip Hop*, and he has written extensively on hip hop culture in periodicals such as *New York, Spin, Rolling Stone,* and *Essence.* He is currently at work on *Pimpnosis,* a coffee-table book on players in the Midwest due out in the spring of 2002.

Kierna Mayo has been down with Brooklyn since jelly jackets, sunflower seeds, and quarter waters (in other words, long before $2,000 rents). She yaps a lot about race, sex, music, movies, and money, sometimes at universities, in print, or while people are watching TV. She has survived much, including the lines in the dead of winter outside of the Latin Quarter, wopping at Union Square, The Garage, Murry Bergtraum ('80s Hip Hop High), Hampton University, '91–'94 at *The Source,* eating off of freelancing (ha), Detroit, a wild marriage, and the still-unsolved kidnapping of her and JD's first baby, birthed only after years of labor pain—push girl, push!–(the original) *Honey* magazine. Today Mayo is a partner of DaM Media (Dingle and Mayo Media Group), a woman-owned and -operated company with big vision and a new, hot-hot urban woman's fashion and lifestyle magazine called *LikePepper...* coming soon. As far as hip hop goes, to paraphrase her boy Jimmy Cozier, "Sometimes she loves it, sometimes she loves it not, although it nags her, and complains a lot, she ain't letting it go. No, no, no." Free the land (and the girls).

Danyel Smith is a former editor-at-large for Time Inc. She is also a former editor-in-chief at VIBE. Currently finishing her first novel, Smith is taking some time off from journalism–an attempt to figure out what's next. ("It'll come to me while I'm walking my dog or something," she says.) A 1996–97 National Arts Journalism Fellow at Northwestern University's Medill School, Smith is a former rhythm-and-blues editor at *Billboard.* She has written for the *New York Times* and has been a columnist at *Spin.* Her work has also appeared in *Time, The New Yorker, Rolling Stone, Us,* and *The Village Voice,* as well as a variety of anthologies. A California native, she was music editor at *San Francisco Weekly* and a columnist at the *San Francisco Bay Guardian.* She attended the University of California, Berkeley.

Greg Tate has been a staff writer at *The Village Voice* since 1986. His essays have been published in VIBE, the *New York Times, Rolling Stone,* the *Washington Post, DownBeat, Artforum,* and in museum catalogues for the Whitney Museum of Art and the Institute for Contemporary Art in Boston. A founding member of the Black Rock Coalition, Tate is also a musician and producer who has released three albums on his own Trugroid label, most recently *Burnt Sugar/The Arkestra Chamber's blood on the leaf, opus no. 1.* Tate will publish two new books in 2002, including *Everything but the Burden, or How Blackfolk Became Fetish Objects,* an anthology on African-American cultural influence in the 20th century that will include essays by Robin Kelley, Hilton Als, dream hampton, Vernon Reid, and Carl Hancock-Rux, and *Midnight Lightning: Race, Sex, Technology, and Jimi Hendrix.*

Mimi Valdés is an editor-at-large for VIBE, former editor-in-chief of *Homegirl,* former editor-in-chief of *Blaze,* and frequent contributor to *The Source* and *Latina.* Her writings have appeared in *The VIBE History of Hip Hop* and *Rolling Stone's Women in Rock.*

Cristina Verán is a journalist, historian, and educator who has documented hip hop extensively. Recent book contributions on the topic include the chapter on hip hop dance in *The VIBE History of Hip Hop* and an old school tour for the *Time Out Book of New York Walks.* Her work covering global news, culture, and politics has been featured on National Public Radio, as well as in VIBE, *The Source, Ms., Latina, New York Newsday, Islands Magazine, News from Indian Country, To2 News* [Mexico City], and other media outlets. She currently serves as a news correspondent to the United Nations. Predating these professional accomplishments, she was a proud member of renowned hip hop collectives, including the Rock Steady Crew, TC5, and the Universal Zulu Nation.

A native of Baltimore, **Margeaux Watson** decided that journalism was her calling after interning at *Baltimore* magazine in high school. As an undergraduate student at Columbia University in New York, she took internships at *Essence* and VIBE, where she also helped edit two books: *Tupac Shakur* and *The VIBE History of Hip Hop.* During a semester abroad in Africa, she interned at the *Sunday Mail,* Zimbabwe's largest newspaper. After graduating from Columbia with a B.A. in African-American Studies in 1998, Watson took an editorial assistant position at *Time Out New York,* and was soon promoted to music writer. Her freelance work regularly appears in VIBE, *Rolling Stone, Spin, O: The Oprah Mag-*

azine, Essence, XXL, and other magazines. Watson is an associate member of the New York chapter of the National Academy of Recording Arts & Sciences. She lives in Brooklyn and is currently writing her first novel, inspired by her Manhattan party-hopping exploits.

You could say **Emil Wilbekin** has majored in Mary J. Blige. The current editor-in-chief of VIBE, Wilbekin has written about the Queen of Hip Hop Soul three times and styled her four times. He even dressed her to the nines for her "I Can Love You" video. When he's not doing something about Mary or being the VIBE visionary, Wilbekin practices yoga, takes Spanish lessons, and serves on the board of directors for the American Society of Magazine Editors and The Design Industry's Foundation for AIDS (DIFFA). When he found out we were doing a book about hip hop divas, Wilbekin demanded he write the Mary chapter. I guess that's what you call "Real Love."

discography
compiled by Serena Kim

VARIOUS ARTIST ALBUMS

B-Girls Live & Kickin' (B-Boy, 1987)

Queens of Rap (Priority, 1990)

Street Jams: Hip Hop from the Top, Volume 1–4 (Rhino, 1992)

Sugar Hill Story (Sequel, 1994)

Wild Pitch Classics (Wild Pitch, 1994)

Old School Rap, Volume 2 (Sequel, 1996)

Mother of All Swing, Volume 2 (Telstar, 1997)

Tommy Boy's Greatest Beats, Volume 2 (Tommy Boy, 1997)

The Sugar Hill Records Story (Rhino, 1997)

Fat Beats & Bra Straps: Battle Rhymes & Posse Cuts (Rhino, 1998)

Fat Beats & Bra Straps: Hip Hop Classics (Rhino, 1998)

Fat Beats & Bra Straps: New MCs (Rhino, 1998)

Vinyl Exams (Sony, 2000)

DJ Red Alert Presents Beats, Rhymes & Battles Volume 1 (Loud, 2001)

THE REAL ROXANNE

Albums:

The Real Roxanne (Select, 1988)

Go Down (But Don't Bite It) (Select, 1992)

Crucial Cuts:

"Bang Zoom" (Select, 1986)

"Real Roxanne" (Select, 1991)

"Romeo" (Select, 1991)

ROXANNE SHANTÉ

Albums:

Bad Sister (Cold Chillin', 1989)

Def Mix #1 (Pop Art, 1989)

Greatest Hits (Cold Chillin', 1995)

Crucial Cuts:

"Roxanne's Revenge" from Marley Marl,

Droppin' Science: House of Hits (Cold Chillin', 1995)

"Cypher Part 3" from Frankie Cutlass, *Politics and Bullshit* (Relativity, 1997)

"Have a Nice Day," from Various Artists, *Droppin' Science: The Best of Cold Chillin'* (BBE Records, 1999)

SALT-N-PEPA

Albums:

Hot, Cool & Vicious (Next Plateau, 1986); certified platinum

A Salt with a Deadly Pepa (Next Plateau, 1988); certified gold

Black's Magic (Next Plateau, 1990); certified platinum

Brand New (PolyGram, 1997); certified gold

Very Necessary (Next Plateau/London, 1993); certified 5x platinum

Crucial Cuts:

"Push It" (Next Plateau, 1987); certified platinum

"Expressions" (Next Plateau, 1989); certified platinum

"Do You Want Me" (Next Plateau, 1991); certified gold

"Let's Talk About Sex" (Next Plateau, 1991); certified gold

"Shoop" (Next Plateau, 1993); certified gold

"Whatta Man" with En Vogue (Next Plateau, 1993); certified platinum

MC LYTE

Albums:

Lyte as a Rock (First Priority, 1988)

Eyes on This (First Priority, 1989)

Act Like You Know (First Priority, 1991)

Ain't No Other (First Priority, 1993)

Bad as I Wanna B (Elektra/Asylum, 1996)

Seven & Seven (Elektra/Asylum, 1998)

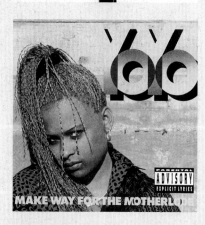

Crucial Cuts:

"I Cram to Understand U" (First Priority, 1987)

"Paper Thin" (First Priority, 1988)

"10% Dis" (First Priority, 1988)

"Cha Cha Cha" (First Priority, 1989)

"Cappucino" (Atlantic, 1990)

"Poor Georgie" (First Priority, 1991)

"Ruffneck" (Atlantic, 1993); certified gold

"Keep On Keepin' On" (WEA/Elektra, 1996); certified gold

"Cold Rock a Party" (WEA/Elektra, 1997); certified gold

QUEEN LATIFAH

Albums:

All Hail the Queen (Tommy Boy, 1989)

Nature of a Sista (Tommy Boy, 1991)

Black Reign (Motown, 1993); certified gold

Order in the Court (Motown, 1998)

Crucial Cuts:

"Wrath of My Madness" (Tommy Boy, 1988)

"Dance for Me" (Tommy Boy, 1989)

"Mama Gave Birth to the Soul Children" (Tommy Boy, 1990)

"Come into My House" (Tommy Boy, 1992)

"U.N.I.T.Y." (Motown, 1994)

YO YO

Albums:

Make Way for the Motherlode (East West, 1991)

Black Pearl (East West, 1992)

You Better Ask Somebody (Atlantic, 1992)

Total Control (Elektra/Asylum, 1996)

Ebony (Elektra/Asylum, 1998)

Crucial Cuts:

"It's a Man's World" from Ice Cube, *Amerikkka's Most Wanted* (Priority, 1990)

"Stompin' to the 90's" (Atlantic, 1990)

"You Can't Play with My Yo Yo" (Atlantic, 1991)

"Romantic Call" with Patra (Epic, 1994)

TLC

Albums:

Oooooooh...On the TLC Tip (LaFace, 1992); certified 4x platinum

CrazySexyCool (LaFace, 1994); certified 11x platinum

Fanmail (LaFace, 1999); certified 6x platinum

Left Eye: *Supernova* (Arista, 2001)

Crucial Cuts:

"Ain't 2 Proud 2 Beg" (LaFace, 1991); certified platinum

"What About Your Friends" (LaFace, 1992); certified gold

"Baby Baby Baby" (LaFace, 1992); certified platinum

"Waterfalls" (LaFace, 1995); certified platinum

"Creep" (LaFace, 1995); certified platinum

"Red Light Special" (LaFace, 1995); certified gold

"Diggin' on You" (LaFace, 1996); certified gold

T-Boz: "Ghetto Love" from Da Brat, *Anuthatantrum* (So So Def, 1996)

T-Boz: "Not Tonight" from Lil' Kim, *Hard Core* (Undeas/Atlantic, 1996)

Left Eye: "Cradle Will Rock" from Method Man, *Tical 2000: Judgement Day* (Def Jam, 1998)

"No Scrubs" (LaFace, 1999); certified gold

"Unpretty" (LaFace, 1999); certified gold

Left Eye: "You Know What's Up" from Donnell Jones, *Where I Wanna Be* (LaFace, 1999)

T-Boz: "Touch Myself" (Rowdy, 1999)

T-Boz: "My Get Away" (Maverick, 2000)

MARY J. BLIGE

Albums:

What's the 411? (Uptown/MCA, 1992); certified 3x platinum

What's the 411?—Remix Album (Uptown/MCA, 1992); certified gold

My Life (Uptown/MCA, 1994); certified 3x platinum

Share My World (MCA, 1997); certified
  3x platinum
The Tour (MCA, 1998); certified gold
Mary (MCA, 1999); certified 2x platinum
No More Drama Herb's Joint (MCA, 2001)

Crucial Cuts:
"You Remind Me" (MCA, 1992);
  certified gold
"Real Love" (MCA, 1992); certified gold
"Reminisce" (MCA, 1992)
"Love Don't Live Here Anymore" from
  Faith Evans, *Faith* (Bad Boy, 1995)
"I'll Be There For You/ You're All I Need
  (remix)" from Method Man, *Tical*,
  (Def Jam, 1995); certified platinum
"Every Day It Rains," from Various Artists,
  The Show (Def Jam, 1995)
"Not Gon' Cry" (Arista, 1996);
  certified platinum
"Can't Knock the Hustle," from Jay-Z,
  Reasonable Doubt (Def Jam, 1996)
"All That I Can Say" (Motown, 1999)
"911" from Wyclef Jean, *The Ecleftic:
  2 Sides II a Book* (Columbia, 2000)
"Hold On" from Lil' Kim, *Notorious K.I.M.*
  (Atlantic, 2000)

DA BRAT

Albums:
Funkdafied (So So Def/Sony, 1994);
  certified platinum
Anuthatantrum (So So Def/Sony, 1996);
  certified gold
Unrestricted (So So Def/ Sony, 2000);
  certified gold

Crucial Cuts:
"Ghetto Love" (So So Def, 1994);
  certified gold
"Funkdafied" (So So Def, 1994);
  certified platinum
"Give It 2 You" (So So Def, 1994);
  certified gold
"Honey" from Mariah Carey, *Butterfly*
  (Sony, 1997)
"The Party Continues" from Jermaine
  Dupri, *Jermaine Dupri Presents:
  Life in 1472* (So So Def/Sony, 1998);
  certified gold

"Sock It to Me" from Missy Elliott, *Supa
  Dupa Fly* (Elektra, 1997)
"Bounce with Me" from Lil' Bow Wow,
  Beware of Dog (So So Def, 2000)
"Gangsta Bitches" from Eve, *Scorpion*
  (Interscope, 2001)
"Survivor (Remix)" from Destiny's Child,
  Survivor (Columbia, 2001)

LAURYN HILL

Fugees Albums:
Blunted on Reality (Ruffhouse, 1994)
The Score (Ruffhouse, 1996);
  certified 17x platinum

Solo Album:
The Miseducation of Lauryn Hill
  (Columbia, 1998); certified 7x platinum

Crucial Cuts:
"Nappy Heads" (Ruffhouse, 1994)
"Killing Me Softly" (Ruffhouse, 1996)
"Fugee-La" (Ruffhouse, 1996);
  certified gold
"Ready or Not" (Ruffhouse, 1996)
"If I Ruled the World" from Nas, *It Was
  Written* (Sony/Columbia, 1996)
"Guantanamera" from Wyclef Jean,
  The Carnival (Sony/Columbia, 1997)
"The Sweetest Thing" from the *Love
  Jones* soundtrack (Sony/Columbia,
  1997)
"Lost Ones" (Ruffhouse, 1998)
"Doo Wop (That Thing)" (Ruffhouse,
  1998); certified gold
"Everything Is Everything" (Ruffhouse,
  1999); certified gold
"Turn Your Lights Down Low" from Bob
  Marley, *Chant Down Babylon*
  (Island/Def Jam, 1999)

ERYKAH BADU

Albums:
Baduizm (Kedar/Universal, 1997);
  certified 3x platinum
Live (Kedar/Universal, 1997);
  certified 2x platinum
Mama's Gun (Motown, 2000);
  certified platinum

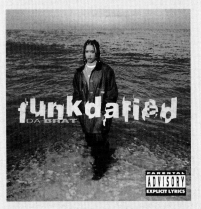

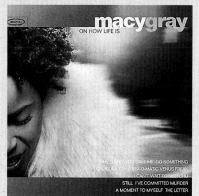

Crucial Cuts:

"On & On" (Kedar/Universal, 1997); certified gold

"Next Lifetime" (Kedar/Universal, 1997)

"Tyrone" (Kedar/Universal, 1997)

"All Night Long" from Common, *One Day It'll All Make Sense* (Relativity, 1997)

"One" from Busta Rhymes, *When Disaster Strikes* (Elektra, 1997)

"Liberation" from OutKast, *Aquemini* (Arista, 1998)

"You Got Me" from The Roots, *Things Fall Apart* (MCA, 1999)

"No More Trouble" from Bob Marley, *Chant Down Babylon* (Island/Def Jam, 1999)

"Hollywood" from the *Bamboozled* soundtrack (Motown, 2000)

"Humble Mumble" from OutKast, *Stankonia* (LaFace/Arista, 2000)

JILL SCOTT

Albums:

Who Is Jill Scott?: Words and Sounds, Vol. 1 (Hidden Beach/Sony, 2000); certified platinum

Crucial Cuts:

"The Rain" from Will Smith, *Willennium* (Sony/Columbia, 1999)

"Funky For You" from Common, *Like Water for Chocolate* (MCA, 2000)

"One Time" from the *Down to Earth* soundtrack (Epic, 2001)

MACY GRAY

Albums:

On How Life Is (Epic, 1999); platinum

The Id (Epic, 2001)

Crucial Cuts:

"Do Something" (Epic, 1999)

"I Try" (Epic, 1999)

"Request + Line" from Black Eyed Peas, *Bridging The Gap* (Interscope, 2000)

"Love Life" from Fat Boy Slim, *Halfway Between the Gutter and the Stars* (Astralwerks, 2000)

"Ghetto Heaven" from Common, *Like Water for Chocolate* (MCA, 2000)

LIL' KIM

Albums:

Junior M.A.F.I.A., *Conspiracy* (Undeas/Big Beat, 1995)

Hard Core (Undeas/Big Beat, 1996); certified 2x platinum

Notorious K.I.M. (Atlantic, 2000); certified platinum

Crucial Cuts:

Junior M.A.F.I.A. with The Notorious B.I.G., "Get Money" (Undeas/Big Beat, 1995)

Junior M.A.F.I.A. with The Notorious B.I.G., "Players Anthem" (Undeas/Big Beat, 1995)

"No One Else (Remix)" from Total, *Total* (Bad Boy, 1996)

"Benjamins (Remix)" from Puff Daddy and the Family, *No Way Out* (Bad Boy, 1997)

"Another" from The Notorious B.I.G., *Life After Death* (Bad Boy, 1997)

"Money, Power, Respect" from The Lox, *Money, Power, Respect* (Bad Boy, 1998)

"Quiet Storm (Remix)" from Mobb Deep, *Murder Muzik* (Loud, 1999)

"Lady Marmalade" with Christina Aguilera, Pink, and Mya from the *Moulin Rouge* soundtrack (Interscope, 2001); certified gold

FOXY BROWN

Albums:

Ill Na Na (Violator/RAL, 1996); certified platinum

The Firm with Nas and AZ (Interscope, 1997); certified gold

Chyna Doll (Violator/RAL, 1998); certified platinum

Broken Silence (Def Jam, 2001)

Crucial Cuts:

"I Shot Ya" from L.L. Cool J, *Mr. Smith* (Def Jam, 1995)

"Ain't No Nigga" from Jay-Z, *Reasonable Doubt* (Roc-A-Fella/Priority, 1996)

"No One Else (Remix)" from Total, *Total*
(Bad Boy, 1996)

"Touch Me, Tease Me" from Case, *Case*
(Def Jam, 1996)

"Big Bad Mama" from the *How to Be a
Player* soundtrack (Def Jam, 1997)

"Too Stoosh" from Spragga Benz, *Fully
Loaded* (VP, 2000)

"Bang Bang" from Capone 'N' Noreaga,
Reunion (Tommy Boy, 2001)

"BK Anthem" (Def Jam, 2001)

MISSY "MISDEMEANOR" ELLIOTT

Albums:

Supa Dupa Fly (Elektra, 1997); certified
platinum

Da Real World (Elektra, 1999); certified
platinum

Miss E . . . So Addictive (Elektra, 2001);
certified platinum

Crucial Cuts:

"Things That You Do" by Gina Thompson,
Nobody Does It Better (PolyGram, 1996)

"Can We" from SWV, *Release Some
Tension* (RCA, 1997)

"Not Tonight" from Lil' Kim, *Hard Core*
(Undeas, 1996)

"The Rain (Supa Dupa Fly)" (Elektra,
1997)

"Make It Hot" from Nicole Rae, *Make It
Hot* (Elektra, 1998)

"My Love Is Your Love" from Whitney
Houston, *My Love Is Your Love*
(Arista, 1998)

"Heartbreaker (Remix)" from Mariah
Carey, *Rainbow* (Columbia, 1999)

"Hot Boys" (Elektra, 1999); certified
platinum

"Get Ur Freak On" (Elektra, 2001)

EVE

Albums:

Ruff Ryders, *Ryde or Die, Volume 1*
(Interscope, 1999); certified platinum

*Let There Be Eve . . . Ruff Ryders' First
Lady* (Interscope, 1999);
certified platinum

Ruff Ryders, *Ruff Ryders, Volume 2*
(Interscope, 2000)

Scorpion (Interscope, 2001);
certified platinum

Crucial Cuts:

"Eve of Destruction" from the *Bulworth*
soundtrack (Def Jam, 1998)

"Ready 2 Ryde" from Snoop Dogg, *Last
Meal* (No Limit/Priority, 2000)

"Caramel (Remix)" from City High, *City
High* (Interscope, 2001)

"Stop Hatin'/Get Money" from Dutch and
Spade, *For Our Family*
(Untertainment/Interscope, 2001)

TRINA

Albums:

Da Baddest Bitch (Atlantic, 2000);
certified gold

Crucial Cuts:

"Nann Nigga" from Trick Daddy,
www.thug.com (Warlock, 1998)

"Shut Up" from Trick Daddy, *Book of
Thugs: Chapter AK Verse 47*
(Atlantic, 2000)

"That's Cool" from Silkk the Shocker,
My World, My Way (No Limit/ Priority,
2000)

"Gangsta Bitches" from Eve, *Scorpion*
(Interscope, 2001)

"I Got It" from Jagged Edge, *Jagged Little
Thrill* (So So Def, 2001)

"Where You From" from Trick Daddy,
Thugs Are Us (Atlantic, 2001)

"Take It to Da House" from Trick Daddy,
Thugs Are Us (Atlantic, 2001)

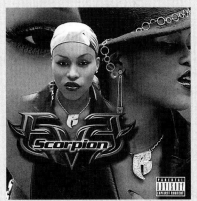

index

credits

Front cover:

Mary J. Blige by Marc Baptiste

Back cover:

Lauryn Hill by Jonathan Mannion

Title page:

Salt-N-Pepa by Ricky Powell

Chapter 2:

Mercedes Ladies courtesy of Sherri Sher

Funky 4 + 1 More: © 2000 Experience Music
    Project

Sha Rock's birthday party handbill: © 2000
    Experience Music Project

Chapter 3:

Roxanne Shanté by David Corio/Retna

Roxanne Shanté boxing handbill: © 2000
    Experience Music Project

Roxanne Shanté by Sue Kwon

Chapter 4:

Salt-N-Pepa by Albert Watson

Salt-N-Pepa flyer with Hurby Luvbug: © 2000
    Experience Music Project

Chapter 5:

MC Lyte by Andrew Eccles/Corbis/Outline

MC Lyte and K-Rock by Jeffrey S. Kane/Retna

Chapter 6:

Queen Latifah by Nitin Vadukul/
    Corbis/Outline

The Super Def Latifah handbill: © 2000
    Experience Music Project

Chapter 7:

Yo Yo by Sue Kwon

Yo Yo and Ice Cube by Steve Eichner/Retna

Chapter 8:

TLC by Seb Janiak

TLC by Ernie Paniccioli

Chapter 9:

Mary J. Blige by Spicer

VIBE covers: © VIBE/SPIN Ventures

Chapter 10:

Lauryn Hill by Jonathan Mannion

The Fugees by Susan Stava/Retna

Lauryn Hill by Jenny Schulder

Chapter 11:

Erykah Badu by Piper Carter

Macy Gray by Fred Prouser/Reuters/Corbis

Jill Scott by Derrick Santini

Chapter 12:

Da Brat by Marc Baptiste/Corbis/Outline

Da Brat and Jermaine Dupri by Fabrice
    Trombert/Retna

Chapter 13:

Foxy Brown by Marc Baptiste/Corbis/Outline

The Firm by S.I.N./Corbis

Chapter 14:

Lil' Kim by Dana Lixenberg

Lil' Kim with Biggie & Puffy by Allen
    Gordon/London Features International

Lil' Kim by Dimitrios Kambouris/Fashion
    Wire Daily/Retna

Chapter 15:

Trina © Sarah A. Friedman

Trina with Trick Daddy: © Sarah A. Friedman

Chapter 16:

Missy by Lyle Ashton Harris

Missy with Tamia by Gary Gershoff

Chapter 17:

Eve by Marc Joseph/Corbis/Outline

Eve with Chivon and Wah Dean and Swizz
    Beats by Dennis Van Tine/London Features
    International

Hip Hop Herstory:

Sequence courtesy of Adler Archives

Jazzy Joyce courtesy of Hot 97

Debbie Harry by L.A. Media/Retna

J.J. Fad by Ernie Paniccioli

Antoinette by B. Oliver/Retna

Ms. Melodie by Ernie Paniccioli

Monica Lynch by Janette Beckman/Retna

Heather B. by Ernie Paniccioli

Monie Love by Justin Thomas/Retna

Rage by Fitzroy Barrett/Retna

Boss by Ernie Paniccioli

Rah Digga by Anthony Saint James/Retna

Mia X by Ronald Cadiz/Corbis/Outline

Gangsta Boo by Jonathan Mannion

Anomolies courtesy of Anomolies

Aaliyah:

Photograph by David LaChapelle-Courtesy of
    Blackground Records